MASTERING
COUNSELLING
THEORY

Ray Colledge

palgrave
macmillan

061327
361.323 COL
COUNSELLING
PSYCHODYNAMIC COUNSELLING
CBT   CMC

First published 2002 by
PALGRAVE MACMILLAN

Palgrave Macmillan in the UK is an imprint of Macmillian Publishers Limited, registered in England, company number 785998, of Houndmills, Basingstoke, Hampshire RG21 6XS.

Palgrave Macmillan in the US is a division of St Martin's Press LLC, 175 Fifth Avenue, New York, NY 10010.

Palgrave Macmillan is the global academic imprint of the above companies and has companies and representatives throughout the world.

Palgrave® and Macmillan® are registered trademarks in the United States, the United Kingdom, Europe and other countries.

ISBN-13: 978-0-333-92243-9
ISBN-10: 0-333-92243-3

This book is printed on paper suitable for recycling and made from fully managed and sustained forest sources. Logging, pulping and manufacturing processes are expected to conform to the environmental regulations of the country of origin.

A catalogue record for this book is available from the British Library.

Library of Congress Cataloging-in-Publication Data
Colledge, Ray.
    Mastering counselling theory / Ray Colledge.
        p.   cm. – (Palgrave master series)
    Includes bibliographical references and index.
    ISBN-13: 978-0-333-92243-9 (pbk.)
    ISBN-10: 0-333-92243-3 (pbk.)
    1. Counseling.   I. Title: Mastering counseling theory.   II. Title.   III. Series.
    BF637.C6 C465 2002
    158'.3 – dc21   2002025185

10   9   8   7
11   10   09

Printed and bound in China

Contents

Part two Humanistic counselling

Part three Existential counselling

Part four   Cognitive therapy and behavioural counselling

Part five   Eclectic and integrative counselling

▪ ⅒ Introduction: what is counselling?

The helping relationship

Those counsellors who regard counselling as a mainly helping relationship usually subscribe to the theory and practice of the person-centred approach. It could be said that a helping relationship is enough to get constructive changes to occur in clients. The core conditions of such a relationship are empathic understanding, congruence or genuineness, and respect for clients' capacity to lead their own lives.

Gerard Egan's influential staged approach has given a practical focus to charting the progress of helping relationships while remaining true to the core conditions. Egan's aim is to help clients to set and achieve goals in certain areas of their lives. In *The Skilled Helper* (1975) he states that effective skilled helpers should also be committed to their own growth, including the social, emotional, spiritual and intellectual aspects of their being. He adds that helpers need to become 'potent human beings' (quoted in Milne, 1999, p. 17); this corresponds to what Rogers calls the 'authentic self'. Potent human beings, says Egan (ibid.), are 'people with both the resources and the will to act'. Egan sets out a list of attributes that contribute to the effectiveness of skilled helpers who do not necessarily work as professional counsellors but have good counselling skills:

- Basic intelligence and respect for ideas.
- Knowledge and competent use of theory.
- Evaluation skills.
- Common sense and social adeptness.
- Easiness with others.
- The ability to feel at home in the social and emotional world of others as well as their own.
- The ability to respond effectively to a wide range of human needs.
- Lack of fear of deep human emotions, both their own and those of others, and a willingness and ability to work at the level of distress.
- A willingness to explore their own feelings and behaviour and to work at recognising and integrating all aspects of the self.
- The ability to interpret non-verbal messages.

Stages in the process of helping

A staged model establishes a framework for helping that grows along with the relationship between helper and client. Egan (ibid.) uses three stages (exploration, interpretation and goal setting/action), while Richard Nelson-Jones (1996) uses five:

- Develop the relationship, identify and clarify the problem(s).
- Assess the problem(s) and redefine in skill terms.
- State the working goals and plan interventions.
- Intervene to develop self-help skills.
- Consolidate self-help skills.

An alternative four-stage model is as follows:

- Comprehend the clients' perspective on their problems and their current situation.
- Explore alternative perspectives with the clients, work on their problems and explore how they would like their situation to change.
- Explore ways of achieving the clients' chosen goals and make concrete plans of action.
- Implement the plan, evaluate the extent to which the goals have been achieved and revise the plan if required.

Interventions

On its own the helping relationship is sometimes insufficient for constructive changes to take place, in which case there is a need for a set of interventions, methods and strategies. These are like tools in a toolbox that the counsellor can select according to the needs of the client and the likelihood of success. These tools will, of course, reflect the theoretical orientation of the counsellor in question. For example a person-centred counsellor will employ person-centred interventions, while eclectic counsellors will use a variety of interventions. Finally, the counsellor's personality and a good client–counsellor match are as important as any of the above.

The psychological process

Counselling is a psychological process in that to a greater or lesser extent all counselling approaches are aimed at changing how people think and feel. Counselling is a movement within and between the minds of client and counsellor, but a great deal of psychological development occurs between sessions and after counselling ends.

Counselling goals and interventions are derived from psychological theories, and many of the best-known theorists are or were psychologists or psychiatrists. Psychological research is an ongoing process and contributes to the creation of new counselling theories as well as adding to the toolbox of existing practices.

The goals of counselling

Naturally, different clients have different goals, for example managing a life crisis, healing a past hurt, handling a transition, making a decision or developing a life skill. Goals can be remedial or developmental, but despite the remedial nature of a lot of counselling the primary focus is on the developmental concerns of the ordinary majority rather than the problems of the severely disturbed few.

Common developmental concerns are becoming independent, finding a partner, bringing up children and adjusting to old age. The counselling process is aimed at overcoming negative qualities and accentuating positive ones. Positive mental health and psychological well-being are the supreme focus of counselling. An excellent example of positive developmental goals is provided by Maslow's characterisation of self-actualising people: autonomy, creativity, social interest and problem centredness (see Chapter 9 of this book).

Whatever the theoretical approach, the emphasis in counselling is on increasing clients' responsibility for their own lives, so it is essential for them to make choices that help them to feel, think and act effectively. They need to be able to experience and express their feelings, have rational thoughts and take effective action in the pursuit of personal goals. Counsellors have done their job when clients are equipped to help themselves when counselling ends.

Counsellors

There are various types of counsellor:

- Helping service professionals: this group includes counsellors, counselling psychologists, psychologists, social workers and career officers.
- Voluntary counsellors: people who are trained in helping skills and are employed by voluntary agencies, youth counselling agencies and marriage guidance services.
- Those who use counselling skills in their jobs: doctors, nurses, clergy, teachers, welfare workers and supervisors, to name but a few.
- Informal counsellors: people in day-to-day relationships who help others such as children, friends and work colleagues to develop their potential.

Counselling theories

Theories provide counsellors with conceptual frameworks that enable them to think systematically about human development and their practice of counselling. This is vital because counsellors constantly have to make decisions and choices about how to view clients' behaviour and how to treat and respond to them during a counselling session. Theories need four elements if they are to be useful:

- A statement of basic assumptions underpinning the theory.
- An explanation of the acquisition of helpful and unhelpful behaviour.
- An explanation of the maintenance and perpetuation of helpful and unhelpful behaviour.
- An explanation of how to help clients change their behaviour and consolidate any gains once counselling is over.[1]

Each theory has a unique language to convey its concepts. However this can hide common elements among the theories. For example in psychoanalysis the term superego is similar to person-centred counselling's 'conditions of worth'. The whole process of counselling is actually a number of conversations using languages. There are usually several types of language in use in any given counselling session, including the inner and outer speech of client and counsellor, and the language of the theoretical framework counsellors are employing – to varying degrees their practice matches their language. The language of counselling is sometimes passed on to clients so that they can better help themselves once counselling ends. Rational emotive behaviour counselling and lifeskills counselling actively encourage this.

Theories are based on and drive research. For example behavioural theory, which is based on both animal and human research, has given rise to counselling practices and then to further research to test the soundness of these practices. It is also the case that theories can provoke research by arousing objections and disbelief. Freud's theories are a superb example of this. It is very important to take great care when designing research, and to avoid overinterpretation of the findings.

Theories are important in providing the frameworks needed to make predictive hypotheses. Every time counsellors make a decision about how to work with a client, they are actually forming a hypothesis. The same is true of clients because they make predictions about the best way to live their lives. The accuracy of their predictions about the consequences of their behaviours are enhanced if the knowledge and understanding of proven counselling theories are made available to them. This also facilitates counsellors' aim of helping their clients to gain greater control over their lives.

Seven sources are drawn on during the development of counselling theory, as follows.

Historical and cultural contexts

To a greater or lesser extent we are all products of the historical and cultural contexts in which we live, and this is true of theorists and the theories they have developed. For example Freud's theories were a response to unacknowledged sexuality in individuals as a result of sexual repression in Vienna in the late nineteenth and early twentieth century. Similarly Rogers' theories were based on individuals' need to overcome the effects of judgemental family upbringing in the first decades of the twentieth century. Existential counselling, on the other hand, was developed in the latter part of the twentieth century when the certainties of society such as family, social class and organised religion were replaced by structurelessness. This meant that people now had to find their own meaning, but many were unable to do so.

Finally, theory is strongly influenced by culture, and this is reflected more and more in multicultural societies where the values of Western and Eastern cultures meet and clash. The theories of Western counselling, for example, reflect the value placed on individualism while people from Eastern cultures place greater value on group harmony through religion and the extended family.

Personal history

Many theorists have drawn on their own experiences when developing their theories. For example Freud gained insights for his *Interpretation of Dreams* by undergoing self-analysis, Frankl developed logotherapy in response to his youthful unhappiness about the seeming meaninglessness of life, and Rogers' counselling theories emphasised the qualities of empathy and non-possessive warmth that his parents had lacked and he had needed for his own personal growth.

Personality

Theories reflect their formulators' own personalities. Rogers' counselling theories reflect his gentle and personal nature. Freud was shy and bookish and this is reflected in psychoanalysis, in which the analyst sits behind the client. A common characteristic of theorists is that they are energetic, creative thinkers and willing to challenge current ways of working.

The desire to write and communicate

All theorists believe they have something worth offering and want to share it. Added to this they tend to have a sense of social interest and altruism, and perhaps experience the sheer enjoyment and sense of achievement gained from contributing to their chosen field of endeavour. Many well-known theorists showed an interest in writing in their earlier years: Beck edited his high school newspaper and was an undergraduate major, Berne's mother was a journalist and he studied English as an undergraduate, Ellis planned a writing career and hoped to be the Great American Novelist, Lazarus helped to edit a body-building magazine, English literature was May's main interest at college, Skinner majored in English and wrote novels and Yalom wrote novels.

Experience

Most of the major counselling theories have been developed by practitioners. Important factors in the development of theories include clinical experimentation, frustration, careful observation and creative insights. The psychoanalysts Beck, Berne, Ellis and Perls had negative experiences in their practices and this led them to formulate their own theories and design new ways of helping their clients. Glasser developed reality counselling as a result of his disillusionment with the psychoanalytic psychology he encountered in training. Similarly multimodal counselling was the result of Lazarus's dissatisfaction with the restrictiveness of traditional behavioural therapy. Rogers discovered that he could achieve better results by listening to his clients than by offering diagnostic understanding and advice.

Research

This is important in theory development and its testing. Counselling theorists are practitioner researchers who form and test hypotheses in their own practices. Counselling theory is based on interviews and/or clinical research – professional experience is one form of interview research. Theorists differ in the extent to which they generate and engage in more formal research such as that conducted by Pavlov (dogs, classical conditioning), Skinner (rats and pigeons, operant conditioning) and Wolpe (cats, counterconditioning by reciprocal inhibition). Heavily researched approaches include person centred counselling, behavioural counselling, cognitive counselling and rational emotive counselling. Less research has gone into existential counselling, reality counselling, transactional analysis and Gestalt counselling.

Other theorists and disciplines

Many theorists have drawn on the work of other theorists, past and present. For example psychoanalysis influenced Berne's transactional analysis, Yalom and May's existential counselling and Perls' Gestalt counselling, while Beck drew on the phenomenal, structural, depth and cognitive approaches to psychology.

With regard to the influence of other disciplines, Freud drew on his medical background, Ellis owed much to the Stoic philosophers and Frankl drew on theology. Anthropology, sociology, politics and social psychology have also been important influences.

The disadvantages of counselling theories

Over-reliance on counselling theories has a number of adverse effects. First, it can lead to limited focus, for example:

- Rogers' sole diagnosis of client problems is that they are not in touch with their actualising tendencies, and that a helping relationship is all that is needed to remedy this.
- Ellis's concentration on irrational beliefs neglects other important facets of thought, such as accurate perception and the use of coping self-talk.
- Traditional behaviourists give scant attention to thoughts and feelings.
- Freud's emphasis on the analysis of dreams to uncover unconscious material neglects the need to form effective behaviours to tackle day-to-day problems.

Second, it can lead to counsellor rigidity in that some counsellors may allow their favourite theory to cloud the accuracy of their assessment and treatment of clients. Although theory gives counsellors certainty and confidence, and this is transmitted to their clients, their confidence might well be misplaced. There are a number of terms for this, such as 'true believerism', 'rigor psychologicus', 'delusions of certainty' and a 'hardening of the categories'. Counselling schools are beneficial in that they promote useful research and training, but they can instil a tendency for theoretical rigidity by giving preferment to those who are loyal to the favoured approach rather than those who are more open-minded. Furthermore the similarities between schools can be masked by the different languages used.

Third, it can result in disservice to clients as many theories tend to focus the problems of clients to the detriment of what is going right in their lives, and can even make their lives seem worse than they are. Psychoanalysts may regard learned ineffective behaviours as a manifestation of underlying conflicts. The value of feedback may be lost if negative feedback is interpreted as resistance and the acting out of negative transference. There is the additional danger that counsellors will put themselves in a superior position to their clients if they operate with a theoretical terminology or language that is not shared with the clients. Ideally language should empower clients to engage in self-help when they leave counselling, but some types of theoretical language fail in this respect.

Fourth, unethical selling may occur when practitioners of varying levels of training market theoretical approaches for their own profit. The development of theoretical schools can be the start of a slippery slope of an unethical approach to selling counselling services. Thus proper psychological services are replaced by counselling certainties.

Finally, it can result in failure to take account of changes in culture and society. Counselling theories make many assumptions about the causes of people's behaviour and how they should behave. Furthermore theorists tend to portray their theories as universally applicable when they are in fact culture-specific. In Western societies there is an increasing need to take on board cultural differences and rapidly changing cultural norms and mores. Moreover counselling theories tend to neglect the effects of poverty, sex-role conditioning, discrimination of various sorts and other disempowering and debilitating socioeconomic and environmental factors. It is also the case that while counselling trainers, students and practising counsellors seem to be aware of the particular needs of gay, lesbian and bisexual clients, most theories assume heterosexuality.

The differences between counselling and psychotherapy

Origins

Counselling emerged from marriage guidance, educational guidance, pastoral care and the work of voluntary organisations, while psychotherapy emerged from Freudian psychoanalysis. For this reason many psychotherapists say that the term should only be used in the context of its Freudian origins. However a clear dividing line is not easy to establish because, for example, the psychodynamic approach to counselling is also grounded in Freudian theory and its core focus is the unconscious and transference.

Training

Normally, psychotherapeutic training takes a minimum of three years, including a year of working in a health care setting or private practice. In contrast a counselling certificate can be gained in a year, as can a diploma, though most diploma courses are now being lengthened to two years. Admission to a diploma course normally requires a certificate in skills and another in theory.

Length of treatment

It is often thought that psychotherapy involves long-term work with clients while counselling is short term and/or crisis based. However, in practice they tend be indistinguishable from each other in respect of length of treatment, with both offering long- and short-term treatment, especially when practitioners are well-qualified and experienced.

Depth of work

The extended training period for psychotherapists is intended to equip them to work in greater depth with clients. Even so they are not exclusively concerned with those clients with the greatest difficulties. They may see their clients two or more times a week, while counsellors tend to see theirs just once. However this is not a hard and fast rule, and a counsellor may see a client more than once a week if the situation warrants it.

Personal therapy

Psychotherapists are required to undergo personal therapy during their training, but this is not the case with counselling training, where personal therapy is merely recommended.

Note

1 Nelson-Jones, R. 1995. Reproduced with permission of SAGE Publications Ltd.

Part One

Psychodynamic counselling

⬛ ⟁ ▌ Sigmund Freud

Freud was born in 1856 in Freiberg, in what is now the Czech Republic. He was the first-born son of his father's second wife, who subsequently had five daughters and two other sons. His father – a wood merchant – moved the family to Vienna when Freud was four years old. Freud was successful at school and on leaving at the age of 17 he was faced with the standard career choice for Viennese Jews: medicine, law, industry or business. He made his decision upon hearing a reading by Professor Carl Bruhl of Goethe's essay on nature, and in 1873 enrolled at Vienna University to study medicine. In 1876 he began his career as a neurologist at Ernst Brucke's physiological laboratory, where he worked with short interruptions until 1882. He then joined the General Hospital of Vienna, where he began to study nervous diseases and was appointed lecturer in neuropathology. He also took and conducted research into the effects of cocaine. For years he had suffered from periodic depression, fatigue and apathy, neurotic symptoms that later were to take the form of anxiety attacks, which he treated by means of his own analysis. Cocaine eased these problems, but all his life he was to suffer from migraine, which defied any treatment. In October 1885 he went to Paris and studied at the Salpetriere hospital for nervous diseases under Charcot Jean Marting until February 1886. He was profoundly influenced by Charcot's work on hysteria, which confirmed the genuineness of hysterical phenomena, hysterical paralyses and contractures by hypnotic suggestion.

He returned to Vienna in 1886 to marry Martha Bernays and to set up private practice as a specialist in nervous diseases. For 10 years he engaged in clinical work with Joseph Breuer, a Viennese physician, using hypnosis to treat hysterias. In 1895 they published their *Studies of Hysteria* (Freud and Breuer, 1956). It was during the 1890s that Freud moved from hypnosis to free association and gradually developed his ideas on psychoanalysis as he had become aware 'of the possibility that there could be powerful mental processes which . . . remained hidden from the consciousness of man' (Freud, 1935, p. 29).

It is interesting to note that at that time he suffered from severe psychoneurosis and he did his most original work when the neurosis was at its worst (between 1897 and 1900). His mood alternated between elation and self-confidence on the one hand and inhibition and depression on the other. At the same time he developed a fear of dying and severe anxiety about rail travel.

Between 1887 and 1900 he developed an intense friendship with Wilhelm Fleiss, a nose and throat specialist who saw sexual problems as central to his own work. This friendship is of particular importance because Freud was encouraged by Fleiss to work on the latter's theories, leading to the development of Freud's ideas on the sexual bases of neuroses. In 1897–99 he wrote his **magnum opus,** *The Interpretation of Dreams* (1976), which contained material obtained by psychoanalysing his own unconscious. During this process he had recognised a childhood passion for his mother and jealousy towards his father; a situation he famously called the Oedipus complex, which he regarded as a pervasive human characteristic.

In the period 1895–1906 Freud worked in isolation, but after that his collaborators and pupils made an increasingly large contribution. In 1938 he left Austria to escape the Nazis, settling in England but dying a year later from the cancer he had suffered for the past 16 years.[1]

The importance of Freud's work to counsellors

Firstly, Freud's psychoanalytic theory provided a deep well of personality concepts. For example Freud's **instinct** theory enhanced the understanding of the biological basis of human functioning, and his ideas on **defence mechanisms** allowed greater understanding of the way in which people sustain self-defeating behaviour.

Secondly, his psychodynamic theory is of special historical importance because of the influence it had on so many other theorists, including Adler, Jung, Klein, Horney, Sullivar, Froman, Winnicott and Bowlby.

Thirdly, psychoanalytical concepts such as transference and resistance, free association and interpretation are important to all counsellors. Finally, some counsellors and a great many psychiatrists employ analytic orientations that range from pure Freudian to modifications of a few of his ideas.

Human instincts

Freud saw instincts as historically acquired and conservative. He believed that instincts are an inherent urge to restore earlier states of things, that they are somatic or biological demands on the mind.

The pleasure principle

The **pleasure principle**, which Freud originally called the unpleasure principle, follows from the hypothesis that the human mental apparatus tries to keep the amount of excitation in it as small as possible, or to keep it constant. Thus everything that increases excitation will be experienced as unpleasurable, while everything that reduces it will be pleasurable. The dominance of the pleasure principle was qualified by Freud, who observed that even though the human mind strongly tends towards the pleasure principle there are forces that oppose it. The final outcome is not always fulfilment of the tendency for pleasure.

According to Freud, human instincts can be divided into two broad categories, namely Eros and Thanatos.

Eros is a group of erotic or life instincts that 'seek to combine more and more living substance into even greater unities' (Freud, 1973, p. 140). Included here are the instincts of self-preservation, preservation of the species, ego-love and object-love. The energy source is the libido. In Freud's view, sexual instincts are unique among the instincts in that they are the only ones that do not try to restore an earlier state of things.

Thanatos is a group of death instincts that oppose the efforts of Eros and, 'lead what is living back to an inorganic state' (ibid.). Given that inanimate things appeared before living things, which arose out of them, Thanatos is a compulsion to repeat the earlier (inorganic) state. Consequently death is the aim of all life. The main representative of the death instinct and derived from it is the aggressive instinct. For Freud, the evolution of human civilisation represents the struggle between these life and death instincts in humankind. He summed this up with a quote from Plautus: *Homo homini lupus* (Man is a wolf to man).

The unconscious and conscious

The mental life of a human being takes place on three levels:

- The unconscious (Ucs)
- The preconscious (Pcs)
- The conscious (Cs or Pcpt Cs).

Freud was strongly influenced by his study of dreams, the interpretation of which he saw as 'the royal road to a knowledge of the unconscious activities of the mind' (Freud, 1976, p. 769). According to Freud there are two kinds of unconscious: the unconscious proper and the preconscious.

The unconscious proper contains repressed material that is not admissable to consciousness. Put another way, very strong censorship prevents material coming into awareness, and it is the job of psychoanalysis to draw out this material. Strong resistance can be provoked during this process, especially because much of what is being repressed has strong sexual connotations.

The preconscious is latent and capable of becoming conscious. It is made up of everything that can move easily from the unconscious state to the conscious state. It is a screen between the conscious and the unconscious, with modifications being made through censorship, as for example in dreams, preconscious material can normally pass into consciousness without the assistance of a therapist.

The conscious acts as a sense organ for the perception of psychical qualities. A state of consciousness is normally very temporary and unlike the unconscious has no memory. Material becomes conscious or flows into the conscious senseorgan from inner excitations or the external world. The human faculty of speech enables internal events such as ideas and intellectual processes to become conscious.

How the human mental apparatus is structured

The human mind has three parts:

- The id is involved in a never ending struggle for the satisfaction of basic instincts.
- The superego represents parental and moral influence.
- The ego applies reality to the demands of the id. The ego has three task-masters, which can be the cause of anxiety, namely the external world, the id and the superego. There are three types of anxiety, one for each of the ego's taskmasters: realistic anxiety, which arises from the dangers posed by the external world; moral anxiety, which results from conflict with the superego; and neurotic anxiety, which results from conflict with the id.

The psychical energy of the human mind is variously distributed between the id, the superego and the ego. These three agencies are in a varying state of harmony or conflict at any given time. Psychological well-being depends on whether or not they interrelate effectively.

The id (in German *das Es*, 'the it') has the following characteristics. It contains psychical processes known as primary processes because they are there from the start. It is the oldest of the mental processes, and is present from birth. Instincts find their mental expression in the id, which is filled with energy from these instincts. This energy means that it ceaselessly strives to satisfy instinctual needs in accordance with the pleasure principle, that is, it seeks the free discharge of excitation. There is no alteration of the id's mental processes during the passage of time. It has no concept of good and evil, morality or values, and it is a person's primary subjective reality at the unconscious level.

The ego (in German *das Ich*, 'the I'), which begins to develop during the first year of life, is the go-between for the id and the external world, and is that part of the id which has been modified by the external world. It represents reason and common sense, and it stops the id destroying itself with instinctual passions. It is derived from bodily sensations, especially those which come from its surface. It serves to substitute the reality principle for the pleasure principle in the id, and although it seeks pleasure and the avoidance of unpleasure, it differs from the id in the methods of achieving this. It controls instinctual demands by deciding the timing and means of gratification, or by suppressing them if they are unacceptable. It does this by introducing thought between feeling a need and acting upon it. If it is weak in relation to the id, it may transform the will of the id into action as if it were its own. The ego deals with external events by means of perception, memory, avoiding excessive stimuli, moderating stimuli and engaging in activity designed to modify the external world to its advantage. A foreseen increase in unpleasure is marked by the arousal of anxiety, thus prompting remedial action.

The superego (in German *das Uber-Ich*, 'the Above-I') is a residue formed within the ego that prolongs parental influences, including racial, cultural and family influences. Parental influences are modified by role models such as teachers. The purpose of the superego is to contain the demands of the id by exerting a moral influence on the ego. A child's fear of loss of love and/or aggression from a parental or other external source causes it to engage in instinctual renunciation. Eventually a secondary situation emerges in which this external influence becomes internalised, whereupon instinctual renunciation is caused by fear of the internal authority or superego. The superego varies from person to person to person, ranging from mild and gentle to harshly inhibiting.

The **ego-ideal**, which is practically synonymous with the superego, is shaped by the admiration the child feels for what it sees as the perfection of its parents, which it tries to live up to. The ego-ideal includes precepts and prohibitions such as 'You should be like this' and 'You should not be like that'. The latter are based on identifications and repressions resulting from the Oedipus complex.

Cathexes and anticathexes

As stated above, central to psychoanalysis is the concept that psychical or mental energy is distributed between the id, ego and superego, and that the id is the source of this somatically (of the body) based psychic energy from our basic instincts. The ego and superego are also charged with energy as they develop.

Cathexes are the charges of instinctual energy that need discharging. The id contains only primary-process instinctual cathexes. **Anticathexes** are charges of energy that inhibit or block the energy of the cathexes. The ego and superego have both cathexes and anticathexes.

Throughout the span of a human life the ego acts as an avenue for libidinal or life-force cathexes to be transferred to objects and into which they can be withdrawn again. Libidinal cathexes have two characteristics: mobility (the ability to pass with ease from one object to another) and fixation (being bound to one object or another).

Sexuality

Freud made a clear distinction between 'sexual' and 'genital'. According to him, sexual life involves the pursuit of pleasure from the erotogenic zones of the body. This does not have to be connected with reproduction and it includes the affectionate impulses that are commonly called 'love'. However he maintained that adult sexual behaviour can be regarded as perversion if it is not aimed at reproduction, heterosexuality and intercourse.

He also distinguished between sexual impulse, sexual object, and sexual aim:

- Sexual impulse is the sexual aspect of libido.
- The sexual object is the person towards whom the sexual attraction is felt.
- The sexual aim is the action (for example touching or sexual intercourse) towards which the sexual impulse strives.

Human beings are sexual from their infancy, although this is forgotten or repressed. By nature they are bisexual, and there is a tendency for perversion in infantile sexuality. There are two main phases of sexual development: the pregenital phase, which lasts until the end of the fifth year; and the genital phase, which starts at puberty and involves the awakening of genital awareness and sexual experimentation with partners. Incestuous object choices are overcome. The period in between is called the latency period.

The pregenital phase

The pregenital phase consists of three stages of sexual organisation: the oral stage, the anal stage and the phallic stages. Children normally pass through these smoothly, but there can be arrested development or fixations at each phase.

The oral stage (0–2 years)

The mouth first of the organs to become an erotogenic zone, so infantile sucking is more than the need for nourishment – it is the pursuit of sexual pleasure independent of that nourishment. This has two substages the first of which simply involves sucking for sustenance. The second substage is the oral-sadistic stage, where the arrival of teeth leads to biting, from which the child derives sadistic pleasure.

The anal stage (2–3 years)

During this stage the anus becomes an erotogenic zone and the child derives pleasure from retaining and releasing faeces. This stage is also known as the sadistic anal stage as there is an impulse for mastery (sadism) as the body musculature strengthens – there is greater control over the anal sphincter, and hence over the release of faeces. The character traits of this stage are orderliness, obstinacy and parsimony. These make up the so called anal character.

The phallic stage (3–5 years)

This is the stage where the male sexual organ and the female clitoris become important. Pleasure is gained from masturbation, and early childhood sexuality reaches its zenith. It is at this time that male and female sexual development diverges.

The Oedipal stage is part of the phallic stage for both sexes. The boy develops a libidinal object cathexis (becomes sexually attached) to his mother and wishes to get rid of his father so that he can take his place with her. However he cannot love her for fear of castration by his father, and he therefore represses his incestuous urges. The situation is resolved by rejection of this object cathexis or attraction. This can lead to identification with his father, which consolidates the masculine side of his character.

The Oedipal stage can be made more complex by the bisexuality (mentioned earlier) that is inherent in human beings. The end result tends to be a mixture of affection and ambivalence, a sort of love–hate relationship with each parent. It is the relative strength of the individual's masculine and feminine dispositions that will decide whether identification is predominantly with the mother or the father. In Freud's view the bisexual Oedipus complex is most pronounced in neurotics.

With girls the mother is again the first object of affection. At first the clitoris is the most important erotogenic zone, but as she develops her attention shifts to the vagina. The object of her love changes too when she discovers the inferiority of her clitoris and the fact that she does not have a penis, for which she holds her mother responsible. This is what Freud called penis envy, which he saw an important feminine characteristic. This is replaced by the wish for a 'penis baby' by the father and a desire to get rid of the mother. As with boys, bisexual disposition further complicates matters. The female Oedipal stage is of indeterminate length and may take a long time to resolve, if at all. However it tends to weaken as time goes by because of disappointment with the father. One noteworthy point here is that although boys are motivated to resolve their Oedipus complex because of fear of castration, this is obviously not the case with girls.

The latency stage (5–12 years)

This stage may be total or partial. It is the time when sexual inhibitions develop and sexual energy is diverted into other pursuits by means of sublimation. At this point libidinous or sexual urges lead to the development of reactions or anticathexes (reaction formations), including such feelings as shame and disgust, and acceptance of a moral code.

The genital phase

This phase starts at puberty and involves a greater increase in libido in boys. However in girls there is increased repression, especially where clitoral activity is concerned. In time, incestuous object choices are overcome and there is more genital awareness. The desire for genital sexual activity with heterosexual partners develops. There is also a break from parental authority and the development of more adult relationships.

Infantile sexuality

Sexual life starts soon after birth, but it lacks a central coordinating focus because of the lack of ego and superego development, and because the genitalia are still immature. The infant finds pleasure in the object of its own body, so it can be said that infantile sexuality is autoerotic.

Freud maintained that there is great tendency for perversion at this age, with normal sexual behaviour developing as organic changes take place, and as a result of psychic repression and the development of inhibitions. The latter mean that people are largely unaware of the dawning of their sexual life; as Freud put it, they experience 'sexual amnesia'.

Early sexual experiences take place at a time when the individual is most impressionable, so they have a vital influence on psychical life and help to determine subsequent development.

Bisexuality

According to Freud the libido cannot be asssigned a sex. Put another way, sexual impulse is independent of its object. This means that it is not originated by chemical attraction.

Homosexual feelings play an important role in normal psychic life. In childhood, and in primitive and prehistoric states, there is free attachment to male and female objects. This forms the basis for the development of both heterosexual and homosexual orientation, or for inverted sexual development to take place. Everyone has a degree of congenital homosexuality as women and men develop out of a child that is bisexual. The final determination of sexuality is the result of constitutional disposition, life experiences and restrictions in one direction or another.

Development of the ego

Identification

Identification is a normal part of development and the ego may be restricted or enhanced according to the nature of the identification. Identification can be viewed as:

- the original form of an emotional tie with an object;
- a regressive substitute for a libidinal object-tie by the introjection of the object with the ego, so that the ego takes on the characteristics of the object, for example a woman or girl imitating her father's cough, facial expression and so on;
- a feeling generated by a person perceiving a quality in common with another person who is not libidinally cathectic.

Defence mechanisms

Defence mechanisms develop to address the conflicting demands of the id and superego. Put simply, defence mechanisms enable individuals to cope with sources of anxiety. In Freud's view the ego could not cope without them.

The development of defence mechanisms is largely part of the child's struggle with its sexuality in its first five years, especially as the ego is feeble during this stage of development. This stage often involves the generation of anxiety because of loss of love or loss of an object – this can continue into later life. Further anxiety arises from fear of castration in the phallic phase, and from the superego during and after the latency period.

However defence mechanisms can cause problems: they prevent the normal functioning of the ego; they divert psychical energy during anticathexis when it could be used elsewhere; and they work unconsciously, so they can continue to hamper realistic behaviour long after they have served their purpose, becoming a form of 'baggage' carried into adult life.

When the ego becomes aware of an endangering instinctual demand it uses the following defence mechanisms to control it:

- **Repression**: the involuntary exclusion of painful, conflicting thoughts, memories or impulses. Repression works in two ways: material in the preconscious (and hence admissable to consciousness) is forced into the unconscious (thus becoming inadmissable); or unconscious material may undergo censorship to prevent it getting into the preconscious. Repression is the basis of all other defences – it is the central defensive mechanism of the ego, for example it may be used to prevent the emergence of latent, sexually perverted impulses.
- **Sublimation**: instinctual sexual activity is repressed and rechannelled into socially acceptable pursuits, such as art and sport.
- **Reaction formation**: is the process of turning an attitude into its opposite, that is, the ego acknowledges an impulse that is contrary to the one it feels threatened by. For example a sexual impulse may be countered by a feeling of shame, disgust or loathing of sexual matters. Likewise, an unconscious dislike of a parent may be transformed into a feeling of admiration.
- **Denial**: non-acceptance of the outside world because it is painful. The reality of the situation is not accepted, for example there may be refusal to accept that a person has died, or denial of criticism by others.
- **Fixation**: caused by anxiety about advancing to the next stage of sexual development, so the libido lags behind. Alternatively there may be fixation to an earlier stage in terms of sexual satisfaction. For example a child may remain dependent on motherly love instead of forming new object cathexes.
- **Regression**: the return to an earlier stage of development at which the person was fixated, for example clinging to a parent. This happens when the individual is threatened. There are two types of regression: (1) a return to an incestuous object first cathected by the libido; or (2) the sexual organisation as a whole returns to an earlier phase.
- **Projection**: an instinctual impulse is externalised because it is unacceptable. For example people may attribute aggressive or sexual impulses to others because they do not wish to acknowledge the extent of these impulses in themselves.
- **Introjection**: the process of unconsciously emulating someone else. For example if a child's parents strongly condemn or ban his or her masturbation habit the child suppresses and condemns it also.
- **Reversal**: a person detaches an attitude from its original object and directs it at someone else. For example the urge to harm one's father could be transformed into a self-destructive tendency.
- **Displacement**: an attitude is detached from its original object and directed towards someone else. For example an Oedipal desire for one's mother could turn into a desire for women or girls with the same physical appearance as the mother.
- **Isolation**: the emotion that accompanies an idea is detached from that idea in order to take away the real significance of the idea. For example someone

who was beaten as a child may recall the beatings in an unemotional and detached way.

- **Negation**: this is easy to confuse with denial and is closely related to reaction formation. It involves negating a disturbing attitude. For example individuals who want to get rid of a brother or sister might develop the idea that they never want to be separated from that sibling.
- **Rationalisation**: false reasons are put forward to justify unacceptable attitudes. For example the false belief that someone deserves punishment provides justification for hurting that person.
- **Conversion**: a psychological disorder is transformed into a physical one. For example if someone had an unconscious feeling of dependency, this could give rise to an illness that would require him or her to be looked after.

Defence mechanisms serve to maintain psychological disturbances because their purpose is to keep such disturbances outside the realms of consciousness. They can work singly or in combination, but specific defences are linked to specific psychological disorders: obsessional neurosis is linked to negation, reaction formation and isolation; paranoia is linked to projection; and depression is linked to reversal and introjection.

Neurosis

A neurotic is someone who is incapable of enjoyment and efficiency. There are three contributory factors, as follows.

The biological factor

Human beings are born unfinished and thus for a long period are helpless and dependent. This causes a fear of object loss, which results in a need to be loved – a need that is never lost.

The phylogenetic factor

This comes from the interruption of human sexual development during the latency period, an interruption that does not occur during the sexual maturation of related animals. In humans most of the instinctual demands of infantile sexuality are regarded as dangers that the ego must guard against. This can result in the repression of sexual awakening at puberty.

The psychological factor

There are three psychological elements that together cause neurotic conflict. First, the ego may repress sexual instincts, especially in infancy and early childhood when the ego is underdeveloped and weak compared with the sexual impulses. The ego realises that the satisfaction of these impulses will lead to danger, so repression takes place under the influence of anxiety. The ego allows a foretaste of the feared unpleasure through a feeling of anxiety. This brings the unpleasure–pleasure mechanism into play, triggering repression of the dangerous instinctual impulse by the ego. This means that the repressed impulse remains outside the influence of the ego because the latter has renounced a portion of its organisation through the very act of repression.

Second, there is a danger that the repressed impulses may not disappear, but will become neurotic symptoms instead. According to Freud, hysterical or conversion symptoms are substitute satisfactions for the frustrated sexual urges. However repression does not always result in symptom formation. Take for example the successful dissolution of the Oedipus complex, whereby the repressed sexual impulse is destroyed and the libido is permanently diverted to other purposes.

Third, repression is quite effective until a child reaches the end of latency, but at puberty its sexual instincts reassert themselves with greater intensity. This can cause intense neurotic suffering. The ego has little if any influence over the transformed instincts of the id unless it is helped to undo its repressions. This situation can be made worse by an alliance of the superego and the id against the ego.

Why and how neuroses are maintained

Freud disagreed with conventional views on sexual morality. In his opinion anyone with self-knowledge is protected against the dangers of morality, and might take up a lifestyle that is at odds with social convention.

Broadly speaking, neuroses are the result of the way in which society tries to regulate sexual activity, as morality or the group superego demands a greater than necessary sacrifice of sexual impulses. Neurotic people are unable to heal their egos and therefore their unhappiness is maintained. This is because the repressions made by their weak childhood egos are unconscious and therefore their egos do not have conscious access to the very material through which the neurosis could be healed. Repression weakens the egos of neurotic people and the functioning of their personality is hindered by psychical energy being diverted into harmful, defensive anticathexes. Continued repression maintains the formation of neurotic symptoms via the rechannelling of frustrated sexual impulses.

This brings us to the process of psychoanalysis.

Psychoanalysis

Psychoanalysis has three major goals: to free impulses, to strengthen reality-based ego functioning (this includes broadening perceptions to include more of the id), and to move the superego away from punitive moral standards and towards more human standards.

Instead of converting their libido into symptoms, neurotics need to be able to bring their egos to bear on real objects, and the energy of the libido has to be available for use by the ego if a person is to function efficiently. Hence the superego must allow libidinal expression. Repressions were etablished when the ego was weak, but now that the ego is stronger it can be re-educated through the psychoanalytic process. Because of the ego's weakness relative to other mental agencies, the conflicts of neurotics are different from normal mental conflicts. Psychoanalysis aims to form an alliance between the analyst and the client's ego. Psychoanalysis was regarded by Freud as suitable treatment for such illnesses as hysteria, obsessional neurosis and anxiety states.

Free association

Encouragement of free association is a fundamental rule for analysts. Clients must tell their analyst everything that occurs to them, even if it is uncomfortable, painful or (seemingly) meaningless. They should share all thoughts, memories, associations, feelings and ideas, and the analyst should encourage them to put all self-criticism aside. The aim of this is to lift repression by making unconscious material conscious.

Transference

Freud found that clients tended to see their analysts as reincarnations of people from their past, and that they tended to transfer onto their analysts the feelings and emotions they had felt for these people. Thus transference is the transformation of the original neurosis into a transference neurosis related to the analyst. Transference love is affection mixed with hostility, jealousy and exclusiveness – it is an ambivalent love.

Transference has three advantages. First, it gives analysts a positive start because their clients want to please them. The clients' weak egos become stronger and they gain out of love for the analyst. Second, analysts gain access to the power that clients' superegos have over their egos when they put their analysts in the place of their father or mother. The analysts become the superego, and can use this situation for what Freud called the 'after-education of the neurotic'. In other words they are in a position to remedy earlier errors in parental education. Finally, vital parts of the clients' life history are reproduced, with defensive reactions and mental attitudes in connection with their neuroses being revealed.

Transference can become negative and hostile when analysts frustrate the erotic demands of their clients by refusing to satisfy them. However this can elicit repressed material that allows insights that enable the clients' egos to be strengthened. Nonetheless analysts must not let transference get out of hand. Clients should be warned that transference might run out of control, and that they should guard against acting out transference issues away from the analyst's room.

Client resistance

Resistance was defined by Freud as all the forces that oppose the work of recovery. The problem is that free association is not really free because clients associate within the context of the analytic setting. They resist reproducing repressed material because everything that occurs to them has some reference to it. Leading on from this, the ego is afraid of the unpleasure that 'digging up' repressed material will cause. Anticathexis protects the ego from the id, so the more dangerous the repressed material, the harder it is to overcome anticathexis. In practical terms, clients' associations become more distant from the repressed material, making the therapists' job that much harder.

There are five types of resistance:

- Repression resistance.
- Transference resistance.
- Resistance to forgoing the gain from illness.
- Resistance by the id to a change in the direction of its fulfilment and the need to work through to a new type of satisfaction.
- Resistance caused by the superego imposing an unconscious sense of guilt or need for punishment. This is the strongest of the five because clients feel they deserve nothing better than to remain ill.

There are three forces that help the analyst to overcome resistance: the clients' need for recovery; any intellectual interest clients might have in the analytic process; and clients' positive transference with the therapist.

Interpretation

Interpretations are constructions or explanations of repressed unconscious material that is brought into the conscious, and of things that are currently happening to clients but are not understood by them.

Analysts have to distinguish between their own and their clients' knowledge. Timing is vital because they will meet resistance if they get it wrong. They must be sure that their clients are near to the moment of insight before interpreting, and that their interpretations are close to what has been forgotten or they might not be accepted by the clients. Analysts use repeated interpretations in the latter stages of therapy.

Analysts use interpretations for the following purposes:

- To understand the impulses of the id.
- To assist the client to understand the defence mechanisms and resistances employed by their egos to cope with repressed material and to evade the efforts of the therapist.
- To understand repressed impulses and the objects to which they have become attached.
- To help clients replace repression by judgements that are appropriate to the here and now rather than their childhood.
- To help the clients' egos to overcome resistance.
- To help the ego take control of repressed libidinal energy.
- To expose unconscious impulses to criticism by tracing their origins.

Analysts obtain the material for interpretation from clients' free associations, parapraxes or slips of the tongue, clients' transference relationships with the therapist, and dreams.

According to Freud, during sleep repression is reduced, which allows un-conscious material to become conscious in the shape of dreams. Dreams are wish fulfilments (that is, the disguised fulfilment of repressed urges) and a compromise between the impulses of the id's and ego's defence mechanisms. A dream can be inserted into the psychical chain and has to be traced backwards in the memory from a pathological idea (pathological in this sense is a mental disorder). The interpretation of dreams involves addressing the latent dream thoughts that are disguised by the process of dream work. During sleep the ego is still able to distort latent dream thoughts to make them less threatening.

Dream work consists of condensing latent dream thoughts into a smaller dream content, displacing the psychical intensity between elements, and the use of symbolism. Freud prepared his clients for dream work by making them pay more attention to their psychical perceptions and abandon criticism of their thoughts (this is part of free association).

The process of psychoanalysis

The psychoanalytic process involves the following:

- Getting clients' weakened egos to take part in interpretation in order to fill in the gaps in their mental resources, and to transfer the authority of their superego to the therapist.
- To stimulate the clients' egos to fight the id's demands, and to defeat any resistance that results from them.
- To restore order to the clients' egos by detecting material and impulses that have intruded from the unconscious.

Freudian therapy requires five key elements:

- Stability: there is considerable emphasis on the frequency and duration of sessions, so much so that late arrival at or absence from a session is seen as relevant to the therapy.
- Anonymity: the therapist is merely a 'mirror' for the client and brings no personal information to a session.
- Passivity: there are long periods of listening without comment, and therapists speak only to interpret. They do not create a social relationship; there is no attempt to persuade, challenge or reassure their clients.
- Free-floating attention: in order to grasp the overall tone therapists avoid analysing the content of their clients' disclosures, rather they simply listen.
- Neutrality: this encompasses most of the first four points – by respecting the client's autonomy and avoiding personal involvement, both therapist and client gain the space needed to look at what underlies the client's symptoms.

With regard to therapeutic style, apart from an introductory handshake there should be no physical contact, and therapists must be outwardly passive when they listen to and then consider the deeper meanings of what their clients say. They should not interfere in client autonomy in any way, so naturalistic attitudes and conventional social modes of interaction are avoided. The rule of anonymity has to be followed, that is therapists must be non-self-disclosing and focus exclusively on their clients' inner world. The only time therapists should speak is to share with their clients what they think is going on in the clients' unconscious (interpretation). Therapists should never reassure their clients, reproach their clients or try to persuade their clients of anything. The aim of all this is to create an atmosphere of safety in which clients feel free to be themselves without the risk of interference or censure.

The only thing there is a direct attempt to change is the clients' level of self-awareness. This process is characterised by a careful, gradual and systematic analysis of resistance, together with increasing emphasis on transference issues. The structure of clients' defences is changed by analysing resistance, illuminating unconscious material and eliminating symptoms.

Freudian therapy consists of three phases. During the opening phase a verbal contract is established, clients' resistances are identified and analysis begins. There is often a honeymoon period of rapid progress, although this is unstable and is not based on real insight. During the middle phase there is a deepening of transference and intensive analysis of resistance. Finally, during the termination phase the gains of the middle phase may be temporarily lost, and there is exploration of important death- and separation-related issues. Much important work is carried out after termination.

Progress can be measured by the elimination of symptoms, increased inde-pendence of spirit, tolerance and passion, and realisation that the human con-dition is contradictory and complex. Clients become more at ease with their own bodily yearnings and those of others.

There are a number of causes of failure to progress. Firstly, in suggestion-based therapy defences can become more rigid and self-deception can increase. Clients are given a model of cure by submitting to manipulation by an external authority, namely the therapist, to modify the way they conduct themselves in the world. Secondly, there is a price to pay for the resolution of symptoms in that buried anguish is brought to the surface and re-experienced. This may prove too much for the clients, who may see neurosis as a lesser evil than making the unconscious conscious. This could be due to the immensity of the clients' pain and/or a dearth of compensation or consolation in the rest of their lives. This is generally true of all human beings, as there is only so much insight we can cope with. Finally, therapist errors can be a frequent cause of lack of progress, so safeguards such as strict analytic self-discipline combined with on-going supervision are needed.

Conclusion

There are a number of limitations to the Freudian approach. Freud claimed that he had created a science of the human mind, but it is more accurate to say that he formed a *potential* science. Psychoanalysis remained isolated from the scientific and philosophical communities for a long time, and so retained an unvalidated methodology that was vague and intuitive rather than being an applied science. The Freudian has no objective approach way of studying basic problems of technique, so new methods of analysing and mathematically modelling psychoanalytic interactions are being developed to put it on a more solid footing. Freudian therapy is lengthy and uncertain, and has a limited range of applications, which means that it is not really cost-effective.

It is worth noting that Freud had a grandiose vision for psychoanalysis. He did not want it to be just one among many therapies; he wanted his teaching to underlie and even to construct culture, including the arts, social science and the bringing up of children. Furthermore he wanted it to replace religion because he saw all religions as a form of neurosis and no more than medieval mumbo-jumbo. His desire to give psychoanalysis total hegemony over the culture, art and education of the Western world amounted to astonishing megalomania. Although he claimed to have created a science, he confessed to Fleiss in 1900 that 'I am actually not a man of science at all . . . I am nothing but a conquistador by temperament, an adventurer (quoted in Howard, 2000, p. 289).'

Given the above, why did his theories have so much appeal? Their appeal lay in his combining mythical themes and pseudoscientific metaphors to produce a theory of human development that filled the vacuum created by the decay of Christianity in the face of the Darwinian revolution and other scientific advances of the nineteenth century. Sadly his contention that societies are essentially oppressive and constraining had been detrimental to the need to nurture, develop and defend civilised society. His preoccupation with the self has narrowed the perspective of both individuals and society. Freud displayed simplistic philosophical attitudes towards personal identity that ignored the progress made in this field since Locke.

Note

1 The author acknowledges the contribution of Richard Nelson-Jones. *The Theory and Practice of Counselling* (1995) to this section.

■ ☑ **2** Alfred Adler

Alfred Adler was born in Vienna in 1870. He qualified as a medical doctor at the Viennese College of Medicine, but after a period of practice he turned his attention to psychiatry. He married in 1897, after which he developed a life-long interest in socialism and sexual equality, and this was reflected in many of his ideas. In 1902, at Freud's invitation he joined the Vienna Psychoanalytic Circle, which had been founded by Freud. In 1917 he published his *Study of Organ Inferiority and its Psychical Compensation: A Contribution to Clinical Medicine*. In 1910 he was made president of the Vienna Psychoanalytic Society, but by 1911 it had become clear that his views had diverged greatly from Freud's and he resigned, along with a number of other members. In 1912 he published *The Neurotic Constitution*, in which he set out his theory of neurosis and the basic ideas behind individual psychology. In 1913 he founded what eventually became the Society for Individual Psychology. He began to develop an interest in children's education, and after the First World War he opened Vienna's first child guidance clinic in order to apply his education theories. He continued to practice and teach in Europe and the USA until 1937, when he died in Aberdeen, Scotland, at the age of 67.

The assumptions and basic ideas of Adlerian therapy

Adlerian therapy takes a holistic, socioteleological approach and is based on Adler's individual psychology. Individual psychology states that people are unaware of their goals and of the logic that powers their progress towards these goals. To explain this further, for Adler the term individual meant that a person is indivisible and cannot be divided into independent mental parts. In other words Adler took a **holistic** approach to psychotherapy. His idea of self-consistent unity contrasts with Freud's theory, which stresses conflicting divisions in the personality.

Secondly, human beings are socially embedded, which means that their actions are only comprehensible when observed within one or other of the groups in which they operate. In other words, they take on meaning in relation to others. Finally, teleological means that humans are goal-driven, that there is a purpose behind all behaviour. Thus it is possible to identify people's short-term and long-term goals. Such goals are of a social nature and they reveal the total personality. In Adler's view, people are unaware of these goals and the private logic that lies behind movement towards them.

Private logic

The ideas and beliefs upon which individuals operate constitute their private logic, which is formed in childhood. These ideas and beliefs are gained by what is known as biased apperception. In psychology, apperception is a process of understanding whereby the newly observed qualities of something are related to past experience. This is not the same as common sense because common sense is understood and shared by everyone – private logic can only belong to one person and it characterises that person's subjective perceptions of his or her experiences. People create their own unique lifestyle out of these inter-pretations, and as a result they are responsible for their own personality and behaviour – they act on what they choose to believe, and these actions have consequences. In other words people are not just passive reactors to life, but creative actors as well.

Lifestyle

According to Adler, people can choose how to respond to their own qualities and to the environment in which they grow up. Their self-concept and concept of life provides a guide or fixed pattern and is called the lifestyle.

Lifestyle is developed by the age of five and is derived from children's unique and creative perceptions of the situations that arise within the family. The scene is set by their parents, their parents' values and the family atmosphere they create. These provide the basis upon which children make assumptions about their world and choose the direction they will take, which is also strongly influenced by siblings and their choice of direction.

Inferiority, superiority, belonging and life's meaning

All people are born with a desire to belong to a family, to larger groups, to society and humanity in general. They all struggle to overcome the fact that they are born into an inferior position, in other words babies are naked, helpless, in the power of others and so on. Adler believed that striving to achieve superiority benefits everyone if it takes place in the context of social interest. There is a positive and a negative side to this struggle. On the positive side, achievement of their potential enables people to regard themselves as equal members of humankind and able to play a useful part in society. On the negative side, if people feel inferior to others their potential and confidence is limited, hampering any contribution they could make.

In summary, behaviour is determined by the meaning we give to life events. We behave in the belief that our perceptions are true, and so life turns out as we believed it would. In a sense we create a self-fulfilling prophecy.

Mental health and social interest

Mental health is measured by the amount of social interest a person has. Social interest is innate in every human being.

Mentally healthy people cooperate with others, are part of a community, are confident of their place in a group or community and contribute to the tasks of the groups to which they belong.

Courage is a characteristic of mentally healthy people. In Adlerian terms courage means activity plus social interest. People are said to be 'encouraged' if they are acting with social interest. They have self-respect and self-confidence because they are acting with social interest other than self-interest.

They aim to belong as social equals and offer a unique, meaningful contribution to the family, larger groups and humanity in general. People included with social interest:

- Treat others as social equals.
- Feel equal to other people.
- Move on a horizontal plane towards others.
- Are task-oriented.
- Behave according to common sense.
- Behave according to the demands of the situation.
- Identify with all human beings because of their feeling of belonging.

Life tasks

According to Adler there are three major life tasks: work (occupation), friendship and love. Rudolph Dreikurs, a young doctor who worked in Adler's child guidance clinics in Vienna in the 1920s, added two more: getting on with oneself and relating to the cosmos. Forming and maintaining an intimate relationship is seen as the greatest test of someone's social interest and desire to cooperate.

Life tasks are achieved by having a social life and friendships, securing an occupation and getting married and having children. These are considered vital to the healthy perpetuation of the human race, although modern Adlerians have expanded the life tasks to cover homosexual/lesbian relationships and unemployment.

When people feel inferior to others, psychological disturbance occurs. This prevents the growth of social interest and prompts a compensatory struggle for personal superiority. This in turn prevents fulfilment of the life tasks because maintaining personal prestige becomes more important than addressing the demands of the situation and contributing to the achievement of tasks. In such a situation movement is away from the group on a vertical plane, which involves withdrawal from some or all the life tasks.

Neurosis, psychosis and psychopathy

When an unrealistic, unattainable goal of personal superiority is set, excuses are needed to explain failure. These excuses are manifest in neurotic symptoms and behaviours, or what Adler called private logic. For example, people who claim to be the best in the class at a particular subject at school may suffer headaches and perform badly in exams because their goal is unrealistic and unattainable. The headaches are a neurotic symptom that prevents their having to admit that they are not as good as they believe. These individuals indulge in self-delusion because they feel inferior, but in fact they are socially equal to all other people. To cure this obsession with self-esteem, personal security and prestige, individuals need to develop their sense of interest and equality, which will free them to concentrate on contributing to the tasks of living. In short, private logic will be replaced by common sense.

Psychotics escape from the logic of social living into a world of hallucinations and delusions that fit their private logic. Both neurotics and psychotics are motivated only by self-interest. Psychopaths openly reject common sense. They too are motivated only by self-interest, but unlike neurotics and psychotics they have no conscience. The psychopath has no need of either neurotic alibis and symptoms or psychotic distorted reality.

When people function adequately they do not develop neuroses. Trouble begins when individuals find themselves unable to cope with the life tasks. Symptoms develop that permit them to explain away their failure with these tasks, and so save face. This can result in their not fulfilling a task (for example, feeling incapable of coping with the task of marriage so breaking off an engagement), retreating from a task (for example, feeling unable to cope with the demands of employment so not seeking a job), or choosing what is known as 'safeguarding behaviour', such as deliberately engaging in one life task to the exclusion of the others in terms of time and energy.

The underlying problem here is a feeling of inferiority. This can be caused by being made to feel inferior during childhood, being spoilt or pampered (see below), being discouraged as a result of neglect, or being criticised and therefore afraid to take risks and make mistakes.

Parenting

Adler uses the terms spoiling and pampering synonymously, but according to Manford Sonstegard, who attended Dreikurs' postgraduate course in child guidance at Northwestern University and then went on to develop his own child guidance centres and parent education, there is a difference (see Dryden, 1991, p. 87): spoiling is giving in to the demands of a child, while pampering is doing things for a child that he or she could do for him- or herself.

In Sonstegard's view, pampering is the most disabling form of parenting. Pampered children seek help from others because they feel unable to complete tasks themselves. As adults they lack confidence because they have insufficient experience of doing things for themselves. They have little or no faith in their own ability to make choices, exert their independence, face hardship and take risks. Parental overprotection has retarded their personal growth. Meanwhile adults who were spoilt as children expect to be served by others and to have their own way. When this does not happen they feel at odds with the world.

The foundations of children's future lifestyle are laid according to their perception of their position in the family, which is determined by the atmosphere and values of the family, as established by the parents. Some children choose goals based on the erroneous ideas or private logic by which they interpret their position in the family constellation. Neither child nor adult is aware of the goals and their underpinning logic.

Competitive family values can produce discouragement in children or cause them to compete against each other. Such children aim for success in differing spheres – each child must be best at something, even if that is being naughty.

Another important factor is the birth order. The eldest child is the centre of attention until the next child is born, when she or he may have to struggle to retain superiority. Younger children may strive to catch up, and if they are successful this may discourage the eldest. Alternatively, if the eldest child is too capable or too far ahead the younger ones may give up. The youngest may be pampered by the older children, who seek to increase their superiority by extending the youngest's baby status. Nonetheless some youngest children become the most successful family members because of their need to strive against their elders.

The consequences in adult life

If people's lifestyle is in harmony with their environment no distressing symptoms or disturbing behaviour emerge. This is the case even when they do not cooperate with others and do not fulfill all the life tasks. However when pampered children become adults they seek rescuers, helpers and advisers to take control of their lives, while spoilt children surround themselves with people who are willing to comply with their demands. Loss of these supporting actors can prompt disturbing behaviour to attract replacement figures. Alternatively individuals may seek therapy for symptoms they regret. They and others may be convinced of their desire to overcome their symptoms, but there is a danger that in the process the symptoms may be aggravated and thus perpetuated. This is because private logic sustains their erroneous and unrealistic life goals.

According to Adler the maintenance of unrealistic and mistaken life goals by private logic leads to a 'yes-but' personality. This means that while individuals recognise their social obligations (yes) they continue with their useless behaviour because of their private logic (but). So life tasks are avoided, and although the symptoms can be cured they will either recur or reappear as other symptoms if the individuals still feel the need to be safeguarded.

How changes can occur

People's perceptions can change if they have an encouraging experience. There may be a revival of social interest, leading to a reduction in their sense of inferiority. Overt behaviour can change without a change in motivation. However behavioural change may be superficial if it is not accompanied by a change in perception and revived social interest. When people change their behaviour they need to gain some insight into the ideas that had caused their problem.

Exchanging unacceptable behaviour for acceptable behaviour cannot be considered to be a change of lifestyle if the people concerned do not feel equal to others. So those who need to be the centre of attention, and who focus on being special and superior rather than on what they could contribute to the fulfilment of tasks and meeting the demands of the situation are only making a superficial gesture by changing their behaviour.

Changes in behaviour can be prompted by encouragement from another person or by a change in circumstances, such as leaving school, passing or failing an exam, getting or losing a job, a change in the attitude of a partner or parent, being left by a partner or losing a parent.

Adlerian therapy

The goals of Adlerian therapy

Adlerian therapy consists of phases, each with its own goal:

- Establishing and maintaining a relationship with the client.
- Discovering the dynamics of the client.
- Giving insight.
- Facilitating reorientation.

Therapy involves reeducating clients to eliminate incorrect perceptions and social values, and to reorientate their motivation. As mistaken ideas and un-realistic goals are a source of discouragement to clients they are helped to gain an insight into these so that change can occur. Once insight is achieved the clients are able to adjust their short- and long-term goals. Hand-in-hand with this goes the readjustment of personal concepts and attitudes. Growing social interest gradually replaces the old feeling of inferiority, and the new sense of equality with other people encourages clients to engage in cooperation rather than strive for personal status.

Criteria for choosing the style of therapy

Adlerian therapy does not have rigid rules on selecting the right approach for individuals. Although clients' choice of therapy will be limited by what is avai-lable, individual choice is respected. Clients who are uneasy about sharing their feelings and beliefs with a group can opt for individual therapy. However, as it is believed that all problems are of a social nature, some therapists prefer to work with a group. For example if a client is a married person the therapist will want the other partner to be aware of the implications of psychotherapy and the changes that may occur as a result of it. Partners can receive couple counselling and individual therapy if needed. Therapists work with the whole family when dealing with children. This is because Adlerian therapy holds that if one child is to change there needs to be change in the family as a whole.

Multiple therapy involves several therapists working with one client. There are several advantages to this approach: the client benefits from the approach of more than one therapist; it provides an ideal training opportunity; discussions and disagreements between the therapists can be educational and encouraging for the client; and clients are treated as equals when explaining their private logic.

Necessary qualities in Adlerian therapists

An Adlerian therapist should:

- Have a feeling of equality with all other people.
- Respect clients without condoning all their behaviours.
- Be able to establish client–counsellor relationship of mutual respect involving honest feedback to the clients and acceptable behaviour by the clients.
- Be warm and accepting of clients, sincerely seeking to understand their lifestyle without being judgemental.
- Be able to act as a social model, but one who is fallible and not afraid to make mistakes.
- Be able to promote social values that help human beings to live together as equals.
- Be able to win people over.

Some clients resist entering an equal partnership because they fear the responsibility. Their relationship with the therapist could be the first they have experienced that is democratic, cooperative and between equals. The therapist should aim to develop a democratic relationship that is free of domination, manipulation or conflict with the client.

Therapeutic style

Therapist and client sit facing each other in chairs of equal height. The aim is to achieve trust and acceptance in the shortest possible time, and this is done by sensitively responding to the client. When the client has introduced his or her presenting problem the therapist starts to gather any information about the client's lifestyle that will aid understanding. Although the approach is directive at this stage it is respectful, because the therapist explains to the client why they have to deviate from the immediate problem and seeks his or her permission to do so. The exploratory stage is conducted as a partnership, with the therapist offering interpretations as the client's story unfolds and thus establishing empathy. The exchange is tailored to the client's particular needs, for example time is allowed for the client to explore his or her feelings, and the client's vocabulary is used when seeking clarification of something he or she has said. The aim is to reveal the private logic underlying the client's lifestyle. The therapist will form hypotheses and tentatively present these to the client for his or her judgement of whether the therapist has made an accurate deduction. Therapist and client must establish mutual goals for the educational phase, but the client has the right to refuse to make changes to him- or herself. The cooperative approach continues into the next phase, which involves task setting and the completion of assignments, the time scale of which varies from client to client. The therapist shows faith in the client by giving him or her total responsibilty for reorientation. Even if a client stays away because he or she feels unready to change, he or she is welcomed back when ready.

The twelve stages of Adlerian therapy

The empathy–relationship stage

This stage is aimed at helping clients to become more cooperative people by learning to cooperate in therapy. Therapists point out any failure to cooperate, although this is done diplomatically and the clients are made aware that the rate of progress will hinge on the degree of cooperation between them. Therapists show understanding, warmth, acceptance and empathy if their clients are distressed, and helpful ideas are sought to improve the situation. Therapists need to 'stand in the shoes' of their clients in psychological terms in order to comprehend their uniqueness. Therapists seek to gain the respect of their clients by showing self-respect, refusing to play games and commenting on behaviour towards themselves that they find unacceptable.

The information stage

During this stage therapists gather information on the presenting problems and their history, their clients' families, early memories, dreams, their clients' level of performances in the three life tasks, and cultural and religious influences. Psychological, intelligence and interest testing may also be conducted. The information gathered will contain distortions, and there will be important omissions.

Any parallel between childhood and present patterns are examined, and the projective material present in early memories and dreams is analysed. The therapists then develop hypotheses about inferiority feelings, lifestyle, private logic and goals.

During the session non-verbal clues are collected – the manner in which the clients enter the room, their body posture, tone of voice and so on – and the therapists may ask about the clients' thoughts on God and ethical and moral beliefs. However the most important question is what would be different for the clients if they did not have their problem. The answer given should reveal the major area of difficulty plus any unrealistic goals.

The clarification stage

Basic beliefs are explored using Socratic questioning, and then the consequences of the clients' beliefs are examined and alternatives explored. The aim is to replace private logic and mistaken notions with common sense, with the therapists tracing their clients' ideas back to childhood to establish how they came to be internalised in the first place. The questioning helps the clients to consider the meaning they give to issues such as love and marriage. It is particularly important for therapists to demonstrate their empathy, and to describe the clients' goals and mistaken ideas in terms that the latter can understand, recognise and own.

Therapists are not required to get everything right at the first attempt, and they even show their fallibility by getting their clients to help summarise their lifestyle. The summary takes the form of 'others are', 'life is' and 'I am'. The therapists explain to the clients how they chose their goals. They do this to help them interpret their lifestyles.

Private logic loses its strength once it has been verbalised, and challenges are made to unrealistic ideas, overgeneralisations and oversimplifications. Therapists use challenging questions such as 'Is this really how people are?' and 'Is it reasonable to expect . . . ?'

Dreams provide clues because, as Adler said, they are the 'factory of the emotions'; in other words they set the mood that instigate people's actions. Remembered dreams reflect the clients' lifestyle; they never contradict it.

The encouragement stage

Clients must find inner courage and therapists assist this by pointing out examples of courage already shown – facing up to the need to go for therapy is a good example. Together they examine steps that the clients could, with a little more courage, take in the way of new behaviour. This is vital because clients come to realise that the disasters they fear are not inevitable if new behaviours are embraced. Each successful effort helps the growth of the clients' courage.

Inferiority feelings are targeted for reduction to manageable levels, and clients are shown that some sense of inferiority can be beneficial in that it can spur improvements. Real self-esteem comes from the conquest of personal difficulties, but clients may firmly believe that esteem stems from other people's praise or approval. Thus small steps are taken one at a time to overcome previously avoided difficulties.

Feelings about the efforts made and the results of them are examined next. One consequence of trying to avoid failure is a decrease in activity. Therapists aim to help their clients to expand the scope and degree of the activity they are willing to undertake. Sometimes a move in the wrong direction is needed as a first step, as then the clients can be commended for showing courage despite making a wrong move, but it is successes that provide the vital springboard for the next stage.

The interpretation and recognition stage

Therapists have to be aware of what their clients have done and are currently doing to fulfil the life tasks. The clients make feeling, thinking and behavioural movements that are a response to their life tasks. The therapists' job is to describe such movements reflectively so that their clients can identify any immediate goals and the final goal. These may include the following:

- Client punctuality: do they arrive at the sessions on time, or late?
- Do the clients talk so much that the therapists can make few responses?
- Do the clients drift off-track during the session?
- Do the clients agree to everything suggested by the therapists but fail to carry them out between sessions?

To raise their self-esteem and punish others for living up to their expectations clients may resort to deprecation and aggression, or adopt a weapon that is likely to hurt others most. It is demonstrated to the clients that such tactics are worthless in the long run and will cause more damage to themselves than to the intended victims. The therapists' challenges will be resisted by their clients because their current way of thinking provides them with certainty about their cherished but childish and egocentric final goals. The reason for their resistance is that the alternative seems to be vulnerability, worthlessness and being a nobody.

Clients' goals are rigid in order to preserve a superior/inferior world view. Clients are therefore helped to see the distinguishing qualities of other people and of events that may have been too subtle to impinge upon the clients' apperception. The aim is to stop the habit of dividing impressions into rigid 'either–or' categories.

If clients' goals are unproductive their emotions will reflect these goals. Such emotions are used as an excuse to avoid resonsibility for useless behaviour. For example, 'I just couldn't help it, she made me so angry.' Therapists have to be precise and sensitive in uncovering the underlying purposes of such emotions because each person's use of emotions is unique. The final goal mirrors clients' expectations of the roles they believe others should play. For example, the final goal is to impress, so others must play the role of impressed people; or the final goal is domination, so others must be dominated/submissive. Clients are helped to recognise this and to understand the effect it has on relationships. The aim is to replace demands on others with self-demands aimed at personal development, thus preparing them to face new situations and the people in them.

The next step is to help the clients to comprehend the driving forces behind their sense of inferiority, their lifestyle and their final goal. This involves exploring early memories, dreams, experiences and family constellations to provide a comprehensive picture. The process requires sensitivity, diplomacy and good timing. The clients should feel encouraged by their success so that they can face the fact that their previous direction in life was wrong. The goal is evaluated so that an assessment can be made of what has been lost and/or gained in its pursuit. The therapists should apply logic, humour, metaphors and so on. There should be vigorous discussion about the meaning of life and the clients' approach to it, plus anything else they could be doing in life.

'Spitting in the Soup' is the term used by Adler to describe the strategy of making a final goal 'taste bad'. So if a client wants to be powerful and frightening, this can be compared to being an unsavoury thug.

The knowing stage

During this stage, rather than therapists interpreting the lifestyles, goals and associated movements of their clients, the clients themselves take on this role and discuss their insights with their therapists. However there is a danger that the clients may decide to end their therapy at this point, confident that they can cope despite not having changed their direction or goals.

The missing experience stage

Childhood memories may cause clients to suffer powerfully negative feelings that can damage both their personal relationships and their perception of their work and role in life. Although they attempt to 'do the right thing' they do not experience affection and/or enjoyment. Therapists should aim either to bring about an emotional breakthrough or to promote change through cognitive interpretation.

To counteract negative family imprints and promote more positive experiences and images, therapists use guided imagery, role play and eidetic imagery exercises (all three of these are discussed in a later section on therapeutic techniques).

The doing differently stage

This is a difficult stage because although clients may be able to address avoided responsibilities and old difficulties by utilising their new courage and insight, they might feel trepidation about taking steps in a new direction. Therapists start by seeing what their clients are willing to attempt, and they encourage them to advance gradually in the direction of social usefulness. The aim is to change their approach to the three life tasks.

The reinforcement stage

During this stage therapists help their clients to abandon the egocentric actions that have provided them with the illusion of self-enhancement and protection. The clients have neglected the needs of others, but now they are encouraged to focus on others, on neccessary tasks and on the demands of the situation. The clients begin to tackle difficulties that have previously been avoided, which brings the added bonus of satisfaction and pride at their brave efforts and positive results. Therapists also provide emotional coaching so that their clients can experience the positive feeings that replace egocentricity.

The community feeling stage

Since their first meeting the therapists have shown their clients their sense of community by accepting their clients as fellow human beings, showing concern for their clients' distress and expressing their desire to help. At first the clients may have had reservations about the therapists' genuineness because their previous experiences made it all seem too good to be true. However as the relationship has developed the clients have accepted and appreciated the sincere care and encouragement being offered. This has boosted their sense of self-worth and enabled them to connect with and cooperate with others, and to contribute to their welfare.

The goal redirection stage

Clients may feel disoriented for a while as they pursue new goals that are socially useful, promote a positive sense of self and attract the esteem of others. The therapists' behaviour is crucial at this point because their clients will observe whether they practise what they preach. It should also be remembered that many clients model themselves on their therapist, be this positive or negative.

Adler believed that people should not aim to become 'normal' or 'average', but should strive to become the ideal human. Again, the therapist will assist in the pursuit of this goal.

The support and launching stage

By this stage the clients will enjoy overcoming difficulties, prefer the unfamiliar, like the unexpected in life, feel equal to others, be eager to develop fully, have a generosity of spirit, want to share their successes, be able to give encouragement to others, function better and feel stronger, and need a self-selected challenge to encourage the development of their self. This challenge could prove to be the 'calling' or 'mission' of their life. The therapists' role is to encourage their clients' search for just such a challenge and to help evaluate those which are considered. The challenge should not be beyond the capability of the client, but nor should it be too easy.

The four therapeutic techniques of Adlerian therapy

Assessment

During the first three stages of therapy a thorough analysis of lifestyle is undertaken. The projective use of early memories is a central technique in this process because, whether true or false, memories contain clients' core beliefs and feelings about themselves and the world. Furthermore they contain echoes of their goals, inferiority feelings, scheme of apperception, courage, sense of community, lifestyle, and level and radius of activity.

The following are also assessed:

- The clients' descriptions of their symptoms and the causes of these, and what the clients would do if they did not have the symptoms.
- How the clients function (now and in the past) in their relationships with their family, friends, schoolmates, work colleagues and lovers.
- The clients' childhood family, its dynamics and constellation, and extended family patterns.
- Health problems, including the use of alcohol, drugs and medication.
- Previous therapy and the clients' attitude towards their present therapist.

The Adlerian client questionnaire is used to collect information, and it also serves to involve the client in the therapy process. It has great value in that it saves time and gives the therapist an enhanced picture because there is a written as well as a verbal testimony.

Socratic questioning

This technique is important because, just as Socrates was the 'midwife' at the birth of new ideas, Adlerian therapists play midwife to the birth of a new approach to life by their clients. Thus the therapists' role is that of a cothinker, not a superior expert.

Socratic questioning has the following characteristics:

- It allows clients to gain insight through a series of questions.
- Its style is gentle, respectful and diplomatic.
- It is a partnership of equals.
- In the early stages it involves gathering information, clarifying meaning and exploring feelings.
- In the middle stages, leading questions expose deeper feelings, private logic and unconscious goals.
- The personal and social consequences of these, both long and short term, are uncovered.
- It generates and evaluates new options.
- In the later stages of therapy it enables the likely impact of a new direction to be evaluated.
- It places responsibility for decisions and conclusions on the client.

Guided and eidetic imagery

Eidetic images are vivid but unreal, especially those remembered from childhood. The therapeutic process brings new feelings to clients, and they may need further work to uncover or change these feelings. Guided eidetic imagery helps clients to break through their emotional blocks. It is used to bring to the surface vivid symbolic images of people and situations that evoke powerful emotions. Clients may have negative images and feelings about childhood family members, and in the middle stage of therapy this technique can be used to heal resentment, guilt and fear.

Clients can thus acquire vivid images of themselves in a happier future even if they are resisting behavioural changes despite knowing that the changes would be beneficial.

Role playing

Clients may have missed out on certain essential experiences, such the approval of parents. Role play addresses this deficiency. It is carried out in the middle stages of therapy in a group setting, which also provides the opportunity to rehearse new behaviours under the supervision of the therapist. The other members of the group play the parts of family members to allow the client to undergo a healing experience, with the added bonus that the rest of the group are able to expand their sense of community by helping the personal growth of their comember. The therapist offers guidance and feedback.

The six principles of Adlerian psychology

1. *Unity of the individual*: human beings are not internally divided or split by conflicting forces; their feelings, thoughts and behaviour are consistent with their lifestyle.

2. *Goal orientation*: human beings are teleological or goal driven; they strive for significance, superiority and success. This is a central personality dynamic that has its origins in the forward movement and growth of life itself. Mentally healthy people aim for superiority over difficulties. Mentally disordered individuals struggle for superiority over others. Childhood inferiority feelings lead to the setting of a compensatory goal, the height of the goal being determined by the intensity of the inferiority feeling.

3. *Uniqueness and self-determination*: the goal is born out of the creative power and thoughts of the individual, and may be influenced by hereditary and cultural factors.

4. *Social context*: human beings are part of a number of social systems: a family, various communities, a nation, a culture, humanity and creation in general. From these they obtain their life tasks: community work and love. However the family, which is the first social system, is likely to provide the prototype of their world view.

5. *Sense of community*: people have the ability to learn to live harmoniously with the rest of society and to develop a sense of interconnectedness and interdependence with the rest of creation. People's personal sense of security depends on a sense of belonging and of being part of the flow of social evolution.

6. *Mental health*: this depends on social usefulness and contribution. The characteristics of mental ill-health are a feeling of deep inferiority, highly uncooperative goals of personal superiority and an underdeveloped sense of community. Therapy aims to promote a sense of equality, bring an end to egocentric self-protection, self-indulgence and self-enhancement, instil a sense of community and foster a desire to contribute to society.

Conclusion

Although Adlerian therapists use a variety of practices their approach is based on a holistic socioteleological view of human beings, with Adler's personality theory enabling a complete understanding of all human behaviour. Much of Adler's individual psychology has been absorbed into other counselling approaches, and it is regarded as being of value to the study of human behaviour.

In addition to the therapeutic methods of Adler and Dreikurs, any other technique that is deemed helpful may be utilised by current practitioners. As well as having insight and skills, Adlerians must have social interests and should use their skills to establish an ideal community. This approach gives counsellors a great deal of insight, but using such insight and understanding of people is very demanding. Many people, including counsellors, have spent their formative years in families where power is used openly, controlling by anger or more subtly by manipulation. Counsellors have to overcome this and equip themselves to work with clients in an equal and cooperative relationship.

Interestingly a lot of clients cannot accept the idea that they are responsible for their own behaviour, and they may well gain insights from their therapy but have no intention of changing. The long-term benefits of such insights may not be noted if the therapy outcomes are reviewed after too short a time. It is sometimes the case that changes occur some years after a lifestyle assessment has been carried out. Although it is always worthwhile helping clients to gain insight, it is certainly not appropriate to attempt to force them to change by whatever method.

Using the Adlerian method in one-to-one situations is more limited in value than observing them in groups. Clients can achieve much by trying out new behaviours in a safe group, and gain a lot from experiencing what it is like to be an equal member of a group whose shared aim is mutual growth.

◼ ꙮ 3 Carl Jung

Carl Jung was born in 1875. He was the son of a Protestant clergyman and therefore grew up in an explicitly Christian environment. His childhood was difficult in that he experienced considerable illness and deprivation. He had strong leanings towards the German idealist and romantic tradition. He studied medicine but it was psychiatry that drew his interest – he wrote a dissertation on a medium and her dissociated states of consciousness. He also read widely in philosophy, language and theology. After receiving a medical degree from Basle University in 1900 he worked at the Burghölzli mental hospital in Zurich. He married in 1903, and in 1909 decided to work in general practice and devote more time to writing. By the time he met Freud in 1907 and joined the Vienna Psychoanalytic Circle he had already formulated a theory of the mind that was distinct from Freud's. He broke with Freud seven years later to pursue his own approach to psychoanalysis, and continued with his writing and practice until he died in 1961. He travelled widely, especially in Africa and Asia, to study different cultures.

Jung's disagreements with Freud

Jung devoted chapters of his autobiography, *Memories, Dreams, Reflections* (1971), to Freud. In it he tells how he was at first overawed by Freud because until then he had not met anyone who could compare with him. Jung was impressed by Freud's sexual theory but had some reservations about it. On a number of occasions he tried to discuss these with Freud, but the latter dismissed his views on the ground that he lacked experience – Jung himself admitted that this was so.

Jung was unable to decide whether Freud's strong emphasis on sexuality was connected with his subjective prejudices, or whether it was based on verifiable experiences. He also found Freud's thoughts on the spirit very questionable. Whenever an expression of intellectual spirituality came to light in a person or work of art, Freud attributed it to repressed sexuality. Jung argued that this meant that culture was nothing but a farce, to which Freud replied 'so it is, and that is just a curse of fate against which we are powerless to contend' (Jung, 1971, p. 173). Jung wrote that the extent of Freud's emotional involvement with sexual theory was astonishing, and that when he spoke of it his tone became urgent, almost anxious. At such times his normal critical and sceptical manner vanished and a strange expression came over face. He asked Jung never to abandon the sexual theory because it was the most essential thing of all. He said 'we must make a dogma of it, an unshakeable bulwark . . . against the black tide of . . . occultism' (ibid.). Jung wrote that he was alarmed by this because a dogma is an indisputable doctrine that is instituted only when the aim is to suppress doubts once and for all. Therefore it has nothing to do with scientific judgement, merely with a personal drive for power. According to Jung, this struck at the heart of their friendship because he could never accept such an attitude. Freud's definition of occultism appeared to include almost all that philosophy, religion, and the developing science of parapsychology had revealed about the psyche.

Jung regarded the sexual theory as an occult in itself. By this he meant that it was just as unproven as any other speculative view. Any scientific truth was just a hypothesis, and although adequate for the moment it might be disproved and therefore could not be preserved as an article of faith for all time. He believed that he was witnessing the eruption of unconscious religious elements in Freud, against which the latter wanted to erect barriers (see also Chapter 11 of this book and Viktor Frankl's concept of *religio*). Jung reasoned that Freud's dogma was a replacement for a jealous God whom he had lost. For Freud the new numen was scientifically irreproachable and free from religious taint. However in essence the psychological qualities of the two incommensurable opposites – Yahweh (Jehova) and sexuality – remained the same. Freud was teaching that sexuality included spirituality, but the terminology he used was too narrow to express the idea. Jung felt that there was nothing to be done about Freud's one-sidedness and that he was a tragic figure, 'a man in the grip of his daimon' (ibid., p. 176).

Jung's approach

For Jung, mental health is characterised by wholeness and unity, and the development of personality is aimed at integration. Jung's theories on psycho-therapy arose from three sources: his student essays, his association experiments and his work on schizophrenia (or dementia praecox as it was called then). Jung called his way of working 'analytical psychology' to differentiate it from Freud's psychoanalysis. To avoid confusion with G. F. Stout's term 'analytic psychology' (as distinct from analytical psychology), Jung's psychology has recently been renamed 'complex psychology'. The term analytical psychology is better known however, and is still in use.

Theoretical assumptions

The *self* is an organismic concept and it provides the matrix for a capacity for psyche that may become available for conscious thought, that is, the mind. The self is the whole individual, the full potential of the individual, bringing together all sides, conscious and unconscious, and opposites.

The psyche consists of the mind, the soul, the spirit and the psychological state of the individual. It is linked to the central nervous system, which is proactive and not merely reactive. It has a relatively limited and stereotyped repertoire of perceptive, cognitive and conative behaviours, and the psyche that results from this, with its conscious and unconscious potential, is similarly stereotyped. The extent to which individuals can relate to these stereotypes determines the extent to which they are able to individuate (to have a certain amount of choice in relation to internal and external necessity, while not rigidly identifying with or denying either). Conation is the aspect of mental processes or behaviour directed towards action or change. It includes desire, impulse, volition and striving.

Archetypes

Jung related stereotyped processes or archetypes to imagery instead of 'object' or interpersonal relations. These archetypes are universal symbols, inherited patterns of the psyche, derived from instincts. Themes from ancient civilisations, folklore, myths and legends and art form the collective unconscious. They are personified in such images as the divine child and the wise old man. Jung found similarities between the visions experienced by schizophrenics and those of mythology but gave no real explanation of how these images matched.

Jung's concept of synchronicity recognises the existence of acausal connections between people, places and world events. He wrote that archetypes are 'Motifs analogous to or identical with those of mythology . . . found everywhere and at all times in Greek, Egyptian and ancient Mexican myths and in dreams of modern individuals ignorant of such traditions' (Storr, 1998, p. 65). This is no coincidence because archetypes derive from the collective experience of humankind as a whole. Examples include the following:

- The mother stands for fertility, wisdom, protection, sin, lust and repression.
- The good mother represents the capacity for renewal.
- The bad mother represents the risk of the loss of differentiation.
- The father stands for the spirit, the devil, sin, lust and repression.
- The self is related to the child archetype, the whole individual, bringing together all sides and opposites, the unconscious as well as the conscious.
- The shadow is the unknown side of the self. It is dark, negative and may be repressed or denied. It is the Hyde in Jekyll and Hyde. It is hidden in the unconscious and is the unacceptable part of ourselves – it is those things we cannot be allowed to do, or do not want to accept that we have urges to do, such as commit murder. It is the primitive, uncivilised, antisocial and uncontrolled part of us that was expressed in childhood until our parents and society taught us that it was unacceptable. It lies dormant and unfulfilled in our psyche and is a potential source of trouble. However it does have the potential to bring light.
- Anima is the woman within a man. It is the feminine personality in the unconscious of a man. It can also be the soul, or true inner sense.
- Animus is the man within a woman. It is the masculine personality in the unconscious of a woman.

In Jung's view, if we are to be whole we have to accept and integrate the anima and animus. He developed this idea from his study of mythology, fairytales and dreams in which women experience their souls as masculine and men experience their souls as feminine. Anima and animus come into play in our unconscious when the shadow elements are accepted and integrated into the opposite sex and other issues have come forward. Figures of the opposite sex, both in dreams and as outer world projections, represent a collective archetype relationship that exists between and beyond individual constraints. The anima and animus are functional to our relationship with the collective unconscious.

The concept of archetype is not limited to processes that are primitive and instinctual. It also relates to the ways in which the experiences of the evolution of the sense of self and its consciousness are represented. This means that Jungian therapists do not regard clients' material as purely defensive, the best compromise between the repression of forbidden desire and its fulfilment. Rather it is the best available expression of the present state of the self and of its desires and ambitions.

Jung and the Oedipus complex

In addition to the Freudian view that the Oedipus complex is the desire to have sexual intercourse with one's natural mother, with all the paranoid anxieties that attend such a forbidden desire, Jungian theory holds that it expresses a desire (and fear) to penetrate the matrix of unconsciousness that is personified by the mother in order to gain an identity. This is attended by the risk of madness (mutilation) and the destruction of consciousness, which is represented by the killing of the father. Jung said that archetypal figures erupt into consciousness as soon as such pathology develops. One such archetype is the 'hero'.

The hero Oedipus is the capacity for emerging and beleaguered consciousness. At Colonnus, Oedipus exercised his choice of when and where to die, and for what purpose. In this respect he represents the individual's ablty to individuate, and to make choices relating to inner and outer reality – to be a mana personality. 'The mana personality personifies the capacity to access freely the frightening and powerful experiences of the unconscious. These are conceived of as "other worlds" with an other-worldly authority.'

Coniuncto Oppositorum is the coming together of disparate elements of the self to achieve a full sense of self. In his later work Jung studied alchemy to gain insights into the 'primal scene' and the Oedipus complex. Parental intercourse personifies the bringing together of conflicting facets of the self, that are manifested in the Oedipus conflict, in a generative and creative way. It is probable that Jung chose to express this through imagery rather than objects from the real world because of the difficulties in his own parents' marriage. This assembling of the different elements of the self is often expressed in what Jung called 'mandala forms', which are symmetrical, harmonious, geometrical designs that represent the wholeness of the self. According to Jung, the self is the God within, or 'a hypothetical point between conscious and unconscious' (quoted in Storr, 1998, p. 19).

Dreams

Dreams are a manifestation of the unconscious mind; in other words they link the conscious and the unconscious parts of the psyche. They contain meaningful information that guides dreamers towards that which might fulfil and nourish them. Dreams are a self-regulating or compensatory mode of communication from the unconscious. They are expressions of unrealised, neglected or repressed facets of a person's true self, and they can be a warning of movement away from the dreamer's proper path.

Jung saw dreams as a medium for purifying and transforming psychic energy, an idea he developed from his study of alchemy. In his view they promote the growth and development of individuals, as well as collectives of individuals when information useful to the whole of humanity is revealed. Jung never imposed interpretation on patients because he believed that it was more important for dreamers to try to understand their own dreams than for the analyst to do it for them. Ideally interpretation should be by mutual reflection and agreement.

The first step towards understanding a dream is to establish its context and unravel the network of relationships it has with the dreamer and his or her life in order to reveal the significance of the images it presents. Each symbol or image is considered in turn, until its meaning for the dreamer is pinpointed as closely as possible.

Jungians do not follow a fixed method of interpretation because every dream is a direct expression of the dreamer's unconscious. Clients record their dreams and illustrate them with pictures and/or wax models. Artistic ability is not important because expressions of the unconscious are frequently very primitive, so that too great an effort to fit them into aesthetic concepts will diminish their power. Working like this helps clients to understand the unconscious and make more real the fantasies that activate them. It also releases tension and lifts their mood. Thus dreams become a source of creative power and not just of information.

In free association interpretation a chain of random associations is followed, no matter where this leads. This method uncovers complexes, but not always those associated with the dream because it usually leads away from the dream.

A series of dreams is better than one when it comes to interpretation because the theme being presented by the unconscious becomes more clear, important images are underlined by repetition and mistakes in interpretation can be corrected by the next dream.

In objective interpretation the dream is linked to events in the environment and people appearing in the dream are taken as real. The relationship between the dreamer and the people in the dream and their potential influence on the dreamer are analysed.

In subjective interpretation, dream figures represent aspects of the dreamer's personality. The subjective aspect becomes more important in the later stages of analysis when personal problems have been identified.

Collective dreams are vivid and have astonishing, often incomprehensible symbols. They have more than personal significance and their relationship to the dreamer is hard to work out. Mythological and historical analogies are used to understand them and to find out what such symbols meant to the people of past times. Jung considered that unconsciously we think like our distant ancestors, and it is important to understand this as it opens up all sorts of possibilities and deepens our experience. While there is no clear boundary between personal and collective dreams, the latter present archetypes from the collective unconscious and are significant not just to the dreamer but to others as well, and the former deal with facets of the dreamer's own life, such as friends, family and daily events. Primitive peoples differentiate between the two and call them 'little' and 'big' dreams, the collective dream being highly valued and used to access knowledge that is not readily available. In some research on the Inuit people there is told of a tribe member's dream about a place with food and shelter. This person led the rest of the tribe over the ice and eventually found the place seen in the dream. Some had turned back before reaching the spot and had died of hunger – the dream had foretold this too.

In antiquity collective dreams were regarded as a prophecy or warning from God. Pharaoh's dream and its interpretation by Joseph is an excellent Biblical example of this. Nowadays dreams are often thought to have physical causes, such as eating a large meal before going to bed. However there is little if any connection between stimulus and dream form. Dreams may reflect the day's events but they usually add or take away something, and they tend to be compensatory.

Jung wrote of a young man whose excellent relationship with his father prevented him from developing his own personality. He then had a dream in which his father was drunk and disorderly, and this was interpreted as his unconscious drawing attention to the fact that his idealistic view of his father was preventing him from maturing into manhood. This can work the other way too, so if we have a low opinion of someone we may have a dream that puts him or her in a better light. Likewise hidden conflicts can come to light by showing an unknown side of the dreamer, for example the ascetic dreams of sexual activity and the gentle person dreams about violence. Conversely in hidden wishes dreams the hungry person dreams of a feast and the thirsty person dreams of a cool drink.

Time and space are the creations of the conscious and are relative. The unconscious does not work according to such concepts so dreams can be prospective or forward looking. For example sleeping people may dream they have got up and dressed when in fact they have slept through the alarm. A stranger example is when someone dreams of something down to the last detail without actually having seen it, but when they do see it the dream proves to be correct, as was the case with the Inuit example. The most striking dreams express a desire by the unconscious to change a conscious attitude. These can be so effective that they change the dreamer without further ado. Other examples of dream types are:

- Warnings of danger: Jung gives the example of a man who dreamt he was climbing a mountain and stepped off into space. He found the dream amusing and chose to ignore it – it later came true.
- Symbolic dreams of death include the mystic 'dying to life' (abandoning worldly matter), the year dying and the lover dying of love.
- Dreams as memories: such dreams recall forgotten experiences, things seen, heard or read.
- Dreaming what others dream: this happens to members of the same family, especially identical twins and husband and wife, and to close friends.

- Sexual symbols: a number of mythical sexual symbols also appear in dreams, for example the horse's hoof, the bull and the ass.

Psychological types

Jung's observations of the differences in temperament and personality between Freud and Adler, and between himself and the other two, led to his work on psychological types. He classified people as extravert or introvert according to their attitude towards life: extraverts incline towards the external world of other human beings and their environment; introverts are the opposite, that is, they are oriented towards their inner world.

Four functions operate the psyche, and these are grouped into two pairs of opposites:

- Thinking–feeling: these are rational because they evaluate experience.
- Intuition–sensation: these are irrational because neither evaluates but depends on perception.

That is, sensation tells you something exists and intuition tells you where it has come from or is going; thinking tells you what it is and feeling tells you whether it is good or not.

The following are Jung's eight psychological types:

- Extrovert thinking: this group includes scientists, and economists, who direct themselves and everyone else by fixed principles and rules. Their focus is on order, reality and material facts.
- Introvert thinking: these are philosophers. They pose questions and want to understand their own being. They ponder their own ideas and neglect the world.
- Extrovert feeling: these are people in public entertainment, such as film and pop stars. They are conventional and adjusted to their time and milieu. They care about personal and social success. They adjust to fashions and are changeable.
- Introvert feeling: this group includes musicians, monks and nuns. Such people are inaccessible, but seem to be harmonious and self-sufficient.
- Extrovert sensation: these include builders and speculators. They are hard-headed, practical and accept the world as it is. The emphasis is on external facts. They are affable and enjoy life. However they have a sensuality that can lead to compulsions, addictions and perversions.
- Introvert sensation: these are the aesthetes and connoisseurs. They are often bemused and unassuming. They live for their senses and are totally absorbed in their own inner sensations.
- Extrovert intuition: this group includes adventurers and PR people. Their unconscious insight keeps them on the trail of future novelty. They can be charismatic leaders or troubleshooters, but they are not suited to long-term stability because of their ruthless adventuring.
- Introvert intuition: these are mystics and poets and follow their inner vision. They are daydreamers and may be clairvoyant. They see themselves as mis-understood geniuses who are wrestling with a unique esoteric experience.

This typology does not portray the full complexity of human beings because each individual is a unique mixture of types. Furthermore individuals can change type at the different stages of life. Nevertheless Jung's psychological types are useful in showing how people respond to archetypal figures. When the different types intermarry they unconsciously rely on the other to take care of his or her inferior function (see Chapter 7).

The psychological types are part of a bigger dynamic of psychic energy involving four archetypal figures. These figures operate in pairs, one of which is conscious and is compensated by its unconscious counterpart.

The first pair: ego and shadow

In his student days Jung dreamt he was out in a foggy night and was struggling to protect his lamp from the wind. A gigantic black shadow began to follow him; it was his own shadow cast by his light. The light and shadow were his Number One and Number Two personalities. Later he identified these as the related archetypal figures, the ego and the shadow. The ego is the fragile, precious light of consciousness, and it must be guarded and cultivated. One of the first steps in Jungian analysis is to make the client aware of the ego–shadow relationship. The shadow is always of the same sex. The ego is a person's sense of purpose and identity. When it is healthy it organises and balances the conscious and unconscious. If the ego is weak the person is left 'in the dark', and faces the prospect of being drowned by chaotic unconscious images. According to Jung the shadow is our dark side and is characterised by inferior and uncivilised animal qualities that the ego wants to conceal from others. He believed that the shadow is not wholly bad, merely primitive and unadapted. Its value lies in its ability to vitalise life if we can but face it. The ego is the centre of consciousness but must not be confused with the self, which is the final goal of the individuation process, being the wholeness of the personality. If the ego identifies with the self it becomes god-like and dangerous. An inflated ego casts its irrational shadow onto others and regards them as evil. Clients face a crisis if they encounter the shadow in the early stages of analysis, and the more they retreat from shadow projections the more the ego is threatened.

The psyche also has a collective shadow and this is structured in the same way as the individual one. It forms the *zeitgeist* or spirit of the age.

The second pair: the persona and the soul-image

The persona is that part of the ego which negotiates with the outer world on behalf of the ego. Persona comes from the Latin word for 'theatre mask'. It is shaped by culture, social class, nationality and job. We use assume different personas to suit different contexts, but have a general persona based on our superior functional type – thinking – simply because it is easiest for us. A well-adapted persona is vital to psychic health and equilibrium because it makes social exchange possible. Dysfunctional individuals identify totally with the persona, and are nothing but the role they play. Those with a 'perfect persona' have a rigid, alienated, one-sided personality. They are afraid of removing the mask and finding nothing real behind it. Neurosis may arise from getting the wrong answers to life, enjoying empty success and having a too narrow spiritual horizon. Neurosis can be overcome by developing a more spacious personality.

The soul-image is the unconscious side of the persona. The male and female names for the soul are animus and anima. The soul-image is always represented by the person's opposite gender. The soul-image is an archetype that can represent the whole of the unconscious, and is inherited, collective and ageless. It is modified by knowledge of the opposite sex, particularly a parent. Soul-images appear in myths, fantasies and dreams and can be projected to present a distorted impression of the opposite sex.

The conscious persona is paired with the unconscious soul-image. The persona is based on the dominant attitude, for example extrovert, and superior function, for example feeling. The unconscious soul-image counterpart is based on the opposite attitude and inferior function. So in addition to an extravert/introvert 'switch' there is the following:

- Thinking persona = feeling soul-image.
- Intuitive persona = sensation soul-image.
- Feeling persona = thinking soul-image.
- Sensation persona = intuitive soul-image.

The overdeveloped thinking person can experience unbalanced moods and upsets. The feeling-type boy may develop thinking characteristics under the influence of a thinking-type parent. This will cause crisis and unhappiness in later life. Hysteria is caused by repressed feeling. Repressed feeling results in compulsions, obsessions and phobias. Mental and physical health require development of the neglected type as all four types are needed to develop a rounded personality.

In Western societies the emotional world is sacrificed to the needs of the intellect. So in the same way that we are inclined towards extravertism or introvertism, we are biased in favour of thinking over feeling, and sensation (sight, hearing, touch, taste and so on) over intuition (information from the unconscious that is independent of sensation).

The process of individuation

According to Jung the European ego-consciousness is inclined to swallow up the unconscious or, if this proves impossible, to suppress it. However the unconscious cannot be swallowed, and it is dangerous to suppress it because the unconscious is life and it turns against us if suppressed, as happens in neurosis. The conscious and unconscious cannot make a whole when one of them is suppressed or injured by the other. Both are aspects of life. Here we have an important difference between Jung and Freud: the latter saw the repressed contents of the unconscious as a threat, while Jung saw them as a partner to the conscious. In Jung's view, if they must contend, let it be at least a fair fight with equal rights on both sides. The conscious should defend its reason and protect itself, and the chaotic life of the unconscious should be given the chance of having its way too, or as much as we can stand. It means open conflict and open collaboration at the same time, and that is the way human life should be. Jung described it as an old game of hammer and anvil: between them the patient iron is forged into an indestructible whole, an 'individual.' Again it is interesting to compare this essentially positive and optimistic view of the psyche with Freud's more negative and pessimistic, even fearful, view of it. This, then, is what is meant by the individuation process. It is a process or course of development arising out of the conflict between the two fundamental psychic facts.

In his *Collected Works* (1953) Jung writes: 'The natural process of individuation brings a consciousness, which unites and is common to all mankind.' Individuation is an inner journey upon which we embark in the second part of our lives. During the first part of life we are concerned with freeing ourselves from parental influence and establishing ourselves as adults through work, marriage/partnering and parenting. Once this is fulfilled, in the second part of life we work to reach a synthesis between the conscious and the unconscious by means of inner contemplation.

Religion and the individuation process

After reading this section, you may wish to turn to the section in Chapter 11 on Viktor Frankl's concept of *religio*.

Jung's study of the archetypes of the collective unconscious led him to a number of conclusions, one of which was that human beings have what he described as 'a natural religious function'. Furthermore he contended that proper expression of this is vital to our psychic health and stability. It is worth noting how this contrasts with the view of so many in the modern world who regard religion as a childish elusion. However in Jung's view the archetypes of the unconscious can be empirically shown to be the equivalents of religious dogmas. Moreover they correspond to all the known religious ideas. This does not mean that the unconscious produces religious dogmas, rather they are the product of conscious thought working on unconscious raw material.

In his *Psychology and Religion* Jung defined religion as:

> a peculiar attitude of mind which could be formulated in accordance with the original use of the word *religio*, which means a careful consideration and observation of certain dynamic factors, that are conceived as 'powers': spirits, daemons, gods, laws, ideals, or whatever name man has given to such factors in his world as he has found powerful, dangerous, or helpful enough to be taken into careful consideration, or grand, beautiful and meaningful enough to be devoutly worshipped and loved (Storr, 1998, pp. 239–40).

It is the dynamism of human religious function that makes it dangerous to ignore. The world and its history are awash with evidence of its work: cathedrals, crusades, witch hunts, persecutions and huge tombs. In the twentieth century a lot of this energy was diverted into communism, fascism, cults and superstition.

With degrees of varying success, organised religion has always tried to provide satisfying forms for deep human needs that find dangerous or banal expression, and to give expression to what Jung described as 'the living process of the unconscious in the form of the drama of repentence, sacrifice and redemption' (Fordham, 1991, p. 72). Dogma, creed and ritual are crystalised forms of the original religious experience, having been refined and developed for centuries into the form they now take. Thus channels are available for the controlling of supernatural influences that are arbitrary and unruly. So instead of being seized by the collective unconscious, people are protected by a living church from the full force of a potentially devastating experience. The ritual in which they take part expresses it sufficiently to 'purge' by its reflection of that collective unconscious.

The most vital and overwhelming image that can be experienced by humankind is the archetypal God-image. Expression of this image depends on the receiving consciousness. In the highest religions it is infinitely refined and developed. In primitive cults it is archaic and simple. A weak consciousness is in danger of being totally destroyed by it, so the image results in not religious development but in some sort of pathological manifestation, even insanity. Examples include the senile person who asks everyone if they been saved, or a woman who thinks she is going to repeat the virgin birth.

The above examples must not be taken as a devaluation of true religious experiences such as those of the mystic. Jung did not belittle religious experience but demonstrated the existence of the religious function in individuals and helped its understanding by reason as well as feeling (ibid.). In his words, 'it is the prime task of all [adult] education to convey the archetype of the God-image, or its emanations and effects, to the conscious mind' (ibid.).

Christian education has tried to do this, but Western attitudes emphasise the object and thus fix the ideal, Jesus Christ, in its outward aspect, thus robbing it of its mysterious relation to the inner man. Such an approach projects onto a remote figure of God everything that is good; and by definition everything that is bad is attributed to the Devil. This takes away the value and meaning of the psyche and leads to the overvaluing of the conscious and the deification of abstractions such as the state. Another problem is the overelaboration of ritual and creed, which have become so refined that they can no longer express the psychic state of ordinary people. In short, religion has been reduced to formalities and externals.

Individuals need to experience the God-image within themselves, and to feel its correspondence with the forms their religion gives it. According to Jung, if this fails to happen a split takes place in their nature, and although they may be outwardly civilised they are actually barbarian and ruled by an archaic god. Furthermore the great events of the world, as planned and executed by humanity, breathe the spirit not of Christianity but of unadorned paganism. This problem originates in a psychic condition that is untouched by Christianity and so remains archaic. In Jung's view Christian civilisation is hollow and but a veneer – people's souls are out of key with their external beliefs. The form is there without substance – image, word, Church and Bible – but never inside where the archaic gods still reign, that is, the pagan unconscious. Inner correspondence with the outer God-image has failed to develop because there is a lack of psychological culture, leaving the inner correspondence trapped in heathenism. Very few have experienced the divine image as the innermost possession of their souls, and paganism in its now threadbare disguise is swamping the world of so-called Christian culture.

Jung believed that dreams could show agnostics that they really are believers, if only they would listen. Many neurotics would be cured if they returned to the Church where they belonged, or experienced a conversion. However he warned that this cannot be imposed; it must come from individuals' inner need, and their awareness and comprehension of that need. Jung also gave thought to the question of what solution existed for those unable to find an answer in Christianity. He found the answer through his work with patients, and borrowed the term 'individuation' to describe it. He found that many of those who completed therapy continued to seek a goal: they embarked on a quest for wholeness that required the forging of a link between the conscious and the unconscious parts of the psyche. This could also be formulated as finding the God within, or experiencing the full archetype of the self.

Being whole involves reconciliation with those aspects of the personality that have not been taken into account. Jung said that these are sometimes inferior because some people do not live up to their inherent possibilities. The intellect must not be developed at the cost of repressing the unconscious. However people cannot exist in an unconscious state.

Jung and neurosis

Neurosis is a psychic disturbance that disrupts the life and health of those afflicted. It is caused by the conflict of two tendencies, one of which is expressed consciously and the other is a complex rupture from consciousness that leads an unconscious and independent existence of its own. Some points to note about this complex are:

- It may or may not have been previously conscious.
- The neurotic does not know that it exists.
- It may erupt unexpectedly into consciousness.
- It may attract energy to itself so that less is available for conscious and directed activity.

Neurosis manifests itself in, among other things, lapses of memory or speech, misunderstanding things we read or hear, misunderstanding the motives of others, and thinking we have done or not done something when this is not actually the case. More extreme examples include physical symptoms without actual physical causes, such as hysterical paralysis, loss of memory, deafness and blindness. Many illnesses that defy explanation have neurotic origins and disappear when the sufferer confesses some dark and forgotten secret, which brings us to an issue of utmost importance in analytical therapy: confession.

Concealment and confession

For Jung the start of all analytical treatment of the soul is with its prototype, the confessional. Although the two have no causal connection they grow from a common, irrational psychic root. Once humanity had invented the concept of sin, humans had to resort to psychic concealment, or to put it in analytical terms, repression. According to Jung, concealment alienates individuals from the community. Such concealment is laden with guilt irrespective of whether or not there is an amoral issue at stake. One form of concealment that can cause serious damage but is practised as a virtue is the concealment of emotions. There are two points here. First, some secrets are essential to our development as individuals – they prevent us from being dissolved into the unconscious of community life. Second, if carried out properly the control of emotion is both necessary and desirable. However self-restraint as a private virtue causes the bad moods and irritability of the overvirtuous. It causes an air of superiority, coldness where there should be warmth, or at best a tepid harmony. Self-restraint should be practised for social and religious ends, and not because of fear or in the interest of personal aggrandisement.

The constructive elements of neuroses

Jung always looked for the constructive elements that can be found in neuroses. He worked on the basis that to look only for infant traumas could be destructive rather than healing as unconscious forces working towards the cure of neuroses could be overlooked or even destroyed. Older people with neuroses need a different approach from that used with the young, particularly in the case of those whose life has been successful until the neurosis develops. There is also a category of middle-aged people who are neurotic but not in the ordinary way – they find life empty and lacking in meaning. This sort of neurosis cannot be defined in clinical terms and can reasonably be said to be symptomatic of the times in which the sufferers live. A third of Jung's patients belonged to this category, so not surprisingly his unique contribution to psychotherapy arose from his work with these patients.

All neuroses are an attempt to compensate for a one-sided attitude to life and the neglect or repression of part of the personality. Thus they are more than the effects of infantile sexuality and the desire for power – they are trying to produce a new synthesis of life, but unsuccessfully (hence the need for therapy).

Jung's contribution to psychotherapy

Jung was adamant that neurosis should not be seen as completely negative as clues to new possibilities for development can be discovered within it. Sexuality and self-assertion are not the only important human drives, and in the second half of life the cultural or spiritual drive is more important. The roots of neurosis can be found in the present as well as the past. The past is important only insofar as it influences the present and causes the libido to fail to overcome an obstacle and thus take the sufferer to a new stage of development. The importance of these points is that when rational explanations have failed and conscious attempts at adjustment have been unsuccessful, the only hope is to tap into the energy of the unconscious to release new sources of life.

The collective unconscious is the true basis of the human psyche. It is not individual but common to all humans as the ancestral heritage of possibilities of representation, and archetypes manifest themselves in visions and dreams to help us to solve problems. The collective unconscious is a reservoir of human experiences and situations for the psyche to draw upon.

Schools of Jungian therapy

There are three schools of Jungian therapy:

- The classical school: this adheres closely to Jung's original methodology. It's main centres are in Switzerland, New York, Los Angeles, Italy and Israel.
- London: in London there is the Association of Jungian Analysts, the Independent Group and the Society of Analytical Psychology. The latter represents the mainstream London view. The society's main thrust has been to put right the absence of a developmental scheme in Jung's original work, to correct the absence of consistent consideration of the child and to remedy the failure to consider the impact of the mother, significant others and the environment upon the child.
- The American group emphasises cultural and mythological phenomena of the mind, avoiding any comprehension of archetypal processes in a way that could be interpreted as suggesting that the 'idea' or *noumenon* can be known as such or related to in what it would regard as any dubiously related developments.

The work of Michael Fordham in London

Fordham was a child psychiatrist working with psychoanalysts such as Winnicott. He addressed developmental issues upon which Jung had done little work, and drew upon Jung's concept of archetypes and Klein's view of innate unconscious ideas. He was largely responsible for bridging the gap between analytical psychology and psychoanalysis, and between innate factors or archetypes and environmental influences, both of which had seemed impossible.

Deintegration

Fordham identified the original and integrated state (the primary integrate) as being the primary self. The primary self holds the archetypal structures or innate schemata with which the self and the environment is explored. Out of this the demands of both internal and external experience can be satisfied. The archetypes or schemata emerge in infancy and become manifest in what Fordham called deintegration.

Deintegration is the process through which archetypes or schemata in infancy 'search' for and elicit the appropriate response from the environment. One example of this is the appeal to be held and fed. If deintegration is successful individuals can make sense of an internal state, and if there is a succession of similar experiences they can modify the archetypal expectation to permit (1) the establishment of their own identity in relation to their experiences, and (2) the progressive acceptance and recognition of experiences that do not fit the archetypal expectation. In other words the person can learn from disagreeable experiences and the natural archetypal responses to them can be modified. For example rage can become an appropriate assertion.

If deintegration is unsuccessful and there is no appropriate response from the environment individuals are unable to make sense of themselves. They are burdened with powerfully fragmenting emotions caused by frustration. That is, there gradually emerges a sense of discrepancy between the ideal situation and the reality, which causes feelings of frustration and disillusion, permitting the integration of loving feelings with hate and destructive feelings. In this schema important environmental objects are the objects of drives and impulses, and they are also their representatives as objects that can be used to personify the self. This is important because the self would not otherwise be available for reflection. This differs from similar psychoanalytic theories (including those of Winnicott and Bion) that assume that aspects of the personality are represented by significant objects in that the latter do not set out to prove the existence of a primary self.

This developmental schema has important technical considerations, particularly in the case of reconstructing childhood fantasies and environmental influences, which are given less importance in classical Jungian theory. Greater importance is attached to the role of transference because it allows counsellors to identify the processes they need to complement. The natural corollary of this is countertransference, in which the objects of the parents (and the counsellor in therapy) eventually reconcile the opposition between an idea and reality in a way that allows the person to be 'individuated'. In other words neither the involuntary function of that person's internal world nor of the external world is left out.

This suggests that the capacity for symbol formation depends on successful object relating, as set out above. Less importance is given to mythology and cultural artefacts than Jung himself would have done. In fact such phenomena could be used defensively to avoid interpersonal conflicts arising from individuation. It is possible that Jung used this compensatory mechanism because his parents, and later Freud, did not mediate between ideas and reality.

The person

The person is a psychosomatic entity with the potential for consciousness and personal identity. Potential, its organisation and coherence are innate in the self. They are realised through the interaction, as mentioned above, between innate potential and opportunities available for the potential to be realised: that is, the ego is seen as the centre of consciousness and is derived from an amalgam of the numerous experiences of such interactions. Pathology that results from overidentification with the environment causes extreme extraversion, corresponding to hysterical personality traits. Pathology that results from overidentification with the innate potential (archetype or idea) causes extreme introversion, corresponding to schizoid withdrawal. Extraversion excessively identifies with the structure that forms the interface between the self and the environment; in other words, the persona. The person can engage a number of mechanisms to relate to the object. In health the person finds a position that transcends exclusive identity with either the natural archetypal disposition or its environmental counterpart.

Health and psychological disturbance

Psychological health means that individuals are free to interact with themselves and their environment without the experience being so uncomfortable that it has to be rejected. Healthy individuals are able to adapt creatively to tasks arising from their environment. At the same time they are emotionally related to their inner world and are nourished by the resulting sense of meaning.

Unconscious processes are repressed (the personal unconscious) because they arise exclusively from impulses that are incompatible with conscious intention. They also arise from innate potential that has yet to be called forth by internal or external needs (the collective unconscious). This means that the individual is disturbed not only by forbidden wishes and memories, but also by unlived aspects of the self. If these are denied or split off, they persist in the form of symptoms. The resulting defences, if rigidly clung to, cause dysfunctional behaviour.

The dysfunctional personality is caused by distortion of the interaction between innate expectation and the environment. This can be due to innate personality factors, inevitable environmental factors such as the death of a loved one, neonatal illness, a congenital defect that interferes with feeding and thus necessitating multiple hospital admissions, or difficulties in the maternal personality that prevent the child from experimenting with emotional experiences.

With regard to the last of these, Jung's mother suffered from depression and his parents' marriage was in difficulty. This seems to have confirmed his fantasy that his destructive feelings were causing damage, thus preventing him from experimenting with aggression in a context where his objects proved their durability; it would be inappropriate and too costly. That is, his innate potential could not be linked to reality (the creative and destructive potential of aggression), so that fantasised damage was not distinguished from real damage. The end result was compensation in the form of idealised creativity, which had to be separated from aggression and thus lost its validity.

With such distortions rigid defence structures can develop, perpetuating the fantasy and making it more and more difficult to test for reality. Dangerous parts of the self are repudiated and attributed to significant others, and then to other relationships. Thus anything done by others might be seen as a product of the repudiated and projected facets of the self, and is therefore treated with suspicion by the dysfunctional individual. For example generosity, kindness, consideration and so on are regarded as attempts to manipulate and seduce. The emotional reality that would correct this paranoid perception of the world is not present, so deprivation is reinforced in a vicious circle that repeatedly justifies the paranoia.

We all have a predisposition to form defensive structures, but good mental health is a reflection of the abilty to be adaptive and flexible in deploying these mechanisms. Adaptiveness is (1) being able to dissociate from certain types of distressing situation, and (2) being suspicious of unscrupulous people or being alert to attack in dangerous circumstances, even though this would be seen as paranoid in safer situations. Everyone, even normal people, have a breaking point if they are subjected to abnormal levels of stress or their adaptive defensive capacity is inhibited in some way.

Change involves the following:

- Recognising maladaptive patterns.
- Recognising the circumstances and environmental failures in which these patterns arose (reconstruction), plus a depiction of the fantasies involved.
- The reparation of distorted object relations to make available the healthy aspects of available objects.

If the above are successful, aspects of the self previously suspended become available and are tolerated, rather than separated from the ego and each other.

Jungian therapy

Jungian therapy has two goals:

- To make it possible for clients to relate adaptively to their internal and external worlds, to cope with them more easily, and to encourage growth and creativity.
- To free clients from overidentification with archetypal processes and/or external objects. This makes the internal and external worlds available for use and mutual enrichment. This is what Jung called the establishment of a compensatory relationship betweeen conscious and unconscious processes.

Suitable clients are those who have the capacity to engage with a counsellor and their own unconscious processes. This is evidenced by a willingness to aid interpretation by releasing conscious and unconscious material. The way in which clients use their counsellor must be open to discussion – this is called transference readiness. Clients must show they have the necessary motivation to change and develop, as opposed to exhibiting dependence and/or using destructive impulses. Important questions are: does the client have the capacity to move in her or his social arena, and will a client who is very isolated find the intimacy of therapy unbearable? Married clients may be required to choose between their health and their partner, and serious consideration is given to counselling anyone who has a psychosomatic illness, has a tendency for impulsive behaviour that might be activated by uncovering unconscious conflicts and other material, or has been actively psychotic.

There are no strict rules on the frequency of therapy. Some clients need five weekly sessions of 50 minutes to maintain continuity and feel they have enough support to risk an encounter with themselves. Others find that attending more than one or two sessions a week causes too much turbulence.

The qualities needed by an effective counsellor

To be effective, counsellors must have undergone analysis and made use of it. Counsellors can only take their clients to the stage they themselves have reached. They must be capable of tuning into their clients' disturbance (counter-transference) in a way that is beneficial to the clients. This needs a considerable capacity to contain any disturbance elicited by the clients and demands a continuing capacity for self-analysis, based on the original analysis. Counsellors must be aware of their personal limitations with regard to the types of patient they can cope with and the number of regressed and disturbed patients they can cope with in their case load.

Counsellors must be accessible as real people without obtruding their views and personality onto their clients. They must be contained, retiring and consistent, and it is important to be attentive to the details of their clients' disclosures. Any invitation by their clients to be more interactive may be an attempt to get them to enact something in the countertransference, for example humour could be a response to an invitation into manic collusion, and self-disclosure could be a response to an invitation to enact a seduction at a primitive level. This does not have to be the case, and it is important for counsellors to be spontaneous.

Clients may become aware of a split-off part of their personality: an auto-nomous complex. They may have great difficulty integrating it because it is totally contradictory to the conscious personality – sympathy and understanding by the analyst are vital here as the powers of their clients' consciousness have to be reinforced until they are able to assimilate this disturbance. The important point is that clients should not be alone in their struggle against what Jung called 'the tyranny of uncontrolled emotion'.

Psychotherapy

Psychotherapy is the treatment of the psyche by psychological methods. Most people would associate it with Freud's psychoanalysis, which explains psychic symptoms in terms of repressed infantile sexual impulses, which implies that neuroses should be traced back to their origins in infancy. Another approach is that of Adler, who explained neuroses in terms of a drive for power to compensate for feelings of inferiority. This is called 'individual psychology'. Jung's analytical psychology is a way not just of healing, but also of developing the personality through the individuation process. However not everyone is looking for this when they attend therapy so Jung recommended varying the treatment according to the client's age, state of development and temperament. He did not neglect sexual or power factors if these played a part in his clients' neuroses, but he found that the approaches of Freud and Adler were usually most appropriate for the young, who needed to give due importance to these instincts while allowing them to function in a socially acceptable way.

Jung's personal experiences caused him to be wary of relying on others and left him with a fear of a regression that would leave him or his patients vulnerable to abandonment. This stemmed in particular from being let down by his parents and the failure of his relationship with Sigmund Freud. As a result his techniques avoided methods that would induce such a regression. He also avoided techniques that would reduce explanations of behaviour to impulses towards the therapist.

Jung favoured a method called active imagination, as opposed to Freud's free association. In this process clients are encouraged to follow through an imaginative train of thought in a directed way. In free association, by contrast, clients allow their thoughts to flow spontaneously. Jung felt that the problem with free association is that clients go back into the complexes that are troubling them. Jung's clients wrote down their dreams in a book, with one column containing their own associations and the other Jung's amplifications (amplifications are references to parallel motifs that might be found in mythological, religious and other cultural material). Jung held sessions comparatively infrequently, perhaps three times a week, and he and his client sat face to face, instead of the client lying on a couch.

Counsellors of the London School have moved away from these practices and developed techniques that allow the most favourable and advantageous level of regression at which to assist the repair of distorted object relations and the manifestation of deintegrative processes at the supposed stage of their inhibition and distortion. Great emphasis is placed on making the setting safe and predictable so that clients can use their counsellor in such a way that the possibility of let-down is minimised.

The couch is frequently used, and there may be up to five sessions per week, depending on the needs of the client. Active imagination is not favoured because there is a danger that clients will use it to avoid interaction with the counsellor. To avoid the danger of compliance and the perpetuation of false personae, dreams are reported but not demanded any more than any other sort of material. Similarly amplification is avoided in case it promotes a competitive or collusive grandness in the countertransference.

Counsellors create a reflective space for their clients to have experiences of the self. It is made clear that events in the session are not subject to a set format, and that both client and counsellor may not know what is going to happen next, and perhaps not understand it when it does.

Counsellors have to be aware that the following may interfere with reflection: unbearable affect, overwhelming anxiety, and defensive manoeuvres such as inconsequential chatter or obstinate silence. They should also take note of quality of speech, as well as silences and their quality.

The content may be straightforward but inferences may need to be made about underlying, disguised fantasies. Intervention is kept to a minimum and counsellors allow impressions to form and reform, together with feelings of countertransference. This allows them to gain some understanding of the session and share their impressions with their clients, including whether something is being blocked. Understanding is always provisional, never final, and it can take anything from a couple of minutes in a session to several months. A client may say nothing for a number of sessions, until some realisation comes to both client and counsellor.

Interpretation is the form in which understanding is shared. In this sense it means translation or making sense of things, and includes reference to the following:

- The symbolic nature of the content, both behavioural and verbal.
- Archetypal structures trying to find expression.
- Fantasies implied by the symbolism.
- Original objects that met or failed the expectations of the person.
- Current relationships and whether they are impaired or improved by the above processes.
- The current relationship with the counsellor, with whom old problems are being relived and new solutions tried.

Most clients quickly lose interest in their presenting symptoms if they have the motivation to change. Instead they focus on the significance of the emotional processes that created the symptoms, and if the symptoms recur they are more interested in their internal dynamic meaning than in accepting them as the external manifestation of some sort of illness. The ability to reflect is developed so that they can exercise choice over their reactions and not be compulsive. This enables them to interact with their environment rather than rehearse prejudices, and to be nourished by this environment and enriched by their experience of themselves.

However the process may well be painful, and clients may feel threatened by their own success in that guilt may make them feel unworthy of relief and reward. They may also be unwilling to give up a psychopathological process that, although painful, gives the illusion of omnipotence. They may fear that if the latter is surrendered they will be left with nothing. These factors may well combine to impair the analysis, and may recur in cycles during the process of change.

It sometimes happens that clients, even when cured, seek to continue the therapy because they cannot do without the person who has treated them. This tenacious attachment is the result of clients transferring the feelings they once held for their parents to the counsellor (this was Freud's special theoretical contribution). As discussed earlier, this phenomenon is called transference. The client suppresses the fact that he or she is like a child, but tries to reproduce with the analyst the family situations of childhood. The analyst may represent any family member, such as a brother or sister, but usually it is the parent of the opposite sex. A considerable amount of repressed material comes to light during such a phase, and fantasies such as incest often appear. The forces activated are predominantly erotic, but 'the will to power', as Adler called it, can also be at work. That is, clients employ childishness in an attempt to dominate the situation and the neurosis is exploited to gain importance.

Only interpretation of the transference can make the clients aware of the situation. As transference naturally changes and develops, this explanation has to be given afresh at every stage. However transference cannot be explained away so clients have to live through it with their counsellor. Obviously limitations are imposed by the conditions of the counselling room and the hours earmarked for sessions, but Jung was insistent that counsellors should treat clients as fellow human beings. There should be equal frankness and a sharing of any suffering. Such a relationship produces therapeutic results that an explanation alone cannot.

Summary of the basics of Jungian analysis

The symbolic

Jung applied the archetypal process in analysis. Clients arrive troubled by fantasies expressed in symbols, but the dictionary meanings of these symbols are empty – it is the emotional response that matters. Clients striving to make sense of disturbing symbols release the unconscious meaning of the archetypes. Jung called this the transcendent function, the archetypal process that brings unconscious content into consciousness and rebalances the psyche.

The transcendent or healing function

Jung favoured a constructive rather than a reductive approach to the process of symbolic expression. This paves the way for the client to gain insight into the process, frequently by searching for helpful parallels to the client's archetypes or symbolism in ancient mythology. The constructive approach reconnects the client 'with the gods' – with the collective archetypes of the unconscious – to allow the healing transcendent function to come into play.

Active imagination

Psychoanalysis uses hypnosis, automatic writing and free association to activate the unconscious mind, but Jung used different approaches and techniques to reconnect his patients with the archetypes experienced through their images from dreams, fantasies and symbols. His experience of drawing mandalas showed him that archetypes could stimulate and regulate creative activity that had a therapeutic effect. Dream symbols could be creatively elaborated by means of drama, dance, writing and painting, which reduced the pressure exerted by the unconscious and advanced the process of individuation.

The centring process

Dream symbols are passive and emerge autonomously from the unconscious. The symbol compensates the dreamer for something lost or unknown. Through the technique of association, clients arrive at the personal context of their dreams. For example if one of Jung's clients dreamt of a sword he employed the technique of amplification, whereby he and his client associated the sword with similar images found historically in myths and fairy tales. The client's own 'weapon' was brought to light by means of excavation or constructive analysis, and she or he could see that the sword, with its crucifix shape, resembled a mandala, which symbolised her or his own centre.

Practice

Analysis is face to face and each case is treated as unique. According to Jung, in the same way that doctors must have clean hands, therapists should be clean of neuroses. He was the first to propose that therapists undergo analysis and receive ongoing supervision.

He saw therapy as progressive rather than regressive, and this necessitated a focus on the client's present position rather than looking for infantile memories. He considered that spiritual issues are important because most who enter analysis after a mid-life crisis do so because of spiritual issues that were neglected during the first half of life. The client's untold secret story is the rock against which he or she is shattered.

Conclusion

Jung's approach to therapy was important in that he encouraged exploration rather than the rigid application of systems. He believed that the reductive approach employed by many theorists, for example their examination of drives and material circumstances, ignored or even denied the very essence of a person's humanity. Taken a stage further, he believed human qualities to be more important than professional qualifications. In this respect it is interesting to compare him with Freud. Freud wanted to be seen as the fount of authority while Jung felt that, as therapy was in its infancy, it was important for therapists to be open about the extent of their ignorance. He also disliked the fact that Freud explained human personality in terms of pathology, because people are not always neurotic. He was fascinated by patients who were not suffering material or psychological problems and were rich, powerful, intelligent and confident. Their problem was that they were suffering from a spiritual crisis for which established religion seemed to have no answer. To find answers Jung thus turned to philosophers ancient and modern, and to religions from the East and the ancient world.

As a result of the above the Jungian approach is more a way of reflecting and thinking than of doing. What happens in the consulting room is the product of the two personalities concerned rather than of therapeutic techniques and approaches. Therapists treat a broad range of problems, including mild neurotic symptoms, life crises, complex disorders and even borderline psychosis. Of course true psychosis can rarely be dealt with by psychotherapy and drug therapies are more appropriate. The real limitation of the approach is clients' motivation to embrace change, and their ability to do so; this is the case irrespective of whether the client is disturbed or healthy. On the other side of the equation, the abilities and motivation of the analyst are also vital.

4 Melanie Klein

Melanie Klein was born Melanie Reize in Vienna in 1882, the youngest of four children in an Orthodox Jewish family. Her father was a Talmud student and her mother was the daughter of a rabbi. This was an important time for European Jews as old prejudices were in decline and professional doors were beginning to open to them. For example, Melanie's father gave up his religious studies and took up medicine, and subsequently practised as a dentist. Melanie later wrote that her family was warm, loving and united. Both parents were intellectuals and she greatly admired Emmanuel, her only brother, who was five years older than her and a medical student. At the age of 14 she decided to study medicine but when she was 17 she became engaged to Arthur Klein, who was an industrial chemist and a friend of her brother. She always regretted not having qualified as a doctor, and this was one of the reasons why the marriage was not wholly successful. She bore three children and before the First World War they all moved to Budapest, where in connection with her interest in medical matters she became acquainted with the works of Freud. She met Sandor Ferenczi, who helped her to develop her ideas and techniques. Dr Karl Abraham, president of the Berlin Psychoanalytic Society, showed considerable interest in her work and invited her to move to Berlin to work. She accepted the offer and took her children, a move that ended her marriage as her husband preferred to live in Sweden because of his business interests. She was later invited to work in London by Ernest Jones, a pupil and biographer of Freud. She flourished in London and continued to work there until her death in 1960.

Theoretical assumptions

According to Klein, life is a series of events that must be experienced, endured and overcome. Kleinian psychoanalysis tries to identify elements of life that start to evolve in the child before it is born. Parents bring to this the capacity they have developed to live their lives in a certain way. The baby has a split persona. At one moment it is a blank page waiting to be written on, the next it is a mass of powerful instinctual drives aimed solely at survival. Klein emphasised the importance of the pre-Oedipal layers of personality development. The two poles of Klein's model of the newborn child are the relationship between the ego, impulses, drives and body feelings on the one hand, and the outside world (the touch of its parents) on the other.

The baby has two conflicting impulses when it is born: love and hate, which battle constantly. The life drive manifests itself in love. The death drive produces envy, hate and destructiveness. The baby has to cope with these desires and has only a short time to develop mechanisms to deal with them. The baby's world is both satisfying *and* frustrating. Good experiences include its mother's breast, a full stomach, a soft warm cot and so on. Bad experiences are cold, hunger and discomfort. Babies do not appreciate that frightening situations such as hunger are only temporary and will soon be replaced by the pleasure of warm milk filling them up. Thus anger and fear change to happy contentedness and back again quite quickly. In short the baby is capable of loving and hating the same object in quick succession; a black or white situation with no shades of grey.

Introjection

As we make our way through this world we not only deal with experiences externally, we also introject or take them into ourselves as part of our inner world, as part of the self. The constant introjection of experiences leads us to believe that we can truly rely on ourselves. It also fosters increased self-esteem and an enduringly positive self-image. Problems can emerge in relation to the strength or weakness of the ego, so that we can fail to take responsibility for our future development. This can happen when we admire certain individuals so much that we would like to have their attributes, and we try to live as they do in all respects.

Projection

Aggressive and envious feelings, because they are bad, are passed on by projection; the alternative being to repress them.

Projective identification is probably one of Klein's greatest contributions to psychoanalysis. The term projection is used in other analytical theories but projective identification is strictly Kleinian. It refers to difficulty in establishing a personal identity and in feeling secure enough to form outward looking relationships. With this form of dysfunction, people who refuse to own their feelings of love and/or hate manipulate others into experiencing them, which leads to visible changes of affect in the behaviour of both parties. This concept deals with therapists' own subjective experiences, and the use to which they are employed when being unknowingly pulled into their clients' fantasy world. A common example is clients' strategy for coping with the deprived part of their own childhood by idealising the parenting process during counselling sessions. This has the following effects:

- It deprives clients of future resourcefulness.
- It may awaken in the therapist a desire for the closeness and dependence of parenthood.
- It reveals the internal world that developed in both the child and the adult as a partial reflection of the external world.

This is a two-way process that continues throughout every stage of our lives, evolving during maturation and maintaining its importance to the world about us. In fact interpretation of reality is never independent of the influence of our internal world.

Splitting

There are a number of stages that are outgrown during normal development but can still be seen in the persecution often felt by paranoid adults. Residual persecutory feelings exist in the sense of guilt that is central to all civilisations. According to Klein, there is a situation in which projected bad objects rebound on children. The bad objects are representations of children's aggressive impulses, such as refusing food and screaming even when they are hungry, or lashing out when they really need to be hugged. Infants need a good mother, and therefore split the two aspects and retain the good one in order to survive. In infancy the objects that surround the child are not perceived in visual terms, they are merely experienced as either good or bad. Likewise the ego is split into good and bad parts that can become obsessional in later life, causing a fragmentation of the self and marking the onset of schizophrenia. With the latter, each split is split again into a multitude of repressions and concessions that ultimately cause chaos. Klein held that this chaotic situation was a psychotic regression to a childhood fear of annihilation.

Hence the first year of life is characterised by paranoid anxieties and the continual splitting of the ego into good and bad parts. There is great contrast between feeling power over the parent and a sudden sense of persecution. Such destructive feelings are of importance to development, but in severe cases can develop into paranoia and schizophrenia. Some anxieties can be dealt with as the ability to think and act develops, but anxiety about murder and madness will always stay in the mind and impoverish the personality. The awful anxiety about annihilation that besets the infant can be repressed into the unconscious, but it remains a threat and might be reactivated. For the personality to grow and develop, some frustration and anxiety is necessary because a balance between the real and fantasised parts of the mind is needed for the growth of the self.

Greed and envy

Klein related these two very disturbing factors first to the infant's dominant relationship with its mother, then to other members of the family and eventually to the various stages of development.

Greed is the need to take everything possible from the mother and family, and it is made worse by the anxiety of being deprived. The greedy infant is temporarily content with what it has, but soon feels robbed of food, attention and other gratifications. An infant greedy for love and attention is unable to give a share to others, which makes its situation worse, and if the mother is unable to provide consolation, for example because of depression, the infant will have murderous feelings towards her. In desiring the death of the person most essential to its survival, the infant is impelled at one moment towards murder and the next towards suicide.

Suspicion is the basis of envy, which is a spoiling pursuit in that if the infant cannot have what it wants it experiences an urge to spoil the object of desire so that no one else can have it. The infant believes that if love, milk or anything else desirable is being withheld its mother must be keeping it for herself, and the result is a disturbed relationship with the mother. The breakdown of natural protective forces highlights the distorted nature of the mother–child relationship in such cases and can lead to the mother suffering postnatal depression.

According to Klein, aggressive envy in infancy can inhibit the growth of good object relations or the child's personal relationship with objects such as toys, which may be perceived as alive and lovable personalities, in need of sympathy and so on. The knock-on effect of aggressive envy is inhibition of the capacity to love. This is because the infant's first object relation is the mother's breast and the mother herself. This is of fundamental importance, because 'if this primal object which is introjected, takes root in the ego with relative security the basis for a satisfactory development is laid' (Klein 1957, p. 389).

Human instinct, fantasy and defence mechanisms

These are best illustrated by projected identification because fantasy can satisfy aggressive impulses and sexual desire, with fantasy acting as a safety net in that it contains and holds the bad parts of the inner self. The Oedipus complex (a boy's desire for his mother and his consequent rivalry with his father) is a facet of murderous fantasy and is rooted in the infant's suspicion of his father, who appears to be taking away his mother's love and attention. This also applies to girls because their relationship with their mother and all women is of paramount importance.

According to Klein, Oedipal feelings are identifiable at six months, when the infant's rage and aggressive feelings are projected onto the parent. Klein agreed with Freud's division of the psyche into the ego, id and superego, but unlike Freud she maintained that all three could be identified almost from birth.

During the months after birth the infant begins to perceive that its mother is a separate entity, divided from it and the source of good and bad feelings that are internalised by the infant. The baby can both love and hate its mother and is as separate from her as she is from it. For Klein, mental pain never goes away, separation being painful and experienced as a situation that is lost forever. This situation is caused by the infant's aggression destroying its link with its mother and leaving it with feelings of guilt, deprivation and utter sadness. The infant's fear that it is the object of destruction is accompanied by the knowledge that it can destroy the person it loves and needs for its own survival.

Klein set out her ideas in *On the theory of anxiety and guilt* (1952), where she states that such depressive anxieties are a normal part of development. Moreover the guilt feelings are part of the imagined harm done by the infant to its love object. The paranoid fears and anxieties of early infancy tend to become modified, with the child offering tenderness to those around it, but the anxieties are easily reawakened during times of mourning in later life. In Kleinian therapy the mourning process is seen as productive because adult depression involves the reactivation of infantile depression, that is, the feelings of a depressed client are regarded as the product of early persecutory impulses directed towards the self.

Change

Klein added to the basic psychoanalytic principle that unconscious mechanisms operating within the human psyche dominate the process of change in human beings. When we are born we have a clean slate onto which the circumstances of our lives are written, and we have to learn with it.

In Klein's view there are two factors to consider. First, when we gain in life we also lose and this causes us to experience ambivalent feelings. For example the infant receives accolades when first weaned, but at the expense of the comfort of suckling its mother's breast. Second, to survive in this world we must accept that every 'have' is counterbalanced by a 'have not'. Change involves the development of a sense of detachment from life, which in turn leads to a sense of personal identity and tolerance, enabling us to cope with whatever comes our way.

Kleinian psychotherapy

The principles of Kleinian psychotherapy are set out in Klein's early work *The Psycho-Analysis of Children* (1932). At the start of therapy, therapists work with their clients' unconscious fantasies about themselves, their relationships with others and the ways in which such fantasies relate to the reality of the outside world and how it is experienced. Psychotherapy is aimed at initiating a process of learning and personal development that advances at its own pace. The whole process is underpinned by the client–therapist relationship.

The primary goal is to reduce the clients' immediate anxiety, which is achieved by helping them to confront their inhibitions and forge a positive relationship with their therapist. With help the clients begin to see themselves as real people in a real world and able to balance love and hate, feelings that alternate in everyone's psyche. When therapy is complete patients should:

- be able to form and maintain normal personal relationships.
- have insight into their personal situation.
- be free from infantile repressions and fixations.
- be sensitive and capable of dealing with problems.
- have less inhibition and be able to enjoy life to the full.
- have stronger egos and the knowledge that they can not only survive the trials of life but also want to survive them.

True reparation or growth takes place when clients recognise their infantile dependence on internal objects or the idealised father and mother, and accept themselves as the product of what was and is. Therapy ends when the clients' persecutory and depressive anxieties have been alleviated and they have a sufficiently strong relationship with the world in general to be able to handle the process of mourning.

To qualify for psychotherapy the clients' problems must be definable in psychodynamic terms, and the clients must have the necessary motivation to change and gain insight into their behaviour. Furthermore they must be equal to the demands of interpretation and confrontation, as well as capable of accepting and maintaining the necessary long-term relationship with the therapist and significant others in their lives.

The qualities needed by a therapist

Training takes years and involves personal therapy four or five times a week, focusing on the personality of the trainee (usually a graduate). Training is divided into three parts: (1) long-term personal analysis; (2) a shorter period of training in analysis at a formal institute; and (3) long-term supervision during work with clients.

Therapists who dogmatically follow the letter of this or that form of therapy are regarded as not having passed beyond the paranoid-schizoid stage. Therapists must be sensitive to the depression within themselves, and should adopt an accepting but neutral attitude, in contrast to the role playing and manipulation used in many therapeutic strategies. Therapists should allow themselves to be used as an object so that they intrude but do not obtrude. The primary means by which clients are helped towards normal functioning is to make clear the transference manifestations that develop during therapy. Klein considered that it is vital to gain a thorough knowledge of the techniques of adult analysis plus considerable experience of the same before embarking on work with pubescent children.

If therapy is to be successful, therapists must be able to control the therapist–client relationship because if clients take control they will continue to be inhibited by the paranoid-schizoid symptoms that caused their need for therapy. The problem of object need is a basic problem in all forms of psychoanalysis, so clients should be able to see their therapists and all aspects of the therapy situation as real. Likewise therapists should regard their clients as real and respond to them as real objects. Clients tend to return to the symbiotic relationship they had with their mother, so therapists should avoid confusing the therapeutic function with the parental function. They should get as close as possible to their clients' life while remaining detached from it. From the outset therapists should help their clients to surrender any hope of receiving gratification from them as idealised objects.

Therapeutic techiques and strategies

The central focus of therapy is the transference situation and its interpretation, with therapists listening to their clients without giving practical advice or reassurance about the life of the clients or their family.

The interpretation of transference involves comprehending how facts and fantasies from previous relationships, particularly figures from the clients' inner world, are transferred onto the therapist; this being in addition to the 'here and now' situation. Current problems and relationships are related to the transference as it unfolds. The therapist considers the way they are handled, their order, their timing, the language used and the amount of interpretation. This facilitates the examination of feelings towards the therapist, both positive and negative. Everyday language is used, and technical jargon is avoided in order not to overawe clients and to ensure that they understand.

There are three points of emphasis in Kleinian therapy: (1) the here and now situation; (2) the totality of all aspects of the setting; and (3) the importance of comprehending the content of the anxiety. Interpretations are given a certain sequence and the past and present are connected gradually. Therapists use preparatory interventions, interpret defences, assess clients' readiness to take on board later interpretations and use language that promotes client understanding.

Interpretations go from what is known or believed about the present, to the situation in the past. Therapy delves into the earliest mental processes as well as later specialised mental operations, which in Kleinian terms are unconscious infantile archaic wishes and fantasies projected towards the therapist as a new source of gratification.

The process of change

Clients learn that aggression and love can be valued, and they acknowledge their inner struggle with these two feelings. Regressive infantile expectations are replaced by rationality. Social relationships are spoilt by jealousy, hatred, greed and rivalry, but therapy equips clients to form more constructive and fulfilling relationships. Knowledge of the destructive elements in the psyche equips clients to acquire clearer judgement and the ability to remain in control, to be less fearful and to be more tolerant of themselves and others.

Change involves the following:

- The desire for reparation and reconciliation.
- Being caring and sensitive towards others.
- Letting go the hurts of the past.
- Believing in the personal ability to love.
- Expecting love in return.
- Making good the imagined injuries received and given in infancy.
- Relinquishing feelings of guilt.

Conclusion

Contemporary standards require scientific examinations of the causes of therapeutic change to incorporate an examination and description of the variables that have facilitated such changes. Then experiments can be devised to test the resulting hypotheses. On this basis the Kleinian approach does not provide the scientific evidence needed to meet such criteria. Furthermore it is becoming increasingly difficult to isolate psychopathology from the changing attitudes and perspectives of the age in which we live. Indeed many Kleinian therapists find it hard to admit to the existence of an outside environment that has been created by their clients and in which they function. Hence Kleinians are separating clients from their social and cultural framework when they attempt to recreate their clients' internal, fantasised world of childhood. It is necessary to remember that clients are unique individuals who have been moulded and developed by a huge number of influences and experiences, but Kleinian psychotherapy maintains that external events are not of primary importance. It is worth contrasting this approach with those in which clients' relationships with others are taken into account, for example family therapy and personal construct therapy.

There are limitations in strictly adhering to a particular type of analytic theory. Nonetheless Kleinian theory can be seen as innovative in that it extemporises and uses new and novel types of psychoanalytic methodology. Kleinians may be tempted to look for affirmation of any novel input from the clients themselves. Melanie Klein held the view that children's free play can be interpreted psychoanalytically, and naturally this provides Kleinians with a store of new material, which in turn leads to constant revision of their analytic theory. This raises a number of questions. When new case material prompts new findings, is it possible that the therapist has made an incorrect interpretation? If the therapist is keen on challenging results, does this mean that the original theory is flawed in some way? We must also ask whether the behaviour of therapists is affected by the assumptions of their theoretical stance, and whether their interpretations dictate their clients' goals. There is a danger that they will look only for what they think they will find. Do they distort clients' information to fit their own expectations? Clients are seen in a strictly controlled analytic setting, and although they report on their daily life, such reports are very selective and often relate to their failures rather than their successes outside the consulting room.

So although psychoanalytic psychotherapy is defined as essentially pre-theoretical in nature, its perspectives are frequently limited by ideological frameworks.

◾ ᴟ **Part Two**

Humanistic counselling

▪ ▼ **5** Person-centred counselling: Carl Rogers

Carl Rogers was born in Illinois in 1902. He was the fourth of six children in a deeply religious family. His father was a civil engineer and owned a construction business. When Rogers was 12 the family bought a farm, where he lived until he went to college. At first he studied agriculture, but changed to history after two years with the intention of entering the Church. While at the Union Theological Seminary he realised that his beliefs were not suitable for a religious career and he became a student at Columbia University. After graduating he worked for 12 years as a psychologist at the Society for the Prevention of Cruelty to Children in Rochester, New York, during which time he developed an interest in social work. In 1940, soon after completing his book *Clinical Treatment of the Problem Child* (1939) he became a professor at Ohio State University. In 1945 he became professor of psychology and a director of counselling services at Chicago University. He was a professor at Wisconsin University from 1957–62 and a fellow at Stanford University from 1962–63. In 1964 he became a resident fellow at the Western Behavioural Sciences Institute at La Jolla, California. In 1968 he and a group of colleagues set up the Center for Studies of the Person at La Jolla, where he was a resident fellow until he died in 1987.

Theoretical assumptions

Person-centred counselling starts from the assumption that both counsellor and client are trustworthy, and that all individuals move instinctively towards the realisation of their inherent potential. Their subjective self-concept is made up of the ways in which they define and perceive themselves, and their single motivating drive is their inherent actualising tendency to maintain and enhance themselves. Individuals start to develop a self-concept very early on in life, and many of the self-conceptions that form the self-concept are based on their own valuing process. Other self-conceptions reflect internalised conditions of worth or the values of others, which are treated as though they are based on the individual's own valuing process. Hence a conflict arises between the actualising tendency and the self-concept (which is a subsystem of the actualising tendency) because conditions of worth impede an accurate perception of inner and outer experiences.

Subception is the mechanism by which individuals discriminate experiences that are at variance with the self-concept. Depending on the degree of threat in an experience, they may defend their self-concept by denying the experience or distorting its perception. Individuals are psychologically well to the extent that their self-concepts allow them to perceive all their significant sensory and visceral (emotional and intuitional) experiences.

The perceptual or subjective frame of reference

Behaviour can be observed from the point of view of outsiders or from the view of the behavers themselves. The former observe from the external frame of reference, the latter from the internal, subjective or perceptual frame of reference. The latter frame forms the foundation of Rogers' theories. The term 'person-centred' arose because the perceptions of clients were and are treated as reality. In Rogers' view there are as many realities as there are people, contrary to the concept of a single real world whose common definition is agreed to by all.

The actualising tendency

The actualising tendency is the basic motivating drive and is always operative. It is an active process that reflects the inherent tendency of all people to develop their capacities in order to maintain, enhance and reproduce themselves. It involves the differentiation of organs and functions, and causes people to engage in self-regulation and self-enhancement. It is a constructive directional flow towards the realisation of each individual's full potential and away from control by external forces. As long as certain definable conditions exist, then people have the ability to regulate, guide and control themselves.

Blockages to the actualising tendency are the cause of all psychological problems, and the purpose of counselling is to clear such blockages. The actualising tendency may involve both deficiency and growth motivations, because in humans there is a basic conflict between growth trends and defensive forces. However, with the right emotional conditions, growth motivations increase in strength.

The organismic valuing process

The organismic valuing process is the continuous assessment of experiences in terms of their ability to satisfy the actualising tendency. This process is central to the idea of a true and unique self. As children we are drawn to experiences that satisfy our sense of security and we reject negative experiences such as hunger and pain; this is because the former enhance our organism and the latter do not. The valuing process is a reaction to sensory and visceral (emotional and intuitional) evidence. As we grow older the valuing process helps us to achieve self-actualisation so that we can be aware of the experiencing that is going on within us.

Experiencing a feeling includes receiving emotional content and the personal meaning or cognitive content as they are experienced together at a given moment. Fully experiencing a feeling means there is a congruence between experiencing, awareness and expression of the feeling. When Rogers wrote about sensory and visceral experience he meant it in the psychological rather than the physiological sense. The total range of experience, both physiological and psychological, is called the 'experiential', 'phenomenal' or 'perceptual' field. Experiencing means receiving the impact of any visceral or sensory experiences coming our way at a particular moment.

Perception and awareness

In person-centred counselling perception and awareness are treated as more or less the same thing. They are transactional by nature, are built on past awareness, and are predictions or hypotheses of the future. They do not necessarily have to correspond with reality or experience, but if they are symbolised accurately any hypothesis can be acted on successfully. Defensive denials and distortions cause awareness to be inaccurately symbolised, and experiences that are unimportant to the actualising tendency will not be perceived. An example of the latter is the bodily sensation of sitting in a chair.

The self and self-concept

The self is the real organismic self, while self-concept is our perception of ourselves and does not necessarily square with our experiencing or organismic self. When facets of the self and self-concept are congruent or synonymous, then self-actualisation can take place because the actualising tendency is able to operate. If there is a desire to actualise the self-concept, this can prevent the actualisation of the organismic self.

The self-concept is initiated in childhood in a series of self-experiences that children discriminate as 'I', 'me' or 'self'. They incorporate all sorts of experiences into their self-concept; for example they negatively value hunger, and as they discover parts of their bodies they incorporate these as facts. Importantly, they interact with significant others who regard them as a separate self, and treat them accordingly. Ultimately the self-concept is made up of their perceptions about themselves and the positive and negative values that come with such self-perceptions.

Conditions of worth

Infants develop a need for the positive regard of others, which can be defined as the feeling of making a positive difference in the experiential field of another person. Certain forms of behaviour prompt a pleasurable experience and attract positive regard, for example smiling at an adult. Conversely children who enjoy hitting a sibling attract the displeasure of their parents, so, instead of internalising the pleasure of hitting they put a negative value on it because of their need for positive regard. An accurate assessment of this episode would be that while they find their action satisfying, their parents find it unsatisfying, so the feeling becomes distorted and they perceive their behaviour as unsatisfying.

Values of this type – based on others' evaluations rather than on the individual's own organismic valuing process – are called 'conditions of worth'. Such conditions are prevalent, according to Rogers, because individuals are culturally conditioned, rewarded and reinforced for behaviours that are contrary to the actualising tendency. This causes them to develop a second valuing process that derives from the introjection (internalisation) of other people's opinions, which impedes the actualising tendency rather than reflects it. The problem is that people tend to believe that decisions based on the second valuing process are in fact the product of their own organismic valuing process, hence they seek or avoid certain experiences to meet false needs instead of real ones.

Parents are able to feel unconditional positive regard for their child only to the extent that they themselves are able to experience unconditional self-regard. Unconditional positive regard means prizing the child despite negative behaviour. The greater the unconditional regard that parents feel towards the child, the fewer the conditions of worth experienced by the child and the greater the level of psychological adjustment. In short, high-functioning parents set up the conditions for the growth of high-functioning children.

Clearly we all differ in the degree to which we internalise conditions of worth. For many people the development of the self-concept enables most of their experiences to be correctly perceived. Nonetheless everyone internalises some conditions of worth. This depends on the following:

- The amount of unconditional positive regard we are given by the significant others in our lives.
- The degree of empathic understanding and congruence shown to us.
- The extent of our need for positive regard, as this governs our vulnerabilty to the introjection of conditions of worth.

The following are common examples of conditions of worth:

- Making money is important and you are a failure if you do not do it.
- Achievement is vital and you are a failure if do not succeed.
- Sexual fantasies are perversions and you are wicked if you engage in them.

Conditions of worth are not just internalised judgements about how we should be, they also include internalised evaluations of how we should feel about ourselves if we consider we are not the way we should be.

Most people's values are largely introjected, they are owned as fixed concepts and are only rarely tested or examined. As a result people are estranged from their experiences, their self-regard is lowered, they cannot fully value themselves and they lower their own sense of self-worth; they become self-oppressors.

Relationships between partners, whether married or not, may have properties that promote personal growth by dissipating conditions of worth and increasing self-regard. The conditions for the development of adequate self-concepts and the reintegration of inadequate self-concepts are basically the same. Both have the necessary characteristics to promote successful and loving interpersonal relationships. Experiences that lead to sound or unsound self-concepts are not restricted to childhood, adolescence or family life and can be found in many human situations. This is important because many people are so hampered by conditions of worth that they fail to be as self-actualising as they really need to be.

It is possible for educational institutions to engineer the emotional climate needed to foster self-concept. Rogers favoured self-initiated experiential learning that mirrored students' concerns (as opposed to the usual emphasis on teachers' and adminstrators' opinions), with a focus on interpersonal and intergroup relationships. Rogers felt that the actualising tendency promoted democratic control and power sharing.

Experience processing

It is important for counsellors to consider not just how their clients came to have the problems they have, but also why the clients maintain behaviour that not only fails to address their true needs but also actively prevents them from being achieved. This problem is at the hub of person-centred theory and practice. Put another way, this approach involves human information processing, or the processing of experiences into perceptions. The conditions of worth mentioned above are a vital part of this process.

Experiences can be ignored in the same way as the sensation of breathing, or they can be perceived quite accurately and organised into a relationship with the self-concept because they meet some need of the self or reinforce the self-concept by being consistent with it. Perception can be distorted to resolve the conflict between self-conflict and experiencing. For example students who have a low opinion of their academic ability but are given a good mark for their work may believe that their teacher has low standards or has not marked their work properly. Individuals may not perceive their experiences at all, and if they do they may deny them. For example they may deny their need for sexual satisfaction because their self-concept has been strongly shaped by a rigid moral upbringing.

Humans have two valuing processes: their organismic valuing process, and an internalised process based on conditions of worth. High-functioning people have fewer conditions of worth than low-functioning people, so they can perceive most of their experiences acurately. Low-functioning people are not in touch with their own valuing process for a great deal of their experiencing, and their self-concepts in affected areas are based on conditions of worth. This causes them to distort and deny much of their experiencing.

Both types are motivated by the actualising tendency, that is they generally tend towards self-actualisation. Self-actualisation causes no major blockage to high-functioning people's actualising tendency because their self-concept permits them to perceive most of their important sensory and visceral experiences. With low-functioning people there is a split and the tendency to actualise may conflict with the subsystem of that motive – the tendency to actualise the self – and their self-actualisation process is insufficiently based on their own valuing process. Unlike high-functioning people they do not have the ability to interact with others and their environments on the basis of accurate information.

A state of congruence exists between self-concept and experience if experiences are accurately symbolised and included in the self-concept. Incongruence occurs when experiences are distorted and denied. This can occur with positive as well as negative experiences and results in low self-concept, distortion and denial of positive feedback from outside and repressed positive feedback from within.

Subception or preperception is the mechanism by which people deny or inaccurately perceive sensory and visceral experiences that are relevant to the actualising tendency. It involves filtering experiences to exclude or change those experiences that are contradictory to or threaten the self-concept. It is a defence mechanism activated by the self-concept when the latter's self-conceptions and structure are threatened. The organism is able to comprehend the meaning of an experience without the aid of the higher nerve centres used in perception and conscious awareness.

Anxiety is the state of tension and unease that arises in response to the subception that an incongruence (a discrepancy between self-concept and experience) is about to enter awareness or perception and trigger an alteration in the current self-concept.

The term intensionality describes the characteristics of an individual who is in a state of defence. It includes the following reactions: overgeneralisation, perceiving experience in rigid, absolutist terms, confusing facts and evaluation, and abandoning reality testing. Extensionality describes the characteristics of a mature self-concept, such as seeing experience in limited, differentiated terms and testing inferences and abstractions against reality.

Although low-functioning people's perception of much sensory and visceral experience is blocked by the self-concept there are occasions when a significant experience suddenly happens in an area of great incongruence. When this occurs, the defence process may be unable to operate successfully. There are three possible consequences of this:

- Individuals' self-concept may be threatened by the anxiety generated.
- The experience may be accurately symbolised in awareness because the process of defence has not been successful.
- Individuals may be faced with more of their denied experiences than they can cope with. This will cause a state of disorganisation that can lead to psychotic breakdown. Once psychotic behaviour begins, the defensive processes may engage to protect against the anxiety caused by the individuals' perception of incongruence.

Summary of self-concept

Self-concept is vital to comprehending how psychological maladjustment is maintained. It is the pattern of the perceptions that people have about themselves and use to interact with life to meet their needs. To perceive experiences realistically, people need an effective self-concept that allows them open access to their experiences.

People may maintain ineffective self-concepts because they see them as a source of personal adequacy and a means of gratifying needs. Ineffective self-concepts contain many conditions of worth that were once functional but have lost their usefulness. The problem arises because they grew out of the need for positive regard, and are deeply entrenched in the self-concept as emotional baggage. The more deeply conditions of worth are embedded the more difficult it is to alter them. This is because the incongruence between self-perceptions and experiencing would provoke anxiety. Conditions of worth lower people's sense of worth and their chance of owning and dealing with their areas of incongruence. The threshold at which low-functioning people are able to assimilate incongruent perceptions into their self-concepts is lower and more strongly defined than in high-functioning people.

Characteristics of self-concept

The self-concept is a unique complex of different self-conceptions. It is people's way of distinguishing and describing themselves. Areas include bodily feelings, emotions, tastes, preferences, sexual feelings, values, intellect, philosophy, work, social life and recreation. The various areas vary in importance between people, and the same is true of the kinds of self-conception they have. For example height may be important to one person but of little interest to another. Self-concept is often revealed in self-referent statements such as 'I'm good at drawing' or 'I get flustered when I have to speak to people in authority'.

The self-concept is composed of different self-conceptions that are related to each other in a variety of ways. It is the process by which we interact with our environment and the means by which we accurately perceive or distort, deny or ignore experiences.

For everyone, some self-conceptions are more central than others. Everyone has their own way of ordering self-conceptions as central or peripheral, and this tends to be implicit rather than explicit.

There is congruence between self-conceptions and experience when self-conceptions match the reality of experiencing. There is incongruence when self-conceptions differ in varying degrees from the reality of experiencing.

If self-conception is based on conditions of worth rather than on one's personal valuing process, then there is incongruence. An example of incongruent self-conception is the person who says 'I want to be an industrial chemist' when their congruent self-conception is 'I want to be a charity worker'. The former might be based on internalised parental values and the latter on the person's own valuing process.

The process of subception is used to deny or distort experiences. This is done to defend existing self-conceptions by preventing us from seeing their incongruence and therefore having to alter our self-conceptions and behaviour.

Intensionality refers to the characteristics of self-concept when in a defensive state. Such characteristics include inadequate reality testing and rigidity. Extensionality refers to the characteristics of a mature self-concept. This involves testing inferences and abstractions against reality, and seeing experience in limited, differentiated terms.

Self-regard is the degree to which people prize themselves – their level of self-acceptance. According to Rogers, when a person's self-concepts are such that no self-experience is more worthy of positive regard than any other, then they are experiencing unconditional positive regard.

Real self-conception is people's conception of what they are. Ideal self-conception is their conception of what they would most like to be. Both are part of the self-concept complex.

Person-centred counselling

Self-actualising, fully functioning people have the following attributes.

1. *Openness to experience.* This equips people to engage in existential living, deal with change and be aware of the range of life choices open to them. The basis of effective functioning is a self-concept that permits all significant sensory and visceral (emotional and intuitive rather than intellectual) experiences to be perceived. Openness to experience allows more efficient behaviour because it encourages a wider perceptual field and a tendency to behave from choice rather than necessity. It also promotes spontaneity and creativity because individuals are unhampered by conditions of worth. According to Rogers there is no need for the 'mechanism of subception' by which people are forewarned of experiences that threaten the self.

2. *Rationality.* Rationality is a feature of openness to experience. People's behaviour is likely to be rational in terms of maintaining and enhancing their organism when they are in touch with their actualising tendency. However, most people's defences prevent them from being aware of just how rational they can be. A characteristic of this is extensionality as opposed to intensionality (see above).

3. *Personal responsibility.* This means that people take responsibility for their own self-actualisation rather than feeling they are responsible only to others. Accordingly they trust in their organismic valuing process, trust the authority within themselves, accept responsibity for their own behaviour and accept that they are responsible for being different from others. An important consequence of this is increased personal autonomy combined with resistance to enculturation. Within the existential parameters of death and destiny, personally responsible people are able to take control of their own lives and their self-actualisation.

4. *Self-regard.* Effective people have a high degree of self-acceptance and unconditional self-regard, based on their own organismic valuing process, as opposed to needing the praise of others. Such people may not prize all their attributes and behaviours, but they prize themselves anyway. An adequate personality is defined not just by the number of positive self-conceptions but also by the importance accorded to them.

5. *A capacity for good personal relations.* People are less likely to be defensive and therefore more likely to be accepting of others if they have achieved self-acceptance. This means that other people are seen as unique, prized and able to be related to both freely and openly. Another feature of this capacity is the ability to communicate a strong and fruitful self-awareness. Such relations are characterised by mutual concern for the self-actualisation of both persons, authenticity, attentive listening and appropriate self-disclosure. The most important factor in the ordinary interactions of life is congruence, genuineness or what Rogers called 'realness'. Empathy is most important when the other person is vulnerable and anxious.

6. *Ethical living.* One of the central tenets of person-centred counselling is that deep down people are trustworthy. This is revealed in self-actualising people in two main ways: they have a strong ability to identify with other people, which

makes them likely to promote other people's self-actualisation as well as their own and to avoid infringing the rights of others while in pursuit of personal goals. They also have the ability distinguish between ends and means and between good and evil. Important qualities in ethical living include indifference to material things such as status and money, trust in internal rather than external authority, closeness to and reverance for nature, and needing and searching for spiritual values that are greater than the individual.

In order to foster these attributes, during counselling clients are directed:

- Away from a preoccupation with keeping up appearances and other facades.
- Away from the internalised sense of duty that arises from externally imposed obligations.
- Away from trying to live up to others' expectations.
- Towards valuing 'realness' amd honesty in oneself and others.
- Towards prizing the ability to direct one's life.
- Towards accepting and valuing one's self and feelings, whether these are positive or negative.
- Towards valuing the experience of the moment and the growth process instead of the endless pursuit of objectives.
- Towards a desire for greater intimacy and the cherishing of relationships.
- Towards a better understanding of and greater respect for others.
- Towards valuing all forms of experience and being open to all experiences, both inner and outer, however unexpected or uncongenial.

Client selection

Person-centred counselling has proved effective with a diverse range of clients, even psychotics, although Rogers felt that it works best with people who are better adjusted to life. People with a rigid and authoritarian attitude towards life and want certainties and secure structures prefer directive counselling, and this makes it difficult for them to relate to a Rogerian counsellor in a way that can help them to get in touch with their inner resources. Logically rational and overly intellectual people often find it difficult to engage in the sort of relationship that is central to person-centred counselling, where the greatest healing stems from facing up to confusing and painful feelings that at first are difficult to verbalise. Both these types of people tend to be referred by GPs, priests and social workers as a last resort, and more often than not they are poorly motivated.

People best suited to the person-centred approach are those who have the motivation and determination to confront painful feelings and are set upon change. Such people, even when afraid of intimacy, are able to trust and are willing to take emotional risks.

Group work

Groups can be large or small, and some have two counsellors or 'facilitators'. Any client who has some measure of self-acceptance and at least some positive aspects of self-concept can be encouraged to join a group. This tends to take place when therapy has produced a measure of self-affirmation and the client is willing to take further risks in respect of relating. Group membership may replace individual counselling, or both may be attended. Whatever is decided, it is the client who makes the decision. It is important that clients with a poor self-concept are not introduced to group therapy too soon as this may reinforce their feeling of worthlessness. Such clients are best served by individual counselling.

In the case of couples and families, counsellors must create the right conditions for the individuals to interact without fear, and this is achieved by painstaking, one-to-one preparatory work with each of them. It is vital for counsellors to be confident that they are capable of authentic relationship with all those involved, and this in turn depends on in-depth preliminary meetings with each of them. In couple counselling it is usual for counsellors to have a number of sessions with each partner before bringing them together to deal with the problems in the relationship. Family counselling is more complicated and therefore preparation is more laboured and time-consuming. As a consequence person-centred family counselling is not very common.

The qualities needed by counsellors

Counsellors must be able to relate to their clients in such a way as to reassure them of their dependability and trustworthiness. Person-centred counsellors must not resort to psychological labelling and diagnosis or to interpretive insights. This is because displays of psychological expertise might hinder the development of clients' trust in their own inner resources. Counsellors must have a high degree of personal acceptance if they are to offer acceptance of the feelings of their clients. This can bring to the surface material long buried in the counsellor, and acceptance of such material is a necessary prerequisite for offering genuineness to the client. The same is true of trustworthiness; counsellors can only be as trustworthy for their clients as they are for themselves.

Person-centred counsellors must be genuine, accepting and empathic – attributes that tend to be found in those who strive constantly to broaden their own life experiences. Continuity, quality and depth of experience are at the heart of professional competence because no counsellor can invite clients to explore further than he has explored himself. It is important to avoid getting stuck in some past self-image as person-centred counselling requires continued growth as a person throughout life, irrespective of age. Finally, it is important for counsellors not to rely too heavily on particular skills as this may cause their counselling style to crystalise into a pattern that is resistant to change.

Creating the counselling climate

Counselling style varies enormously between counsellors but they have a common desire to create a facilitative climate in which clients can start to develop their capacity for self-knowledge, change their self-concept and abandon self-defeating behaviours. Without such a climate there is no hope of establishing the type of client–counsellor relationship needed for therapeutic progress. Four core conditions are required for the process to succeed.

1. *Genuineness.* This includes authenticity, realness or congruence and it hinges on counsellors' ability to get in touch with the feelings, attitudes and thoughts they will experience as their clients reveal theirs. It is equally important for clients to be able to recognise their counsellors' capacity for humanity, so another skill required by counsellors is the ability to know when to communicate what they are experiencing to the client, and when to keep quiet. Body language and facial expression often reveal this anyway, thus minimising the need for verbal communication. However it is done, counsellors should communicate their desire to be deeply and fully involved in the relationship without exhibiting professionality and pretence.

2. *Total acceptance.* This is vital because conditions of worth may have damaged clients' self-concept to such an extent that it has little relation to the actualising organism. This is the direct result of conditional and judgemental attitudes imparted by significant others in the clients' lives, compounded by cultural and societal norms. Counsellors should counteract this by offering positive regard and non-possessive love, that is, unconditional acceptance of their clients as they are. This cannot be offered by people who feel threatened by their own inner feelings. Nor is it possible to simulate it. True acceptance is unaffected by differences in background and beliefs, and social, moral and ethical factors have no part to play. This must be fully communicated so that clients will feel safe no matter what they are going through. Counsellors have to remember that their clients may have never experienced this degree of acceptance and will test it from time to time. Counsellors' response to this can be quite subtle; a smile, nod or gentle squeeze of the hand often says far more than words could ever do.

3. *Empathic understanding.* This is the most trainable of the core conditions. It centres on clients' subjective perceptual world because counsellors must have a strong understanding of their clients' inner world in order to come alongside them and be regarded as a reliable element in their life. It would be foolish for counsellors to enter the perceptual world of their clients if they are not secure in their own identity and therefore fear being overwhelmed. Once there, counsellors must be gentle and tentative because feelings and meanings that their clients have yet to become aware of could drive them away from therapy if realisation comes too soon. Rogers referred to such blunders as 'blitz therapy'.

4. *Tenderness.* This is marked by the abilty to move without strain between the emotional, physical, mystical and cognitive worlds.

Strategies and techniques

No single strategy or technique could be said to be integral to the person-centred approach. It is based on experiencing and on communicating attitudes. Many people believe that person-centred counselling is just a matter of reflecting clients' feelings or repeating the last thing they said. On the contrary, counsellors must have the highest possible sense of self-knowledge and self-acceptance, and to communicate this requires great skill that is unique to each counsellor. Merely imitating Rogers or the counselling trainer is not enough.

There are three distinct stages in counselling:

- Securing the trust of the client: this can take months, or it can happen after only a few sessions.
- The development of intimacy: clients reveal their deepest levels of experiencing at this stage.
- Increasing mutuality between counsellor and client: at this stage counsellors engage in more self-disclosure and risk more of themselves in the relationship.

The process of change

Clients move from a state of poor self-concept, as expressed in behaviour that reinforces their negative self-evaluation, into a state where they are closer to the real worth of the organismic self. This is followed by a change in behaviour that reflects this improvement and further enhances their self-perception. At the end of successful counselling clients will have learnt how to be their own counsellor.

By experiencing the core conditions from their counsellor clients are motivated to adopt the same attitude towards themselves. Being cared for causes them to believe that perhaps they are worth caring for after all, and as a result they treat themselves with more respect. Likewise being listened and attended to causes them to listen to themselves and lose their fear of delving into what is going on inside themselves, leading to increased understanding of personal meanings. Clients eventually come to define themselves and realise they do not have to accept the definitions and judgements of others. Their sense of self-responsibility increases, so they feel able to make their own personal choices.

Conclusion

The limitations of this approach essentially reflect the limitations of the counsellor, which vary from counsellor to counsellor and are unlikely to be constant. There is also a danger of this approach limiting itself by its traditional emphasis on the here and now and its reliance on verbal interaction. Such tendencies are reinforced if the counsellor's congruence is at a low level. The more that counsellors are able to give to the clinent–counsellor relationship the more they will be able to trust their own intuition or hunches during counselling sessions. This invariably proves to be highly beneficial to the therapy. Clients suffering from behavioural disorders such as obsessive-compulsive neuroses and phobias are unlikely to benefit from this approach unless they see their problems as resulting from their way of being in the world. Those who regard their problems as disabilities that need curing will benefit more from a behavioural approach.

■ ⋎ 6 Gestalt: Fritz Perls

Fritz Perls, the originator of Gestalt counselling, was born in Berlin in 1893. He was the son of a Jewish wine salesman and grew up with his two sisters in a disturbed family atmosphere caused by frequent fights – physical and verbal – between his parents. He studied at Freiburg and Berlin Universities and obtained a medical degree in 1920. He then studied psychoanalysis in Berlin and Vienna. In 1926 he joined the Institute for Brain Damaged Soldiers in Frankfurt. In 1933, when the Nazis rose to power, he moved to the Netherlands. The following year he went to South Africa to work as a training analyst, and in 1935 he set up the South African Institute for Psychoanalysis. In 1946 he moved to the United States, where he and his wife founded the New York Institute for Gestalt Therapy and the Cleveland Institute for Gestalt Psychotherapy. In California he became resident associate psychiatrist at the Esalen institute at Big Sur. In 1969 he moved to Vancouver, Canada, where he established a Gestalt community. He died in 1970 after a brief illness.

Theoretical assumptions

Gestalt is a German noun meaning 'form' or 'shape', and the verb *gestalten* means to shape, form, fashion, structure and organise. Gestalt holds that human nature is organised into patterns or wholes and is experienced by the individual in these terms. That is, humans do not perceive things in isolation but organise them into meaningful wholes.

The figure is the focus of interest, for example a pattern or an object, and the ground or background is the setting or context. The interplay between figure and ground is dynamic, which means that any given ground may give rise to different figures if there are differing interests and shifts of attention. A figure may become background or ground if some detail of its own becomes a figure or replaces it as the focus of interest.

Holism versus dichotomy

In line with Perls' view that the human organism is a unified whole, an important element of Gestalt is rejection of dichotomies or divisions. For example mental activity is viewed as an activity of the whole person, but at a lower energy level than physical activity. In short, mental and physical activities cannot be dichotomised or divided.

Gestalt also rejects any separation of the self from the external world because individuals are not autonomous from the environment in which they live. In fact the individual and the environment are what they are because of their relationship to each other and the whole. They do not create each other. For example there is no sight unless there is something to be seen, and nothing can be seen unless there is an eye to see it.

Other rejected dichotomies are the infantile/mature dichotomy, as the lack of some childish traits can devitalise adults, and some so-called infantile traits are actually introjections of adult neuroses; plus emotional (subjective)/real (objective), love/aggression, conscious/unconscious and biological/cultural.

Homeostasis

Homeostasis or organismic self-regulation is the process by which the organism restores its balance when its equilibrium is disturbed by a demand or need. This striving for balance is a basic tendency in every organism, but internal needs and external (environmental) demands cause continuous imbalance. When there is homeostasis the individual has good health, whereas a prolonged state of disequilibrium means ill-health. Death is the result of the total breakdown of the homeostatic process.

If individuals experience several needs at the same time a selective process takes place based on the need to survive and self-actualisation. These come before any other needs. The most urgent need will always come to the forefront, although there are always hundreds of unfinished situations at any one time. The object is to satisfy needs; to complete or close incomplete 'gestalten'. Thus people have to be able to sense what it is that they need and manipulate themselves and their environment to satisfy these needs. This process goes on throughout life, with new gestalts appearing as old ones are satisfied.The organism maintains itself by the homeostatic process. According to Perls the only law that is constant is the forming of gestalts – wholes or completeness. He saw gestalt as an organic function, an ultimate experiential unit. In fact, in his view we can dispense with instinct theory and consider the organism as a system that needs to be balanced if it is to function properly.

The contact boundary

The organism and the environment have a relationship of mutuality. The contact boundary is the boundary between the organism and the environment, and it is there that psychological events take place. For Perls, psychology is the study of the operation of the contact boundary. This involves sensory awareness and motor behaviour.The sensory system provides the organism with orientation, and manipulation is provided by the motor system. Once orientation has taken place the organism manipulates both the environment and itself until balance is restored and the gestalt is closed. It is at the contact boundary that all feelings, thoughts and actions take place.

Contact can be seen as acceptance; withdrawal as rejection of the environment. Contacting the environment means forming a gestalt, withdrawal means closing one. Although the means of contact and withdrawal are normally present, neurotic people have a reduced capacity to judge which is appropriate and consequently their behaviour is less effective.

The self and self-actualisation

The self is the system of contacts at the contact boundary. It forms figures and grounds; it integrates the senses, motor coordination and organic needs; it finds and makes the meanings that we live by; and it is the system of identifications and alienations at the contact boundary, for example we identify with friends and feel alien to strangers. Self-actualisation is showing appropriate identifications and alienations.

Healthy functioning involves identifying with one's organismic self, not inhibiting one's creative excitement, and alienating what is not organismically one's own. Healthy functioning is hindered by all external controls, including internalised external controls.

Self-actualisation is based on the principle that you are what you are and should accept it. Low-functioning people live according to an image of what they should be rather than accepting what they are. The 'you should' of life hinders healthy functioning. So the only controls on life should be those demanded by the current situation. People learn to cope with life when they understand the situations they are in and let these situations control their lives. The last word on self-actualisation is Perls': 'Lose your mind and come to your senses' (Perls, 1970).

Excitement and emotion

In Gestalt counselling excitement means the energy we create. The physiological purpose of excitation varies hormonally according to the situation: sex hormones for erotic situations, adrenalin for anger. The energy of excitement not only powers the motor system and muscular activity, some of it also works on the senses. This is a healthy situation, but in unproductive thinkers much of the energy of excitement is diverted into fantasy and self-image actualisation.

Excitement is converted into specific emotions that are suited to the situation that has to be addressed. These emotions mobilise the sensory and motor systems to satisfy needs. Emotion is immediate and is not regulated by thoughts and verbal judgement. It is also a continuous process because everything we do has elements of the pleasant or unpleasant in varying degrees. Emotions make us aware of our concerns and therefore are vital to Gestalt counselling.

Aggression, assimilation and introjection

For an experience to be assimilated as the organism's own, an aggressive response to that experience is needed. Every organism grows by selectively taking in new matter and destructuring or digesting it. This matter can take the form of food and drink, parental influences or lessons.

Not all experiences undergo this process, and introjections are absorbed or swallowed whole without proper digestion. This means that the undesirable as well as the desirable is retained, and this weakens the organism. For example hateful parents inflict experiences on their children that are swallowed whole or introjected even though they are detrimental to the organism. In contrast loving parents provide experiences that are readily assimilated because they are beneficial to their children's progress from environmental dependence to self-support.

Frustration and manipulation

At first babies are absolutely dependent on their parents. However they soon learn to bite, crawl, accept and reject. This is part of the process of learning to realise their potential for existence. Growth is the process of overcoming frustrations by mobilising personal resources to manipulate the environment. Manipulation in this sense means the ways in which people use the environment to satisfy their needs. Healthy and unhealthy organisms both manipulate the environment, but healthy organisms manipulate it to achieve self-support while unhealthy organisms seek environmental rather than self-support.

Frustration is important because without it there is no reason or need to mobilise personal resources to do something on one's own. Perls considered that children learn to manipulate the environment in order to avoid or escape the pain of frustration. Put another way, the right sort of frustration teaches children to manipulate the environment in such a way as to meet their needs and maintain their organismic balance.

Lack of frustration produces spoilt children. If they are unable to cope with their frustrations or block them they may engage in play-acting – including flattering and pretending to be helpless, stupid and weak – in order to manipulate their environment. As a result they alienate parts of themselves, such as the ears, eyes and genitals.

Interruptions of contact and zones of awareness

There are interruptions in the contact provided by the organismic processes. These processes lead to self-support if left alone, but humans are brought up to rely more on knowledge gained from education than on biological instincts. This means that our animal intuition of the correct procedure to follow is blocked and replaced by composite procedures developed over the generations. Such procedures are mostly to do with social contact, for example ethics, manners and protocols. As these are not biologically based they result in the contact interruptions mentioned above. Common examples we have all experienced are 'Don't do that!' and 'Don't touch!' Withdrawal may also be prevented: 'Stay at the table and concentrate on your homework!' Parental interruptions may become introjections: 'A real man doesn't cry'. Neurotics self-interrupt and need to be made aware of this, as well as what it is they are interrrupting.

One way in which adults interrupt their children's contact is by suppressing emotion. Adults of this type tend to have been brought up in an environment where significant figures feared emotion, and as a consequence they tend to disapprove of and suppress their children's emotions. This results in the latter failing to develop and differentiate naturally and is usually accompanied by overemphasis on the external world and reality and by the ridiculing of emotions and other organismic needs. Children adjust to this antipathy by dulling their body senses, with an attendant loss of vitality.

All this is counterproductive because emotions are inherent in the make-up of human beings, undesirable emotions are not destroyed by the general suppression of emotions, and it disturbs the intricate organism/environment field by setting up situations that are actually emotion-arousing. There are three zones of awareness: the outer zone, which is made up of awareness of the world and the facts and processes that are available to all; the self zone, which is our authentic, organismic self; and the intermediate zone, which lies within the self zone and is usually called the conscious or the mind. The latter prevents people from being in touch with themselves and the world. Perls had two ways of describing this: 'mind fucking', or the activity of the intermediate zone preventing people from coming to their senses; and *maya*, an Indian word that equates fantasy and illusion with a dream or trance-like state.

Anxiety

The word anxiety derives from the Latin *angustia* (narrowness). It is caused by a physiological or psychological response to the conflict between control and excitement. There are two definitions of anxiety in Gestalt theory:

- Physiological: anxiety is the experience of breathing difficulty during a period of blocked excitement. That is, energy mobilisation increases and breathing quickens whenever there is powerful contact and concern. It is a normal and healthy response during exciting or energetic pursuits such as sport, sexual activity or creative activities. It is not healthy to try to control this excitement by attempting to breathe at the rate that was adequate before the excitement began because this causes a narrowing of the chest and forces the person to exhale, thus creating a vacuum that will precipitate an inrush of fresh air.
- Psychological: anxiety is the gap between the now and the later. It could also be described as stage fright. It is the result of fantasy activity in the intermediate zone, the fantasy being a rehearsal for a future of which we are afraid. According to Perls, humans do not want to contemplate the future so they fill the gap with sameness, insurance cover, the *status quo* or anything else that will do the job.

People who are in touch with their senses tend not to suffer anxiety. This is because their excitement is spontaneously funnelled into inventive and creative actions to resolve unfinished situations. Their contact with themselves and their environment is not restricted by *maya* (fantasy), apprehension or prejudice. Such people are willing to take reasonable risks in their lives.

There are two types of fantasy: catastrophic fantasy, which entails overprecaution; and anastrophic fantasy, which entails too little precaution. Some people manage to balance the two types of fantasy and thereby achieve perspective and 'rational daring'.

Neurosis

With neurosis there is a constant fight between *maya* and reality. This contrasts with psychosis, where the sufferer loses touch with reality and adopts *maya* instead, with a sense of worthlessness or megalomania being paramount.

Neurotic people permit society to impinge overly on their lives and are unable to identify their own needs. They perceive society as larger than life, and themselves as smaller. Society consists of groups such as the family, colleagues, friends, the state and so on, and if the neurotic and one of these groups experience different needs the neurotic cannot decide which need is paramount. This prevents him or her from making good contact or good withdrawal and results in contact boundary disturbances, which in turn hamper personal growth and self-recognition. It should be noted that not all disturbances in the organism–environment balance constitute or are evidence of neurosis. Language can represent and help to sustain boundary disturbances, as discussed below.

There are four mechanisms of contact boundary disturbance: introjection, projection, confluence and retroflection.

With introjection, instead of being properly assimilated external material is swallowed whole, complete with its undesirable elements. The results of introjection are the undigested feelings, thoughts and behaviour known as introjects. In short, introjection is the process of owning as part of oneself what is actually part of the environment. In language terms, 'I' is used when the real meaning is 'they'.

There are two outcomes of introjection: dealing with introjects results in people being unable to get in touch with their own reality; and incompatible introjects can contribute to personality disintegration. Introjectors do as others want them to do.

Projection is the opposite of introjection in that individuals see what is actually part of the self as part of the environment. This involves shifting onto others those parts of themselves they dislike and devalue, rather than recognising and dealing with them. Projections are associated with introjects in that people tend to devalue themselves in relation to introjected self-standards. The self-evaluations deriving from this process are then projected onto the environment.

Projection takes place when they disown the parts of themselves from which undesirable impulses emanate. For example an urge or emotion is given an objective existence outside themselves, and they blame it for their problems. They say 'It took control of me' or 'It seemed to have a life of its own', and in so doing deny that the so-called 'it' is actually a part of themselves. In language terms, the pronouns 'they' and 'it' are used in place of 'I'. Projectors do to others what they accuse others of doing to them.

With confluence there is no boundary or distinction between the self and the environment. When individuals are unaware of the contact boundaries between themselves and others they are unable to make good contact or to withdraw if necessary. Confluence cannot tolerate difference and insists on likeness. Examples include parents who cannot see that their children are different from themselves, or husbands or wives who cannot accept that their spouse is different from them. In language terms the pronoun 'we' is used when in fact there is differentness. People in confluence do not know who is doing what to whom.

Finally, **retroflection** means 'to turn sharply back against'. With retroflection individuals redirect their activity inwards, making themselves rather than their environment the target of their behaviour. They fail to discriminate between themselves and others accurately in that they treat themselves as they want to treat others. So angry people who have had an awful time turn their destructive urges against themselves.

Retroflection does not have to be viewed as neurotic because it may be to people's advantage to supress their urges or responses. It is pathological only when it becomes habitual, chronic and out of control. In language terms the reflexive 'myself' is used, for example 'I am ashamed of myself' rather than 'I am ashamed'. Retroflectors do to themselves what they would like to do to others.

There are five layers of neurosis:

- The cliche layer: this involves meaningless greetings such as handshakes or saying 'Alright then?'
- The Eric Berne or Sigmund Freud layer: here people use counterproductive manipulations in false games and roles. Typical examples are the important person, the good girl, the cry baby and so on.
- The impasse or stick point: this involves avoiding or escaping from authentic living. Suffering is avoided, including frustration and the pain of impasse or being stuck and lost. This is an important feature in the maintenance of neurosis.
- The death or implosive layer: people with this form of neurosis fear death or have a feeling of not being alive. They compress and contract themselves.
- The explosion: explosions connect with the authentic, organismic person. The strength of explosions depends on the amount of energy invested in the implosive layer. There are four basic kinds of explosion from the death layer: grief (individuals work through a loss that has not been assimilated), orgasm (occurs in sexually blocked people), anger and joy.

An example of the last two layers of neurosis is a woman whose husband has died of a heart attack, and who is struggling to face her grief and nothingness so that she can return to normal life and make real contact with the world.

Gestalt counselling

Gestalt counselling is aimed at people experiencing an existential crisis. The goal is to assist clients to progress from environmental support to self-support. At first the emphasis is on problem solving and on getting clients to acknowledge their expert status, that is, that they are the authors of their own lives. If this is not possible at the start of counselling it becomes a focus of the therapeutic process. Counsellors work to promote their clients' sense of freedom and responsibility, that is, to increase their 'response ability'.

Personal development of this sort requires increasing awareness of sensing, feeling and thinking at any given moment – in fact it has been said that the only goal of Gestalt counselling is awareness. It also requires clients to gain self-support or inner strength so that they are not dependent on the environment for their functioning, to have an integrated way of operating so that they use and experiment with more of their potential and recognise when they are at odds with themselves, and to identify how they relate well or badly to others and acknowledge their status as social beings.

Personal maturation is never completely attained in that there is always a chance of making further progress as the years progress, but people tend to stop when they have found a satisfactory way of functioning in the world. According to Perls, 90 per cent of people seek therapy not for a cure but to be more adequate in their neuroses! Gestalt counselling is not a normative process aimed at fostering well-adjusted behaviour in the conventionally accepted sense; instead it helps each client to discover unique solutions to his or her particular situations. There is emphasis on the unique nature of each client's personal history, values, needs, preferences and circumstances. Personal solutions using personal resources are pursued even if this means flying in the face of commonly held values, for example with regard to the accumulation of wealth. This includes radical criticism of society and its norms and institutions.

To be effective counsellors must undergo prolonged personal and group therapy. This form of counselling is not based on theoretical knowledge – it requires counsellors to be aware of their own psychological processes; it must be internalised and become part of the counsellor's life and work. Counsellors vary greatly in terms of their professional and personal qualities, but they must be authentic and open about their feelings and reactions, and competent in handling all facets and manifestations of interpersonal relations. They must be able to step outside their problems and preoccupations so that they can be fully there for their clients. Just as importantly, they must be able to recognise when they cannot do this and are therefore unfit to counsel. They must be non-exploitive and have respect for the integrity of the counselling process. A strong ethical base is integral to the work of Gestalt.

Therapeutic style

Counsellors work to provoke and support their clients' exploration of their 'here and now' experiences. This includes relating to their counsellors or their fellow members in a group situation. Such open-ended enquiries must have a 'dialogic' realtionship based on an 'I–Thou', person-to-person dialogue, with client and counsellor meeting each other as people and not as 'roles'. Counsellors let themselves be themselves, and clients are expected to do the same.

The validity of clients' reality is honoured, and although counsellors share some of their own life experiences and feelings, they do not attempt to impose any views and values of their own. Honesty is more important than constant softness in these dialogic relationships.

Experimentation and playful creativity are encouraged. For example metaphorical and intuitive thinking is encouraged because most people are less adept at this than at verbalisation and explanation. Physical expression is encouraged, for example dance and dramatisation, and dialogue between the parts of the self is promoted to increase clients' awareness of their inner states and the whole mind–body system.

Good counsellors adapt their style to suit their clients, the individual situation and the stage of therapy that has been reached. Such choices are grounded in skill and experience. Counsellors' responses depend on their degree of inventiveness when working to increase their clients' level of awareness:

- They may be challenging and confrontational in order to show their clients that their own behaviour is self-destructive or manipulative.
- They may set up a channel of support if this is what clients need in order to take a risk.
- They may listen caringly when clients recall a trauma they have never told of before.
- They may openly yawn at yet another repetition of the same old story, with the intention of provoking some new realisation or shift in the client.

Creative, spontaneous responses are needed when attending to clients' unfolding reality and unique experiences. Fixed techniques, stale routines and stereotyped reactions will not do. Responses are also influenced by the clients' previous experience in therapy, the severity of their disturbance, the stage reached in the therapeutic relationship, the degree of support available to the clients, clients' confusion at the contact boundary and concerns such as the amount of time available.

Gestalt counselling techniques

The awareness technique

This is an experiential rather than a verbal or interpretive approach. Gestalt counsellors are awareness experts and actively stimulate clients to explore their ongoing present experiences, such as feelings, images, sensations and so on. Counsellors are naturally aware of their own experiences, so the counsellor–client dialogue is a shared exploration of each other's experiences. Data on the ways in which clients interrupt their contact with life are collected and assessed. Counsellors also investigate their clients' changing sense of reality. The following questions are asked: What is happening? What are you aware of? What are you doing now? What did you feel when you said that? Questions deliberately begin with 'What' and 'How' in order to focus attention on the specifics of experience. They do not use 'Why' because this provokes explanation and generality. It is important that clients understand their present manipulations, understand their contact boundary disturbances, and reexperience the unfinished business of past problems and traumas.

For Perls the phrase 'Now I am aware' is the foundation of Gestalt counselling. Now, because it keeps counselling in the present and experience can only take place in the present. Aware, because this gives the best picture of clients' present resources. Clients are asked to become aware of their body language, breathing, tone of voice and so on. The emphasis on 'now' does not exclude what has happened in the past, but clients' recollection of it is happening now and therefore it must have some significance for the present. Likewise memories do not crop up randomly; they relate to incomplete gestalts from the past, to needs that were unmet and persist into the present to drive present behaviours and internal feelings.

Clients find it difficult to remain in the here and now so the awareness technique is used to promote concentration or what is often called 'focal awareness'. This involves clients learning to experience each 'now' and each need. They also learn how their feelings and behaviour in one area are related to feelings and behaviour in others. This reveals that they are interrupting their contact with themselves and the world, what it is that they are interrupting, and that they are doing it through neurotic mechanisms such as projection and introjection.

Finally, homework is set that requires clients to review the session in terms of systematic application of the awareness technique.

The sympathy and frustration technique

It is not enough merely to empathise with clients because this means that counsellors are withholding themselves. Sympathy is also needed, but sympathy on its own spoils the client. The best combination is a mixture of sympathy and frustration, that is, clients must be frustrated in their endeavour to control their counsellors by means of neurotic manipulation. Instead clients' manipulative power is redirected to enable them to meet their true needs. Clients are taught to avoid becoming phobic when they become uncomfortable, and instead to be more aware.

Perls set up situations that resulted in clients being stuck in frustration. He then frustrated their avoidances even further so they were forced to mobilise their own resources. In other words he frustrated clients in order to bring them face to face with their blocks. The important point here is that frustration eventually reveals that phobic impasse exists in fantasy and not in reality, and that clients are stopping themselves from using their resources because of their catastrophic expectations. Frustration helps clients to express their needs directly rather than masking them with neurotic manipulations. The primary form of communication is the imperative because clients who are able to state precisely what they need and mean what they say have made the most important advance in counselling.

The fantasising technique

This is used to speed up counselling. Fantasising can be verbal, written or acted, and there is often a strong transference element, representing projected attributes.

Drama techniques

Firstly, monodrama or monotherapy is a type of psychodrama in which individual clients play all the roles in a drama of their own creation and under their own direction.

Secondly, the shuttle technique involves clients shuttling their attention from one area to another. For example a client may shuttle from the visualisation of a memory to the reliving of it in the here and now. Another useful application of this technique is to get clients to shuttle between talking and listening to themselves. After each sentence they are asked if they are aware of what they have said. The object is to stop them talking compulsively because this prevents them from hearing what others have to say and from experiencing themselves.

Thirdly, with the hot seat technique the hot seat is occupied by one of the clients taking part in a group session and the counsellor works with that client in front of the group.

Fourthly, the empty chair technique involves clients changing chairs as they shuttle between parts of themselves or between the different people in a monodrama, or to complete unfinished business. For example clients might be asked to imagine that a deceased person from their past is sitting in the chair, and then to say all the things they would like to say if that person were really there. The imagined person might be an abuser or some other person who has hurt the client.

Finally, top dog–underdog dialogues involve chair shutling and fantasy work. Many people have self-torture fantasies in which they are fragmented into a top dog or inner controller and an underdog or the controlled. The top dog is the superego and is characterised by the issuing of authoritarian and righteous 'shoulds' and 'should nots'. This top dog is a perfectionistic manipulator that threatens dire consequences if its demands are not met.

The underdog is the intra-ego and is cunning. It manipulates by being apologetic or defensive, by wheedling, by being a crybaby and so on. Typical underdog statements are 'My intentions are really good', 'Mañana' and 'I really do try my best'.

Counsellors get their clients to shuttle between these two polarities so that they can understand how their behaviour is structured. The aim is to reconcile the two adversaries by enabling clients to be more in touch with their organismic self.

Dreams

According to Perls, dreams are the royal road to integration. They are not just unfinished situations, symptoms or current problems, they are existential messages. If a dream is repetitive, then an important existential issue is likely to be involved.

There are four stages to dreamwork. In the first stage the dream is related by the client. The second stage involves the client retelling the dream, or part of it, in the present tense so as to make it into a drama. For example 'I was walking along this country lane' becomes 'I am walking along this country lane'. In the third stage the client becomes the stage director, setting the scene and talking to the various actors. Finally, the client becomes the actors, the props and everything else involved. The empty chair technique is valuable in the final stage as it facilitates a dialogue between the different characters, parts of the self and so on that are encountering each other.

Dreamwork promotes the integration of conflicts and reidentification with alienated parts of the self, especially the assimilation of projections, and it reveals holes in the client's personality. The latter show up as blank spaces and voids, accompanied by confusion and nervousness.

Group counselling

There are six basic rules for Gestalt groups

- The 'now' principle: communications in the present are encouraged, for example the question 'What is your now?' might be asked.
- I and thou: this involves sending direct messages to the other. The personal pronoun 'I' is used rather than 'it'.
- Responsibilty language: this involves changing statements such as 'I am unable to do that' to 'I refuse to do that'.
- The awareness continuum: rather than the usual 'why' of behaviour, emphasis is switched to the 'now what' and 'how' of behaviour.
- No gossiping: communication should be directed at the people concerned, as opposed to talking about others when they are present.
- Changing questions into statements: instead of asking questions that serve to manipulate the environment to gain support, group members are encouraged to exchange passive questions for active, self-supporting statements.

A number of games are used by counsellors in group sessions. In the 'I take responsibilty' game every statement made by a client is accompanied by the phrase '. . . and I take responsibilty for it'. For example 'I am aware that I am walking forward, and I take responsibility for it'. In 'I have a secret' every person in the group thinks of a personal secret that fills them with shame and guilt and (without sharing it) imagines (or projects) what others might say about it. Games of dialogue are used for splits in the personality, such as the top dog–underdog scenario. Others include masculine–feminine and nice guy–rogue. In 'Making the rounds' a theme or feeling is elaborated by a client. For example 'I don't trust anyone in this room' is turned into a specific statement to each person. 'Unfinished business' requires clients to complete unfinished business with parents, friends, colleagues or siblings. Unfinished business includes feelings such as hurt, resentment and anger.

In 'Playing the projection' a client who has difficulty with, for example, trusting others is asked to play an untrustworthy person in order to identify and assimilate his or her own untrustworthiness. A lot of human thought constitutes a rehearsal of social roles, so in 'Rehearsal' group members are asked to share their personal rehearsals. The main principle behind 'Reversal' is that overt behaviour is frequently the reverse of latent/underlying impulses, so in this game the considerate young man is asked to play someone selfish and uncaring, and so on. 'Exaggeration' focuses either on verbal statements or on movement and gesture. Clients are asked to exaggerate the statement or behaviour in each case. Finally, in the 'Marriage counselling' game partners sit opposite each other and say 'I resent you for . . .', followed by 'What I appreciate in you is . . .'. The next step is to get partners to relate to the reality of each other, rather than their fantasy of them. So partners describe each other in sentences that start with 'I see . . .'.

Changes to gestalt counselling since the death of Perls

Nowadays there is less emphasis on confrontation and frustration in Gestalt counselling. A softer approach is taken and clients' perceptions are emphasised. Counsellors are more likely to make disclosures about their own defensiveness, personal problems, life experiences, confusion and fears, but only if it helps the client to take the next step. Physical contact takes place, and to enhance contact with clients and improve client focusing counsellors make 'I' statements. Psychoanalytic formulations are openly voiced to describe character structure. Counselling is carried out on an individual, group or joint basis, and increased attention is given to theoretical instruction, theoretical exposition and general work with cognition. Finally, Gestalt techniques have been integrated with other approaches, such as transactional analysis, which is discussed in the next chapter.

Conclusion

The most worrying aspect of the Gestalt approach is that it went through a period of being fashionable, during which time it was simplified and distorted by therapists from other approaches who used Gestalt after just a few days' training. The scarcity of research and literature contributed to the trivialisation of the approach and the lack of understanding of its theoretical content. This was also the result of a regrettable propensity to minimise the use of the intellect. Fear that a rigid structure might emerge caused a disinclination to move on from the early phase of innovation and improvisation to develop a solid theoretical and organisational base. Another problem was that practitioners failed to take the founders' insights into new areas in a way that was consistent with the approach's principles. The result, especially in Britain, was that many Gestalt therapists felt isolated and lacked a professional network. The consequence of all this was variable standards among Gestalt therapists. However the problems have been addressed and Gestalt has survived because, at its best, it enables clients to make sense of the world. It is therefore a theory that fits the functioning of human beings.

⬛ ☑ 7 Transactional analysis: Eric Berne

Eric Berne was born Eric Lennard Bernstein in Montreal, Canada, in 1910. He grew up in a poor Jewish quarter of Montreal, where his father was a GP and his mother a professional writer and editor. He studied English, psychology and premedicine at McGill University, Montreal, gaining a BA in 1931. He obtained his MD and Master of Surgery degree in 1935 from the same university. He then went to the School of Medicine at Yale University, where he became a psychiatric resident. He changed his name to Berne to avoid the anti-Semitism of the period and began a private psychiatric practice in Norwalk, Connecticut. He served as a psychiatrist in the Army Medical Corps during the Second World War, after which he went to California and resumed his practice. He also accepted a position as consultant in psychology and neurology to the US Army. He began working on group therapy during the 1950s, and underwent training analysis with Erik Erikson. He continued his writing and private practice until his death in 1970.

Theoretical assumptions

Berne's approach differs from other approaches in that it is based on child, parent and adult ego states, and the dividing line between what is and what is not transactional analysis (TA) rests on whether or not human behaviour is explained in terms of such ego states. Berne was strongly influenced by Freud, but the theory and practice of TA are very different from those of psychoanalysis. TA is both a theory of personality and social interaction, and a method of counselling.

The fundamental 'OK' position

Berne had a positive view of human nature, as expressed in the TA statement: 'I am OK; you are OK'. In Berne's view 'Every human being is born a prince or a princess; early experiences convince some that they are frogs, and the rest of the pathological development follows from this' (Berne, 1966, pp. 289–90).

Related to the basic assumption of human 'OKness' are two further assumptions. First, almost all human beings possess the complete neurological apparatus for adequate reality-oriented or adult functioning. The only exceptions are those with severe brain injuries. The therapist's task is to strengthen this apparatus so that it can take its normal place in the client's psychic organisation.

Second, people have a built-in drive for mental and physical health, and the therapist's job is to help nature by removing obstructions to patients' emotional and mental development, thus letting them grow in their own direction.

Ego states

The notion of ego state is central to TA. In Berne's words, 'An ego state may be described as a coherent system of feelings related to a given subject, and operationally as a set of coherent behaviour patterns; or pragmatically as a system of feelings which motivates a related set of behaviour patterns' (Berne, 1961, p. 17).' Though not always emphasised by Berne, ego states involve thinking as well as feeling and behaviour. All people exhibit three kinds of ego state, and at any given moment all individuals in a social grouping will predominantly exhibit one or other of these states, which are discussed in turn below and depicted structurally in Figure 7.1.

The parent ego state

The parent or exteropsychic ego state is a set of feelings, thoughts, attitudes and behaviours that resemble those exhibited by parental figures. It is both an accumulation of data and a way of relating to people. The parent ego state takes one of two forms:

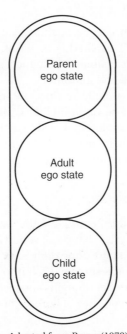

Source: Adapted from Berne (1978), p. 12.

Figure 7.1   Structural diagram of a personality

- The controlling or prejudicial parent is manifested as a set of seemingly arbitrary and rigid rules, usually prohibitive, that may agree with the rules of a person's culture.
- The nurturing parent is manifested in sympathy and care for another individual or for oneself.

Hence the parent can be overcontrolling and inhibiting, or supportive and growth enhancing. The parent ego state may also influence a person's adult or child ego states. The function of the parent is to conserve energy and to diminish anxiety by making certain decisions automatic.

The adult ego state

The adult or neopsychic ego state autonomously and objectively appraises reality and makes judgements. Berne likened the neopsyche to a partially self-programming probability computer, and stated that its adequacy can be judged by the use that individuals make of the available data. The characteristics of the adult ego state include organisation, adaptability and intelligence.

The child ego state

The child or archaeopsychic ego state is a set of feelings, thoughts, attitudes and behavioural patterns that are archaic relics of a person's childhood. According to Berne we all carry within ourselves a little boy or girl who feels, thinks and responds just as we did when we were children of a certain age. The child ego state takes two main forms (Figure 7.2):

- The adapted child, which can be further divided into the compliant child and the rebellious child. This child is manifested in feelings and behaviour that inferentially are under parental influence, such as sulking, compliance, rebelliousness, withdrawal and inhibition.
- The natural child, which is manifested in spontaneous expression such as self-indulgence or creativity. The natural child is the most valuable part of the personality. The proper function of a healthy child is to motivate the adult to provide it with gratification. It does this by letting the adult know what it wants and by consulting the parent about its appropriateness.

Structural analysis of ego states

This involves diagnosing and differentiating betweeen the different ego states. Second-order structural analysis (Figure 7.3) subdivides these states, for example the parent is divided into two parts, one derived from the mother and one from the father, and the child absorbs some of each into its own ego states, including how each parent showed his or her thoughts and feelings when expressing values. The parent, adult and child ego states of both parents are found in second-order structural analysis.

When the child decides on its life script the parent, adult and child ego states are already in place in the child's ego state. The parent in the child is called the

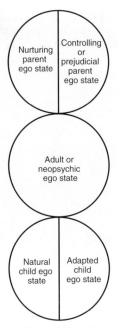

Source: Adapted from Nelson-Jones (1996), p. 71.

Figure 7.2   Structural diagram of the personality

'electrode' because when it 'pushes a button' the person does something negative, such as turn off sexually if feeling strongly aroused, drink excessive amounts of alcohol or engage in uninhibited gambling. This is called the 'pig parent'.

The adult in the child was regarded by Berne as a keen and perceptive student of human nature. In TA the adult in the child is called the 'professor' or 'little professor' and is the source of creative and intuitive thinking. However it is also the source of delusion because it is not always right.

The child in the child is the origin of inner wants and feelings and is characterised by a spontaneity that is sometimes destructive.

Psychic energy and cathexis

TA uses the concepts of psychic energy and cathexis (the distribution of energy). For this reason it is regarded as a dynamic theory of personality. The ego state that is most strongly cathectic at any given time is in control. The flow of cathexis causes shifts in the various ego states, each of which has a semipermeable boundary separating it from the other states. Shifts in ego states depend on three factors: the forces acting on each state, the permeability of each ego state's boundaries, and the cathectic capacity of each of these states. The degree of balance between these factors determines the clinical condition of the individual and this in turn determines how counselling should preceed.

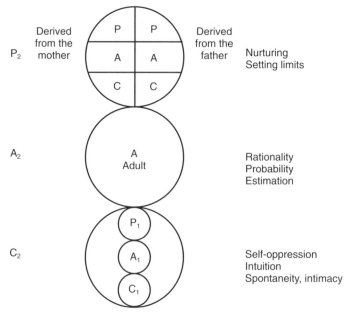

P₂ Derived from the mother

Derived from the father

Nurturing
Setting limits

A₂

Rationality
Probability
Estimation

C₂

Self-oppression
Intuition
Spontaneity, intimacy

P = parent;　A = adult;　C = child

Source: Adapted from Berne (1978).

Figure 7.3　Second-order structural diagram of personality

Social interaction

There are three types of hunger, drive or motivation. First, stimulus hunger applies especially to physical intimacy. Second, recognition hunger can be viewed as a partial transformation of infantile stimulus hunger. The term 'stroking' refers to any act that conveys recognition of the presence of another, including a simple nod of the head and short verbal greetings such as 'Hi'. Even negative recognition is preferable to no recognition because everyone needs strokes of some sort. Third, structure hunger is people's everyday quest to organise their waking hours and is concerned primarily with the time spent with others, or social time.

Time structuring

Any two people can engage in six types of time structuring or social behaviour:

- Withdrawal: here there is no communication and individuals are absorbed in their own thoughts. Examples include waiting in a queue and sitting in a train or bus.
- Rituals: these are dictated by tradition and social custom and are stylised signs of mutual recognition, such as saying 'hello'.
- Activities: in this context activities mean work and earning a living, but they are also socially significant in that they provide a framework for recogntion

and satisfaction. Transactions in this area are adult-to-adult and are mainly oriented towards external reality.

- Pastimes: these are mainly socially programmed and are semiritualistic topical conversations. They last longer than rituals and their focus is external to those concerned, as opposed to being directly self-referent.
- Games: these are a series of overt or covert transactions based more on individual than on social programming, and which lead to a payoff or predictable outcome. Payoffs are called 'rackets' if they involve negative feelings such as depression or anger. Collecting racket feelings is referred to as collecting 'trading stamps'. These can be cashed in for behaviours that range from crying or going on a shopping spree, to attempted suicide and divorce. All games have a motto that makes them recognisable, examples being 'If it weren't for you' and 'Why don't you – Yes but'.
- Intimacy: this includes (but is not restricted to) sexual intimacy. It is the most satisfying way of dealing with stimulus, recognition and structure hunger. It is instinctual and individual programming in which ulterior motives and social programming are largely absent. It is a candid, game-free relationship, with mutual giving and receiving and no exploitation.

Transactions

The fundamental unit of social interaction is the 'stroke', or unit of recogntion. Exchanging strokes is a transaction, and in a transaction one of the three ego states is predominantly cathected or energised. In other words, transactions take place between ego states, and so at the basic level TA involves analysing ego states that are engaged in stimulus and response exchanges. There are three types of transaction: complementary, crossed and ulterior.

Complementary transactions are those in which individuals receive a response from the ego state they have addressed. Examples include:

- Parent–parent: talking about the state of society.
- Adult–adult: discussing work.
- Child–child: playing together.

There are nine complementary transactions: PP, PA, PC, AP, AA, AC, CP, CA and CC. As long as transactions are complementary they will progress smoothly.

In crossed transactions the response comes from a different ego state from the one addressed, and/or may go to an ego state that is not the one that sent the original stimulus. Communication is broken off when a crossed transaction occurs – this may only be slight and momentary but it can be a complete break. There are 72 types of crossed transaction, though few occur frequently.

Finally, with ulterior transactions a covert, risky communication is disguised as an overt and more socially acceptable one. A lot of human interaction has more than an overt social meaning; it has a deeper psychological agenda too. By definition a psychological game is an ulterior transaction. For example someone might say 'Thanks for the lift home, would you like to pop in for a drink?' and the other person says 'Yes please, I could do with one'. The first person is offering an opportunity for seduction and the second one has accepted.

Scripts

Scripting is the process by which individuals, normally in childhood, make far-reaching decisions that influence or shape their future life experiences. A script is a preconscious life plan by which individuals structure their time. Such scripts determine their approach to relationships and tasks, and are based on infantile illusions that can persist for a lifetime. Individuals might believe they have personal autonomy but in fact they are acting out the orders of the script. An identity crisis can be caused by questioning the script, and even the removal of barriers to genuine autonomy may not always solve the problem.

Five factors play a role in people's script decisions:

- Lack of power.
- Inability to handle stress.
- Immature capacity to think.
- Lack of information.
- Lack of options.

The script matrix

The script matrix (Figure 7.4) is a diagram that is used to aid understanding of the development of an individual's script. It shows the messages, influences and prohibitions from parents and significant others. It is usually the parent of the opposite sex that tells the child what to do, but the parent of the same sex shows them how to do it. It is the child in the parent who gives restrictive orders, and the adult in the parent who gives the child the pattern or programme of behaviour.

Injunctions

Positive parental directives are nurturing and conducive to the child's emotional development, while negative parental directives are restrictive and reflect the fears and insecurities of the child in the parent. This manifests itself in scripting where growing individuals limit their capacity for awareness, spontaneity and intimacy in order to survive. This equates with acceptance from caretaking figures in both the practical and psychological sense. Normal developmental processes are inhibited by script decisions made when individuals are immature and their mental capacities undeveloped.

Injunctions are expressed as messages that begin with 'Don't'. They can be highly restrictive or mild. There are five injunctions for blocking intimacy:

- Don't give strokes if you have them to give.
- Don't ask for strokes when you need them.
- Don't accept strokes when you need them.
- Don't reject strokes when you don't want them.
- Don't give yourself strokes.

The above are causes of depression, while others can prevent thinking and feeling.

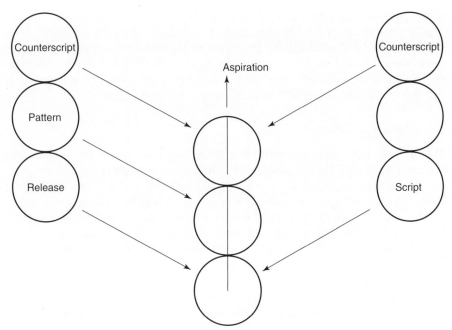

Notes: Script: negative inhibiting messages such as 'do not have good intimate relationships'. Counterscript: positive instructions about how to live one's life, for example 'work hard'. Release: an external intervention or condition releasing someone from their script, for example a heart attack. Aspiration: autonomous aspirations such as the desire for intimacy and health. Pattern: the modelling of significant figures such as the father whose devotion to work ruined his family life.

Source: Adapted from Berne (1975/1978), p. 128.

Figure 7.4   Script matrix

Attributions

These involve telling children how they are feeling, what they are and what they have got to do. Children are punished if they do not follow the attributions, but if they do they are rewarded, with what are called 'family reinforcement schedules'.

Discounts

In general terms, a discount is the minimisation of some aspect of oneself, or another person or situation. It is a crossed transaction in which someone says something from an adult ego state to another person's adult ego state, but that person responds from his or her child or parent ego state.

Decisions

The infant utilises early transactions to develop a view of the world. These early transactions are related to feeding, toilet training, family relationships and weaning. The infant is less likely to form restrictive scripts if it is given unconditional protection. The child may obey parental wishes even at the expense of autonomy if its parents make nurturing conditional on submission to injunctions and attributions. Decisions of this sort are normally made in preschool years and are as realistic as the capacity of the adult in the child ego state or the little professor. The result is that children take a negative position and develop scripts, although some of these can be winners' scripts.

Life positions: OKness

This is the fundamental assumption of TA and is expressed in the life position/statement 'I'm OK – You're OK'. There are three 'not OK' positions: 'I'm not OK – you're OK', 'I'm OK – you're not OK' and 'I'm not OK – you're not OK'. Each of these reflects and maintains impaired ego state development. They hamper the development of intimacy and are the bases on which people play out their games. The need to justify a basic life position can be a motivator, but it is probably more accurate to regard position hunger as a refinement of the other motivators (stimulus, structure and recognition hunger).

An example of a decision leading to a life position is given by Berne (1966), who tells of a little girl called Rita who always greeted her father when he came home from work until his drinking made him reject her. A bad row between her mother and father made Rita so upset that she vowed never to love any man and maintained her decision by regarding her father as fundamentally bad even when sober. After childhood she generalised her position to most other men, whose not-OKness was summed up as 'All men are beasts'. This became a game in which she used seductive behaviour to provoke men, who she then rejected. Her manoeuvring was an attempt to form an intimate relationship she was unable to pursue.

Development games

Rituals, pastimes and activities that fit life situations are part of children's upbringing and stem from experiences in family life from the earliest days. An example is the child who pleads illness (a social transaction) in order to get out of doing something (an ulterior or psychological transaction). Games are imitative and are deliberately initiated by the neopsychic adult ego state (the little professor) in the child from the ages of two to eight. Such games are often used to justify a life position.

Counterscript messages

These come from the parent's parent and are usually transmitted from grandparents. 'Work hard' and 'Be good' are typical examples. Script injunctions and counterscript prescriptions may conflict and the life course can switch from one to the other. Counterscripts can mean a change from unhappy life plans to happy ones, but script injunctions always prevail in the end. Even so the chance of a winner's script is always possible. An alcoholic's parent ego state may issue a counterscript to be sober, but the parent in the child ego state says 'Don't worry about it, have a drink'.

Script payoffs

The script payoff is the ultimate goal and marks the end of a life plan. For example the little girl discussed above (Rita) had a script payoff that manipulated men into behaviour that confirmed her position that men were not-OK. Games not only have the social function of time structuring, they also maintain the health of some individuals because the doggedness with which they hold their life positions means that any tampering with payoffs or removing them can cause anxiety and even psychosis. A common example is the game with the payoff 'if it weren't for you', whose main features are as follows. A person claims that another person, such as a husband, wife, child or employer, is preventing him or her from pursuing a desired goal, but this is a way of not facing the possibility that he or she might not be capable of achieving this goal. The script payoff is validation of the life position that others are not-OK.

Autonomy

Autonomy is the capacity for reversible non-script behaviour; it is the opposite of script behaviour. It has no special timetable; it is developed in later life and is not under parental influence. It is the freedom to make important decisions about behaviour. It means being free of one's parents and their influence, so that they can be visited from time to time but can no longer exert their influence. Gaining autonomy requires the overthrow of three things:

- The influence of a tribal or family historical tradition.
- The parental, cultural and social background.
- The pursuit of ulterior payoffs from games.

Illusion of autonomy

Illusion of autonomy is when individuals believe that their feelings and behaviour come from the adult ego state and do not acknowledge feelings and behaviour coming from the child and parent ego states. Few people can live without illusions, and the most difficult to give up is that of self-determination or autonomy. A person who has achieved autonomy knows: what is adult and practical, what she or he will accept from others, and what she or he does that is determined by early impulses.

There is a difference between delusions and illusions: delusions are parental directives and prejudices that individuals believe to be their own, while illusions are the child's wishful thinking and urges that are seen as adult and rational. The illusion of autonomy means that individuals are unaware of the above and have not acquired the motivation and insight to be able to change. The answer is to adjust the adult ego boundary to permit the correct processing of information. The effectiveness of the adult ego state depends on the quality of the information it has access to, and on whether it has developed the necessary skills of effective adult functioning, such as the ability to acquire and correctly assess information that is relevant to it.

When ego boundaries lack sufficient definition the parent and/or child ego states contaminate the adult ego state. In individuals with true autonomy the ego boundaries are strong but sufficiently permeable to permit the movement of psychic energy between the various ego states.

Exclusion refers to the condition where one ego state is strongly cathectic while the other two are sidelined. Thus there is a constant parent, constant adult or constant child ego state. The excluding ego state may defend itself, for example by means of intellectualisation in the case of the excluding adult.

Transactional analysis

The aim of transactional analysis is for the client to reach the 'I'm OK – you're OK' life position. Berne used the analogy of princes and princesses being turned into frogs by life's experiences. The goals are to become more comfortable as a frog, (meaning to get better or progress), and then 'to cast off the frog skin and continue development as a prince or princess' (Berne, 1966, p. 290). This is achieved by securing autonomy and becoming the integrated adult. In the integrated adult, child-like and parent-like qualities are integrated into the adult ego state in a positive and non-contaminating way.

There are three basic capacities in the fundamental OK position:

- Awareness: this is the ability to hear directly rather than in the way in which we have been brought up to hear. It involves living in the here and now, and receiving sensory inputs from the environment.
- Spontaneity: this means feeling directly and expressing feelings directly, rather than in the way in which we have been brought up to do. Spontaneous people have the ability to select their feelings from any of the three ego states.
- Intimacy: this means relating to others in a game-free way that is loving, aware and spontaneous. This is a function of the uncorrupted natural child.

There are four methods of ego state analysis:

- Behavioural diagnosis: this is based on gestures, tone of voice, observable words, expressions, attitudes and posture.
- Social diagnosis: this is based on the reactions that the person elicits from others.
- Historical diagnosis: this relies on what is called historical validation, that is, validating that a past experience really did happen.
- Phenomenological diagnosis: this requires subjective self-examination, especially of intense experiences.

Contractual goals

The contract contains definitions of the treatment goals and the mutual responsibilities in achieving these goals. The goals include:

- Psychological matters such as impotence, and any **phobias**.
- Physiological changes such as the lowering of diastolic blood pressure.

- Behavioural changes such as not consuming drugs and alcohol or hitting children, keeping a job for a given time, increasing earnings, passing exams and so on.

Contracts can be amended as necessary and the goals are constantly changed and updated. For example an analyst investigating a client's archaic attitudes towards parental figures may first set a goal of alleviating the symptoms, but later update it to include changing the client's attitude towards parental figures. The ultimate goal may be different from the set of operational criteria for improvement set out in the initial goals. Determinants are kept under observation by the analyst as the counselling proceeds.

Egograms

The egogram is a bar graph that shows the distribution of a client's energy between the five functional ego states. It reveals the client's likely problems and their strengths and weaknesses. The amount of psychic energy in a person remains constant, so if one ego state yields energy, that energy is available for another ego state. Through therapy the adapted child ego state will yield energy to the adult and free child ego states.

Each person has different ego state imbalances, and a variety of techniques and exercises are used to raise or lower the energy cathected in specific ego states:

- Energy low in adapted child: strive to compromise and get on with other people.
- Energy low in free child: creative and intuitive activities.
- Energy low in critical parent: assertiveness techniques.
- Energy low in nurturing parent: empathy techniques.
- Energy low in adult: thinking exercises.

Psychological disturbance

There are three ways of conceptualising psychological disturbance.

1. The confusion model

In this model psychological health is defined as integrated adult functioning. High-quality information and a problem-solving ability are vital to the efficiency of the adult ego state. Adult functioning is shackled by traumatic experiences, limiting beliefs and learnt physiological and emotional responses. In TA this is known as contamination, which happens when the parent ego state intrudes upon the adult ego state, resulting, for example, in prejudices. It can also happen when the child ego state intrudes on the adult ego state, resulting, for example, in phobias. Both parent and child ego states can intrude on the adult ego state in a double contamination. These problems restrict effective functioning and reality testing. The goal of therapy is an integrated adult ego state free of unresolved experiences from child ego states or from the influence of internalised significant others, that is, parent ego states.

2. The conflict model

In this model there are intrapsychic 'stuck points' between the ego states, such as when the parent ego state is driving the client to work harder, whereas the child ego state needs to play more. If the child ego state has inhibited the expression of feelings, then an 'impasse' or conflict will occur when the client decides to be more assertive. Mental health requires the resolution of such impasses and a return to normal functioning without the suppression of emotions, needs and values.

3. The developmental deficit model

Here the disturbance is seen as being caused by pathological, neglectful or inadequate parenting at any of the stages of a child's development. For example: someone with a narcissistic personality disorder will have had insufficient reflecting or mirroring to allow a healthy sense of self; the child of an alcoholic could need the corrective experience of relationships with consistency of response – a reparative relationship with the analyst is needed; and schizophrenics in reparenting can regress and redo the various child development stages and introject a new parent ego state at the same time.

Perpetuating psychological disturbance

This happens when individuals seek the same strokes that were familiar in childhood (motivation). Also, they may interpret current situations in ways that match the preconceived needs of the script (cognitive meditation). Disturbance takes the following forms:

- The racket system provides a visual model for observing the script in operation and focusing on the self-reinforcing nature of the script as it operates in the life of the client.
- Script beliefs: this refers to early decisions and their related self-limiting beliefs about the self, others and lifestyle.
- Racket displays: these are behaviours that result from script beliefs
- Repressed feelings: feelings are repressed at the time of script decisions.
- Reinforcing memories: this is conducted by clients to back up their script position.

The process of change

The change from dysfunction to sound mental health is conceptualised as a manifestation of 'Physis' or growth towards autonomy – in the journey through childhood and adulthood people grow under the influence of Physis.

If this self-actualisation process is disrupted and the individual is trapped in a self-reinforcing, destructive life pattern a major development is required to correct the situation, that is, a religious conversion, love, a crisis, education or psychotherapy.

Change involves changing the course of clients' lives, with new characters, roles, plots and payoffs. Feelings, thoughts and behaviours also change, and as a result most of the symptoms besetting the clients disappear. There are a number of stages to the process, as follows:

- Motivation: clients' unhappiness motivates them to do something about it. They seek information about what TA has to offer, and the nature of the change process. Based on this a conscious decision is made to pursue change.
- Awareness: clients make themselves aware of what it is they want to change. With the help of their therapists they become aware of unresolved archaic issues in the child ego state, and of unassimilated parental ego state material. This is all part of the process of decontaminating the adult ego state.
- Treatment contract: in order for clients and therapists to assess the goals an operationally verifiable TA contract must be agreed. The terms are stated specifically and the contract is reviewed regularly throughout therapy until the clients have achieved autonomy.
- Deconfusing the child ego state: this stage addresses the unmet feelings and needs of the particular ego state that was suppressed at the time the script decision was made. It is vital for clients to have a sense of internal safety to underpin any redecision in the next stage.
- Redecision: this involves gradually changing the decisions that gave birth to the script. The redecision is made in the child ego state but with full adult comprehension of the consequences of change. If necessary the clients will also come to redecisions in the parent ego state.
- Relearning: here the clients, supported by their therapist, practice the new behaviours. Any redecision must be integrated into the functioning and general life of the clients if it is to be successful. The therapists monitor progress and provide information and feedback to the clients.
- Termination: once the reorientation and reintegration goals are reached the clients are ready to teminate therapy. Clients and therapists together assess the fulfilment of the contractual goals.

The qualities required by effective therapists

Therapists should have a sound theoretical background in TA and the ability to apply and explain different TA approaches. They should be able to set up clear contracts and treatment approaches, and to establish a safe environment for their clients. They require perceptual and cognitive clarity for client assessment. They should be aware of distortions of reality and incongruities, of the range of options for therapeutic interventions, and of both the privileges and limits of training. They should adhere to ethical principles and act as a model of psychological well-being and healthy living.

Therapeutic style

TA values uniqueness and difference, so the use of only one approach is frowned upon – therapists should have a flexible approach to a range of strategies. The core condition for TA therapy is for therapists to have self-respect and respect for the client as this forms the basis of the contractual therapeutic relationship, that is, the 'I'm OK – you're OK' position. Therapists should be active and interventionist, and their clients should be questioning, active and informed on their own behalf. The therapist's involvement varies from client to client and depends on the stage of therapy reached or the situation in question.

There may be a need for crisis intervention in the case of clinical depression, as well as neutrality, confrontation, the giving of information, the use of humour and the relating of personal experiences. Clients should be involved in their own treatment planning and goal setting; this includes reading to gain psychological knowledge if this is appropriate to their needs. Working with transference can form the pivot of in-depth, long-term therapy in TA.

A reparative relationship may be assumed by the therapist in order to provide what was lacking at the outset, correct developmental deficiencies or overcome trauma. For example, as a child a client might have suffered a long-term illness and was overprotected by anxious and worried parents, so the therapist provides the core conditions for the resulting inhibited adult to experiment and take risks. The core relationship is an integrated adult-to-adult relationship between client and counsellor, and is based on the idea of the therapist being available as a genuine and authentic person in an 'I–thou' relationship with the other person.

Finally TA offers an umbrella for a wide range of practitioners, ranging from short-term counselling by counsellors with a specific focus and a narrow range of skills, to long-term, in-depth work by psychotherapists who are restructuring their clients' personalities in the context of transferential relationships.

Therapeutic strategies and techniques

Contracting

Contracts are a distinctive feature of this type of therapy. They are important because they limit the destructive effects of psychological games in the therapeutic relationship. In order to provide clarity and avoid misunderstandings they set out the responsibilities of both client and therapist in specific terms, the outcomes of which are both observable and measurable. There is emphasis on client responsibility for the therapeutic process, which encourages cooperation and provides motivation for the client. Underpinning the contract is the assumption that the client has an active desire for health, which can be contrasted with client resistance to change. The therapist aims to find ways of actualising the client's positive forces for growth, and attention is paid by therapist and client to the survival functions of the defences developed by the latter over the years.

Decontamination

This strategy is designed to strengthen the integrated adult ego state by dealing with unintegrated material from the other ego states that may be hampering effective functioning. Parental beliefs that are irrelevant to the client's situation have to be highlighted and dealt with because contamination from the parent ego state is outside the client's conscious awareness. A major problem here is that parental beliefs are often regarded by a child as inviolable truths, so a male client may have internalised a belief by his father that women are not trustworthy, resulting in a succession of casual sexual relationships that end in disaster.

There may also be traumatic archaic child ego states and unresolved fears from infancy that are blocking the adult ego state reality testing. Transference interpretation and symbolic enactment are two of the techniques used to separate the contents of the different ego states, which enables therapists to increase their clients' awareness of the nature of reality, and of automatic assumptions about themselves and other people. All transference interpretation is decontaminating because it separates archaic experiences from the reality of the present. There are eight techniques for decontamination.

- Interrogation: questioning the client in order to collect vital information for therapy.
- Specification: putting the relevant information into clear categories.
- Confrontation: using the above information to show the client where there are inconsistencies.
- Explanation: telling the client what the therapist's adult ego state thinks is happening.
- Illustration: comparisons, anecdotes and similes are used by the therapist to strengthen explanations and confrontations.
- Confirmation: new confrontations are used to reinforce previous confrontations of the same issues.
- Interpretation: putting forward ways of understanding a situation in order to correct distortions and regroup the client's experiences.
- Crystallisation: summarising the client's position to aid decision making.

Impasse resolution in the conflict model

As already stated, TA assumes that the script decisions of early childhood determine individuals' subsequent behaviour. This script decision is a protective measure taken by children in response to pressure from their parents or the environment and carried into adult life, with all the consequences that this entails for the individuals concerned. Thus individuals may be psychologically disturbed, generally unhappy and unaware of the chance of change. If they develop a desire for healthy growth or gather energy the different ego states will clash as a consequence. If the situations worsens the individuals hit a 'stuck point' or impasse and it is at this point that they are most likely to seek therapy.

Redecision therapy

Here clients reverse the script decisions that are blighting their lives, thus resolving the impasse between child ego states and parent ego states and the different facets of the child ego states. Therapists are able to access historical child ego states because their clients relive them in their original vividness. If clients spontaneously regress to a child ego state this can be used in redecision making. For example a client might see the therapist as a 'withholding father'.

Clients relive the traumatic events of the past so as to cathect the particular child ego state that led to their script decision, and to deal with the unaddressed needs and hurts of that time. The advantages and disadvantages of keeping to the decision are examined and fresh decisions are made to replace them, witnessed by the parent and the decontaminated adult ego states. The therapists validate the constructive decisions made by their clients in the interest of survival in childhood. Finally the clients practice the redecisions both during and outside the therapy sessions until these new behaviours and their attendant feelings are absorbed into their personality. In the worst cases a complete overhaul of the child ego state is required, which involves rehearsal, experimentation and self-monitoring.

Techniques of parenting and reparenting in the deficit model

Clients' inner child is equipped with the parent experiences that were lacking in childhood. Reparenting is based on reparenting work with schizophrenics, in which psychotic clients who have regressed and are reliving early childhood experiences are 'reparented' by positive parents. Less disturbed clients can benefit from replacement parents in that they can replace restrictive directives from their natural parents with permissions and positive messages from their therapists.

Time-limited reparenting

This provides the therapy needed to repair an early deficit in a child ego state that is causing a current dysfunction. During childhood a client may have been unsupported during some trauma, so the missing support is provided during therapy in a symbolic reenactment.

Radical reparenting

This technique is often used with psychotic patients. A wide array of techniques and strategies are employed to equip clients with adequate parent ego states, accompanied by complete regression to allow the clients' child ego to progress more soundly through the usual developmental cycle. This involves the withdrawal of energy (called decathexis) from the original dysfunctional parent ego state and the adoption of a new, pre-agreed parent ego state, normally that of the therapist. Subsequent therapy is aimed at integrating this new parent state into adult functioning.

Self-reparenting

In contrast to the previous therapy, with self-reparenting clients provide their own new parent messages without introjection or incorporation from the therapist. This can be done with non-psychotic clients because their personality is more integrated than that of psychotics, whose parent ego state is destructive and fragmented. Such an approach assumes a normal level of adult ego functioning.

Working with the parent ego state

Changes to the parent ego state are brought about by decontamination, redecision and parenting techniques. Parental figures from the past are treated as if they are real people and can be interviewed. This method is used to restructure the parent ego states.

Conclusion

The success of this approach can be limited by the limitations of the counsellor. Either the client or the person referring the client should enquire about the practitioner's own experience of personal therapy and his or her previous professional work, for example teaching or psychiatry, in order to determine his or her suitability to take on the case.

TA is blessed with a rich repertoire of techniques, but there is much scope for the development of more theoretical and applied approaches to bodily awareness, affective work and transpersonal perspectives. A great strength of TA is its accessibility. This is because its concepts can be translated into simple language that ordinary people can comprehend and apply. The downside, of course, is that there has been an unfortunate popularisation of misconceived ideas that are not based on an adequate study of primary TA literature, and there is a dearth of knowledge on up-to-date theoretical developments. The written material on TA does not properly convey the complexity, subtlety and sophistication of clinical practice. It would help if veteran clinicians put their experiences into print for the benefit of trainees, less experienced colleagues and practitioners of other approaches. It would also benefit TA if major trends in mainstream psychology and developments in other approaches to therapy were absorbed and integrated.

▾ 8 Reality counselling: William Glasser

William Glasser, a California-based psychologist, developed reality counselling in the 1950s and 1960s. He grew up in Cleveland, Ohio and in 1953 received an MD from Western Reserve. He received his psychiatric training at Brentwood Hospital, and also studied at the University of California at Los Angeles. He became head psychiatrist for the California Youth Authority at the Ventura School for Girls. In 1968 he opened the Institute for Reality Therapy in Brentwood, Los Angeles.

Originally reality counselling was based not on a systematic theory but on the assumption that people should be responsible for what they do. Glasser added control theory during the early 1980s to provide his practice with a theoretical foundation. Its basic tenet is that human behaviour is an attempt to control the world, and ourselves as part of that world, in order to best satisfy our needs.

Theoretical assumptions

Control theory

Control theory, upon which reality counselling is based, has five main elements: active language, basic needs, pictures in the head, total behaviour and people as control systems.

Active language

Behaviour has three components – *thinking, doing* and *feeling* – and people choose how to do them. Verbs are used to express doing and thinking, for example swimming and contemplating. Adjectives are used to express feelings, for example 'excited'. Nouns are also used, for example 'depression'. However feelings do not just happen, people choose to feel a particular way, so Glasser does not use nouns and adjectives when he refers to feelings, he uses verbs. 'Active language' describes the behaviour chosen by people as they strive to control their environment to satisfy their needs. Examples are 'angering' for anger, 'depressing' for depression, 'anxietying' for anxiety, 'phobicking' for phobia and 'headaching' for headache.

Basic needs

The basic needs that drive us are genetic. All of our behaviour is aimed at trying to control our environment to meet these needs, which are never ending because when a need arises we have to satisfy it, and when we have succeeded in this other needs arise. Life is the endless striving to satisfy our various needs and to reconcile the continual conflicts between them. There are five basic needs:

Survival and reproduction: this is located in what is called the 'old brain', a group of structures at the top of the spinal cord (Glasser makes a distinction between the small, unconscious 'old brain' and the huge, conscious 'new brain' or cerebral cortex, which evolved later). Our genes tell the 'old brain' to execute the necessary survival activities to promote health and reproduction. There is constant communication between the two brains, the 'new brain' being the source of awareness and voluntary behaviour. Together they satisfy our survival needs. A large part of life is devoted to satisfying the more complex and conflicting needs that emanate from the conscious new brain.

Because we have to satisfy our genetic instructions psychologically rather than physically, Glasser refers to these new brain needs as psychological needs. These needs are still biological and are just as urgent as the physical needs of survival and reproduction.

The remaining four needs are psychological needs:

- Belonging–loving, sharing and cooperating: satisfying this need can involve a combination of any of the following – family, friends, groups, classes, pets, plants and even computers, boats and other inanimate objects.
- Power: satisfaction of this need is achieved by the acquisition of status, recognition and the obedience of others. This can conflict with the need to belong because the latter leads to relationships that can easily become power struggles.
- Freedom: we all need some freedom of choice about how to live our lives, or at least some parts of it, for example choosing friends, how we express ourselves, choice of occupation. Again this can conflict with other needs, such as the need to belong as a husband or wife, as a parent and so on. It is also fundamentally important that when satisfying needs our behaviour does not prevent others from doing the same.
- Fun: for higher animals, fun is the result of basic genetic instructions designed to assist learning. It improves motivation and takes away the drudgery of learning.

Mental picture albums

From our earliest days we develop a series of albums that contain pictures of the things required to satisfy our needs. For example hungry screaming toddlers might be given a bar of chocolate, and this restores them to happiness. Accordingly a mental picture of the chocolate bar is then filed away to look for when hungry again. Our senses combine to form a sensory camera that takes pictures of sounds, sights tastes and textures. Glasser uses the word pictures rather than perceptions because 80 per cent of the contents of personal albums are visual.

Personal picture albums are a small, selective part of the total memory bank and form what Glasser calls the 'quality world'. It contains very definite pictures of the things that satisfy our needs for worth, love, fun, success, freedom and so on, so it contains more than a vision of an ideal world. There is at least one picture for each of our needs, and it is practically impossible to have a need without a picture to satisfy it. Conversely we often have pictures that cannot be satisfied in the real world, and some pictures may be incompatible with each other, or irrational. Pictures can be added, and those which do not satisfy needs can be removed.

Our lives are changed when we change important pictures, but a picture can only be replaced by one that meets the same basic need. For example a battered woman may stay with her partner and endure a lifetime of misery because she is unable to replace her picture of him with that of another partner. The same applies to a woman who remains with an unfaithful partner. It is difficult to change our own pictures, and even harder to change other people's – this can only be done by discussion and making compromises. People do what they do because of the pictures in their own heads, not those of other peoples.

Pictures are essential to comprehending the control theory view of motivation because behaviour always begins with the pictures in our heads, and the difference between the pictures in our heads (what we want) and what is actually happening in the real world (what we have) determines our behaviour. When there is a difference we act to reduce this difference. This process is biologically driven, but what we do is usually our choice.

Total behaviour

According to control theory, behaviour is how people try to control the world to meet their needs rather than being a response to stimulation. 'Total behaviour' is Glasser's term for his expansion of the concept of behaviour. Total behaviour is always the sum of four components:

- Acting: this involves active behaviours such as swimming and walking, in other words anything that involves the voluntary movement of some part of the body. Routine activities are accompanied by involuntary actions, for example we swallow when we eat.
- Thinking: this has two aspects – voluntary thoughts, and involuntary thoughts such as dreams.
- Feeling: this consists of the pleasurable and painful feelings we generate.
- Physiology: comprises voluntary and involuntary body mechanisms involved in the feeling, thinking and doing parts of behaviour, for example sweating.

Depressed people are said to be depressing or choosing to depress the acting component (the client sits around lethargically), the feeling component (this involves misery, unhappiness and pain), the thinking component (thoughts such as 'my position is hopeless', 'what's the point?' and soon) and the physiology component (inability to sleep, bodily pains and soon). In order to deal with this clients must recognise the following. Behaviour is not a response to stimulation, it is how individuals try to control the environment to satisfy their needs. It is more than action and conduct, hence the term 'total behaviour'. The feeling component is just one of the four components in total behaviour and verbs such as 'depress' should be used when describing the behaviour. When clients admit to choosing to depress they are admitting they have a choice, that they could behave differently, and better.

Glasser likens total behaviour to a four-wheel-drive car, each component being one of the wheels. Acting and thinking make up the front wheels, feeling and physiology the rear wheels. The engine symbolises the needs, and drivers steer as closely as possible to the favoured picture in their album. Drivers have total control over where to steer the front wheels, and therefore can steer their life cars in a better direction than the one currently being followed. They have greater control over the front wheels (thinking and acting) than over the rear wheels (physiology and feeling), so reality counselling is designed to help clients to change their thoughts and actions (front wheels).

People as control systems

All living organisms have basic needs that are genetically built into their systems, and they are constantly trying to control the environment to satisfy those needs. As control systems, people act upon their environment and themselves in order to secure the picture they want. There are two ways of controlling the environment:

- The input dimension: people have to perceive what is available in their environment to secure the picture they think will satisfy their needs.
- The output dimension: they need to control (to act on) what they see as fulfilling their needs.

For example hungry people must first perceive what hunger is and how it can be satisfied by food. Then they satisfy their hunger by controlling or acting on their environment to search for food. If the preferred type of food is not available, then another type will be substituted.

According to Glasser there are few genuinely stressful situations in the outside world, and a situation is only called stressful when individuals cannot control it with their chosen behaviours. As control systems, people need to be in control – no control system wants to be controlled. People choose to rebel if others attempt to control them, or if they attempt to control themselves in ways that result in their needs remaining unmet. Rebellion can be direct or indirect. Indirect rebellion manifests itself as choosing to be ill or to depress, or migraine. People cannot be controlled unless they can be persuaded that this will satisfy one of their pictures.

Acquiring knowledge about needs and accumulating pictures

When babies are born they know how they feel, but they do not know what their basic needs are, or how to satisfy them. When their needs are not satisfied they do not like how this makes them feel, and by means of such feelings they build up a knowledge of their needs. For example babies are not aware of concepts such as eating, food, survival and so on. However they do not like hunger or discomfort, and when they are fed and/or have a nappy change they feel contented. In this way they accumulate knowledge about food, and later about eating and their need for survival.

Psychological needs include belonging, freedom and fun. When these are satisfied people feel better. Although they may be unsure of what their needs are, by striving to feel good they try to satisfy those needs.

As children grow older they file in their personal picture albums everything they decide will satisfy their needs. Glasser estimates that by adulthood they have thousands of pictures to satisfy each need. Some pictures are decidedly dangerous, for example alcoholics usually picture satisfying their needs with alcohol, and anorexics picture the desirability of being thin.

Acquiring total behaviour

Individuals know from infancy that survival requires them to make every effort to control their environment in order to satisfy their needs, hence the behaviour of angering.

Angering is how babies inform the world that their needs are unsatisfied. Mothers sooner or later refuse to allow their babies to control them with angering, and this has the effect of encouraging independence. Babies learn quickly, and if they cry but nothing happens they try different behaviours to control their environment. These include smiling, making endearing noises and so on. Learning is usually assisted by imitation, and the most effective teachers are people whom children care for and respect. Environment-controlling behaviours are also learnt from television, at school, by reading and so on.

From their earliest years children add negative behaviours to their repertoire, including sickness, misery, craziness and dysfunctional angering behaviours such as fighting. In order to control and manipulate adults they will sulk, depress and pout, or they may fight to control their peers. In Glasser's words, they add 'angering' and 'miserabling' as control methods of satisfying their needs. However these behaviours only deliver short-term payoffs and in the long term they reduce the degree of control that people have over their lives in that they tend to produce negative consequences for themselves and others.

Bringing up children

In Glasser's view parents should 'try as hard as possible to teach their children to gain effective control over their lives' (Glasser, 1984, p. 198). However it is common for parents to attempt to mould their children to their own pictures, and therefore power struggles develop because children want to live according to their own pictures, not those of their parents. Parents need their children to picture them as loving people, but children may take advantage of parental love to control them.

There is a difference between doing things for, to and with children on the one hand, and leaving them alone on the other. When parents do too much for their children they cause them to have less control over their lives in subsequent years. Problems also result from parents doing too much to their children, such as punishing them for not conforming to parental wishes or just shouting at them, and too little with their children, such as not chatting about mutual interests or playing together. Children are not left alone enough to make their own amusements, or to work through a tantrum. If they are encouraged to achieve their goals alone, this fosters a feeling of success that fulfils their need for power. All this boils down to children learning how to control their own lives from adults who do things with them but allow them to do things for themselves.

Discipline and punishment

It is human nature for children to challenge their parents' authority and break the rules in the quest for power, and negotiation and compromise are the best way of dealing with this.

Control theory differentiates between discipline and punishment. The bedrock of discipline is teaching children to follow fair rules established by negotiation. They are shown that there are better pictures and behaviours within the rules. In contrast punishment begins and ends with coercing children into obeying rules by threatening retribution if they do not comply, even if the rules are unreasonable. This is characterised by the absence of negotiation and failure to examine other pictures and behaviours that are within the rules. This causes children to suffer a great loss of power and control.

Instead parents should do as much as possible with them, and fewer things for and to them. If children refuse to change or negotiate, then sanctions appropriate to their age should be imposed, but these should not be so strong that they lose their willingness to alter their behaviour. No sanctions should be imposed without first explaining the consequences of failure to comply. This provides some element of personal choice: children can choose either to comply or to face the consequences.

The maintenance of unhappiness

According to control theory, people in need of counselling have chosen some form of self-destructive behaviour as part of their quest to regain control of their lives. They are not awake to the fact that they can better meet their needs through behaviour other than depressing, headaching and guilting.

At around the age of two children start to look for alternatives to angering because they realise that this is not getting them what they want. When their desires are frustrated they may choose to keep their anger under control by using depressing from their collection of behaviours. Depressing is unpleasant but it is safer than anger and more effective at gaining control over others. A whole repertoire of painful behaviours is developed to replace angering by the time adulthood is reached.

Depressing is a powerful way of attracting help – many people open themselves to control when they become the target of depressing behaviour. Alternatively it can shield people from awareness of the need to tackle their problems. Depressing and other forms of pain and misery are common excuses either for being too frightened to do something or for doing nothing, or a mixture of the two. Depressing also masks the fear of failure, which could make their lives even harder to control. Finally, people may choose to depress in order to control their parents, offspring, spouse and so on. They know that the targeted person may, for example, choose guilt. When targeted people choose to guilt they are actually using this as a way of controlling their own anger.

One of the main reasons why people continue to engage in unhappy behaviour is that they are unaware of choosing to do so. But even if they were to accept that unhappiness is a choice they would not want to be responsible for doing something about it. There are three reasons for this.

First, short-term feelings can be mistaken for long-term feeling behaviours. There are two stages to what people feel. At first there is 'pure feeling', or the immediate experience of a feeling. Pure feelings have their origins in the early evolutionary need for people to be alert to threats to survival and to be aware of whether or not they are in control. These feelings are not chosen and dissipate as soon as they arise. They are replaced by a long-term feeling behaviour to prolong the unhappiness or pleasure started by the pure unchosen feeling. Typical feeling behaviours include depressing and loving.

Second, a thwarted child often consciously engages in sulking or angering, but by adulthood this process has become automatic and subconscious. Painful behaviours such as headaching number about twenty, but the majority of people limit their repertoire to four or five that have proved their worth. Pleasurable behaviours are more likely to be acknowledged as conscious choices than negative ones.

Finally, so great is people's need for power and self-esteem that they fail to acknowledge they have chosen painful feelings. If they could acknowledge that they have the option of choosing other behaviours and changing their pictures they could regain control of themselves and others.

A cornerstone of control theory is never to let people control you with the pain and misery that they have chosen. People can give control to others with a control agenda of their own. People need to understand that controlling people have chosen the misery they are complaining about. Control can be retrieved by separating oneself from the other person's control. For example if the problem is an 'ill' relative who habitually demands attention, then regular visiting times should be set and demands for 'emergency' visits should be refused. Collusion should also be ended; this is done by ceasing to let people take control by asking them 'How are you feeling today?'

Reality counselling

The principle aim of reality counselling is to teach clients to take control of their lives – as Glasser says, all counselling is teaching. Although there are no strict rules, counsellors should always have a clear control theory reason for everything they do. The goals are as follows:

● To teach clients the control theory framework for comprehending their behaviour.

- To raise clients' awareness of their choosing behaviours and the way in which they control their environment through them.
- To help clients take responsibilty for making choices that work for them. In tandem with this they are taught that they do not have to be victims of past and present choices.
- To help clients to identify and understand their needs in respect of survival, power, belonging, freedom and fun.
- To help clients to develop realistic pictures in their heads to satisfy their basic needs.
- To teach clients to evaluate how effective their total behaviour is in achieving what they want, and to adopt new behaviours as needed.
- To help clients to develop and engage in behaviours that will help them to satisfy their needs now and in the future.
- To help clients to avoid being controlled by the negative controlling behaviour of others.

The client–counsellor relationship

Most clients are lonely so the first step is to befriend them. It follows from this that counsellors need to be involved and caring human beings whom clients will feel supported by and to whom they can relate. The key qualities are acceptance, patience and compassion. This carries with it the need for honesty about how much involvement counsellors can permit, including the length of sessions and the rules about contact between each session. Both counsellor and client are encouraged to use humour as long as it does not trivialise their work together.

Counsellors must be honest when explaining to clients that their needs must be met and their problems solved. Counsellors must avoid being controlled by the behaviour that clients use to control others. This includes anxietying, angering and depressing. Clients are not allowed to dwell on past traumas, although counsellors will show sympathy for what has happened. This is sometimes allowed to happen so that the relationship can be strengthened for follow-up work on present choices that are perpetuating problems. Eventually clients come to realise that they cannot control their counsellor, and that the counsellor will, as Glasser exhorts, 'Never give up'.

The teaching of control theory

During the initial structuring process clients are given hope by being told that they will learn to make better choices that will give them control over their lives. It is also emphasised that they will need to work hard to secure and sustain such control.

Control theory concepts are taught by getting clients to remodel their problems within these concepts, which include basic needs, pictures in the head and total behaviour. Work is carried out on the assumption that the only behaviour clients can control is their own, and they are taught that changing their behaviour is their best shot at controlling themselves and their environment to meet their basic needs.

Clients are also asked to read Glasser's book *Control Theory* (1984) and to discuss it with their counsellor. Together they analyse the clients' problems in the light of control theory.

The identification of wants and needs

It is important for counsellors to find out what their clients are really 'controlling for'. The less in touch clients are with what they want, the more difficult it is to work with them. Counsellors try to get them to describe the pictures in their head of what they want now. If their focus is on changing someone else, this focus will be shifted to how they can change themselves because their behavioural systems cannot control others. The emphasis will then be on what it is possible for them to achieve.

The control theory concept of basic needs is explained to clients so that they can explore which of their essential needs they want to satisfy. The 'needs tray' technique involves asking the client 'If I had a tray of needs and you could have one or more of these before you leave today, which would you choose – love, personal power, fun or freedom?' The answer given determines the focus of the counselling sessions.

Evaluating total behaviour

Once clients have worked out what they want, counsellors have to find out what they are doing now. Clients may well talk as though they are victims of circumstance and of other people. They may say that they want to be loved, and yet stay at home with the feeling behaviour of depressing and the thinking behaviour of 'I'm so depressed I can't be bothered to do anything'. These are accompanied by physiological symptoms such as the inability to sleep properly.

To help clients and counsellors to gain a better understanding of the clients behaviour, significant others whom the clients feel controlled by or are trying to control are asked to join in a session. Such people may themselves gain from the experience.

The action and thinking facets of total behaviour are focused on because they are the most amenable to change. Counsellors ask about the times when their clients have functioned effectively, and highlight any effective behaviours in the clients' repertoire. This not only helps the latter to comprehend their assets, it is also easier to develop behaviours that are already in their repertoire than to develop new ones. The main questions are:

- Is your behaviour getting you what you want?
- How is your behaviour helping you?
- Is this what is best for you?

The purpose of the questions is to show clients that their behaviour is not getting them what they want, for example a lonely client who stays at home lacks company because staying at home precludes the possibilty of finding company.

Planning and changing total behaviour

The first step is to look for alternative behaviours. Clients are willing to look for alternative ways of regaining control as soon as it dawns on them that their present behaviour is preventing that end. Because they are amenable to being told what to do, questions are asked that will encourage them to identify better behaviour for themselves.

The next step is to negotiate plans which can satisfy important pictures in the clients' heads outside the counselling sessions. Clients develop their own plans rather than their counsellor doing it for them. Their plans focus on the doing and thinking facets of total behaviour and include new and satisfying pictures. However they should be within the ambit of the clients' ability and motivation, and because clients need small successes to build up their confidence on the road to regaining control the plans should not be too ambitious during the early stages. During the formation of the plans counsellors ask questions to clarify specific details, and the more this is done the more likely it is that the plans will be successful.

Once the plans have been finalised there must be a commitment to carrying them out. When counsellors are seen as need-fulfilling people in the internal world of their clients the latter will take their commitment to them seriously. In doing so they are making a commitment to themselves, and the stronger the commitment the more likely the chance of a strong follow through. Furthermore the making and following through of plans enhances clients' feeling of control.

Next the counsellors work with their clients to develop the behaviours necessary for carrying out the plans. For example if a client has a job interview coming up the counsellor can role-play a mock interview with the client.

The actual carrying out of plans is set as homework, with the counsellors checking their clients' progress. It is assumed that a reasonable plan can always be carried out, so counsellors are interested in when and how their clients carry out the plans, not in why they cannot – no excuses are accepted. Clients are helped to focus on what they are capable of doing now, and to avoid losing control by finding reasons to be unhappy and ineffective. If necessary they are asked when they are going to get on with their plans, or told that they cannot control their counsellor with their usual manipulative behaviour. If a plan turns out to be genuinely unfeasible, client and counsellor work together to produce a better one. Succesful implementing of a plan is praised by the counsellor. Negative reactions are seen as a punishment, weakening clients' involvement with their counsellor and making their failure identities even worse. Negative consequences that derive from failure to implement plans are regarded as totally distinct from punishment.

Other applications

Marital counselling

Here the focus is on how a couple can sustain their marriage without controlling each other. They have to evaluate the advantages and disadvantages of continuing the marriage and decide whether they do want it to continue.

Groups

Counsellors often act as joint leaders of groups, with the members helping each other to assess the effectiveness of their current behaviours in satisfying their needs and pictures, and to find alternative behaviours and commitments.

Education

Reality counselling and the principles of control theory are widely used in educational settings. Much of the recent work in this field has concentrated on helping administrators and teachers to establish suitable environments for students to learn to take control of their lives.

Conclusion

Reality counselling arose from Glasser's dissatisfaction with psychoanalytical psychiatry and its emphasis on clients' feelings and past history. He believed that there should be more emphasis on what clients were doing, and what they were doing about what they were doing. His private practice was not successful owing to a lack of referrals so he took a position with the California Youth Authority as head psychiatrist at the Ventura School for Girls. Reality counselling developed from his work with delinquent girls, private outpatients and physically injured clients at a rehabilitation centre. He went on to do considerable work in the education system and concluded that the answer to failure among students was to shift education towards involvement, relevance and thinking. After he discovered William Powers' *Behavior: The Control of Perception* (1973) and Powers' theory of how the brain acts as a control system, Glasser realised that people with psychological disorders are failing to control the world in order to get what they need. Thus the thrust of his work has been to show clients how to gain control of their lives.

■ Ṽ 9 Maslow's theory of human motivation

This chapter outlines a useful psychological theory that can be used by counsellors in combination with those of Rogers and Frankl and other approaches to counselling.

Maslow was a member of the Chicago school of psychologists and sociologists, and like his colleague Carl Rogers he believed that actualisation is the driving force of human personality, as explained in his book *Motivation and Personality* (1954). His great contribution was to put actualisation into a hierarchy of motivation. Self-actualisation, as he called it, is the highest drive, but before individuals can turn to it they must satisfy their lower motivations, including hunger and thirst, safety and belonging.

Maslow describes people's motivation as an inertia that aims to satisfy a number of different needs. These needs are not equally important at any one time, rather they are organised hierarchically with each level of needs resting on the assumption that the ones below have been satisfied. When each group is satisfied the ones above come to the fore. Maslow asked:

> What conditions of work, what kinds of work, what kinds of reward or pay will help human stature to grow healthy, to its fuller and fullest stature? Classic economic theory, based as it is on an inadequate theory of human motivation, could be revolutionized by accepting the reality of higher human needs, including the impulse to self-actualization and the love for the highest values (quoted in Hoffman, 1989, p. 255).

The hierarchy of needs is dynamic in that the dominant need is always shifting, for example an artist may be absorbed in the self-actualisation of painting, but will eventually grow tired and hungry and will therefore have to stop. A single behaviour can incorporate several levels, for example having a meal can be both physiological and social. The hierarchy does not exist by itself but is subject to the situation and the general culture. According to Maslow a satisfied need can no longer motivate, for example when hungry people are fed they are no longer motivated by the prospect of food, but when hunger returns they are remotivated.

Maslow's research among the Blackfoot Indians

In 1938 Maslow carried out anthropological research among the Canadian Blackfoot tribe. He found that the Blackfoot's idea of wealth was not how much money, possessions and property people had but how much they gave away as this brought individual status, prestige and security to the tribe. He relates the story of a Blackfoot called Teddy Yellow Fly, who was the only person in the tribe with a car and willingly lent it to anyone who wished to use it.

Likewise at the annual Sun Dance ceremony those who had accumulated a great deal in the way of blankets, food and other possessions gave them away to widows, orphans, the blind, the ill and others with some sort of misfortune. For them wealth was meaningless unless it met the needs of somebody else. In our society money in the bank is a hedge against an insecure future. The Blackfoot did not feel insecure about the future because of their custom of sharing their wealth.

Maslow found that his dominance test could not be used on the Blackfoot because it assumed a strong drive for power and the Blackfoot lacked this. However his security/insecurity test did prove useful. He found that some 80–90 per cent of the tribe rated as highly in ego security as the most secure people in our society, who make up 5–10 per cent of the population at most. The Blackfoot seemed to suffer less from self-doubt and self-consciousness than people in our more competitive, impersonal society.

Maslow's findings led him to abandon his concept of cultural relativity. He said that every human being comes into society not as a lump of clay that is then moulded by society, but as a structure that society may build upon, or warp and suppress. He concluded that the Blackfoot were human beings first and Blackfoot Indians second. Their society contained the same range of personalities as ours, but with a very different distribution curve.

Talent as a drive

In 1938 Maslow's views on therapy reached a turning point when he took on a college woman as a client. Her presenting problems were lack of appetite, insomnia, irregular menstruation and chronic boredom. Nothing gave her pleasure or aroused her interest. She had graduated from Brooklyn College a year earlier and taken a well-paid but boring job as a personnel supervisor in a chewing gum factory. At that time the USA was still in economic depression and she was supporting her family, all of whom were unemployed. She told Maslow that her life had no meaning as her family's financial difficulties had forced her to abandon her studies in psychology. At first she had tried to convince herself that she should be grateful for having a well-paid job, but the prospect of a lifetime of such work eventually got on top of her.

Maslow did not employ the classic Freudian approach but relied on his intuition. He was not interested in the conflicts, fantasies and repressions of her childhood. Rather he felt that the real problem was her feeling of meaninglessness and wasted talent. He suggested to her that she was frustrated and angry because she was not utilising her intelligence and fulfilling her talent for psychology, and as a consequence she was bored with her life and the normal pleasures of life. He said that any talent, any capacity was also a motivation, a need, an impulse. She agreed so he suggested that she continue her studies after work in the evenings. This was successful and she became happy, and most of her physical symptoms had disappeared by the time he had his last contact with her.

There is a tendency to regard a talent as just a possibility or potentiality of developing a skill, but for Maslow there is more to it than that. Talent is also a drive, an innate need, an impulse to develop a skill or skills. Every talent has an intrinsic tendency for development if the right conditions are present. This conclusion formed an important part of Maslow's motivation theory, which will be discussed below. He believed that personal failure consists solely of failing to live up to one's potential, and 'in this sense every man can be a king and must therefore be treated like a king' (Maslow, 1969, p. 99).

Maslow's hierarchy of human needs

In 1943 Maslow published a paper entitled 'A Theory of Human Motivation', in which he described the hierarchy of needs mentioned earlier. We shall consider each set of needs in turn.

Basic physiological needs

The basic physiological needs are those which must be met to stay alive, including food, water, action, rest, sex and enough resources to raise children. Both humans and animals have these needs, but Maslow considered that studying animals could not provide an adequate understanding of human motivation because animals have few motivations other than physiological ones. In Maslow's words, 'Too many of the findings that have been made in animals have been proven to be true for animals but not for the human being. There is no reason whatsoever why we should start with animals in order to study human motivation' (ibid.). Maslow therefore based his theory solely on humans.

Safety/security needs

Once the basic physiological needs are satisfied a new set of needs emerges: protection from danger, security, shelter, stability, structure and boundaries, and in the modern context, security from job loss. The latter includes a safe working environment, and employers who provide this open the way for the next set of needs to be activated.

The nature of safety needs can best be studied in children and infants because these needs are more simple and obvious among the young. When adults feel that their safety is being threatened they may not show it, but infants react overtly if they are disturbed, dropped, startled by a loud noise, a flashing light or any other unusual sensory stimulation, as well as to rough handling, loss of support or inadequate support. Children require an undisrupted routine or rhythm and a predictable, orderly world. Inconsistency, injustice and unfairness on the part of parents cause children to feel anxious and unsafe, often because such treatment makes their entire world seem unsafe, unreliable and unpredictable. Children appear to flourish better if there is a system with at least some degree of rigidity and a firm routine or schedule, something that can be relied upon not just in the present but also in the future.

This has important implications in that failure to satisfy the safety needs means that the higher drives have less chance of operating. In other words, people whose safety needs continue to be paramount are inhibited with respect to higher drives. However, because society usually ensures that its members are reasonably safe from wild animals, extremes of temperature, criminals, assault, murder, tyranny and so on, people no longer have any safety needs as active motivators and therefore one must turn to neurotic or near-neurotic individuals and social and economic underdogs in order to witness such needs directly and clearly.

Other manifestations of safety needs are a common preference for familiar rather than unfamiliar things, and for the known rather than the unknown. Safety-seeking also provides a partial motivation for the tendency of mankind to turn to some or other religion or world philosophy that organises the universe and the people in it into some sort of coherent whole. According to Maslow the neurosis in which the search for safety takes its clearest form is obsessive-compulsive neorosis. Obsessive-compulsives make extreme efforts to order and stabilise their world so that no unexpected, unfamiliar or unmanageable danger can materialise.

Love, affection and 'belongingness' needs

These are about our need for affectionate relations with others. As Maslow points out, human beings need to be liked, loved, respected and cherished in their own right if they are to avoid social anxiety, alienation and loneliness. According to Maslow, in our society failure to secure these needs is usually manifest in maladjustment or severe psychopathology. In his view love and sex are not synonymous as the latter is purely physiological. Ordinarily sexual behaviour is determined not only by sexual needs but also by love and affection, and fulfilment of the love need involves both the giving and the receiving of love.

Esteem needs

There are two esteem needs. Higher esteem is the self-esteem generated by our own sense of achievement, self-respect, self-sufficiency and independence. Lower esteem comes from the respect of others for what we achieve and includes attention, status, appreciation and dominance. It is the need to know that one is relevant to the outside world. It is similar to the need for love and belongingness, but it is not quite the same thing. Continuity over time is important in esteem needs, whereas the need for love has more to do with momentary experiences. Maslow identifies two subsets of needs:

- The desire for strength, achievement, adequacy and confidence in the face of the world, and for independence and freedom.

- The desire for reputation or prestige, that is, the respect or esteem of other people, together with their attention and appreciation. Adler and his followers paid attention to these needs, but Freud and other psychoanalysts tended to neglect them.

Cognitive needs

These involve curiosity, exploration and the search for meaning and knowledge. According to Maslow (1943) 'The desire to know and to understand are conative, ie, have a striving character, and are as much personality needs as the "basic needs".' Maslow is not clear about where this cognitive drive should be placed in the hierarchy of higher motivations, but it could be placed after the need for love and self-esteem and before the need for self-actualisation.

Knowledge is a prerequisite for self-actualisation because a certain amount of knowledge is essential to the discovery of innate talents and life planning motives. When individuals have ascertained the direction in which self-actualisation can be found, additional learning will be motivated by the need for self-actualisation. However at an earlier stage the urge to know and comprehend a world for which a sympathy has developed will lead individuals to uncover their deeper self. In Maslow's opinion, learning and understanding is pointless without embeddedness. Knowing and understanding require a bedrock of affective connectedness with the world.

Self-actualisation

Self-actualised people are those who are living the life to which they are best suited. Self-actualisation is the realisation of one's full potential. As Maslow put it: 'A musician must make music, an artist must paint, a poet must write if [s]he is to be ultimately happy. What a [wo]man must be, [s]he must be. This need we may call self-actualization' (ibid.). Maslow equates self-actualisation with 'growth motivation' – the continuing desire to be all that we can be. Self-actualised people are reality-centred in that they can tell the difference between what is genuine or real and what is dishonest or false. They are also problem centred in that they focus on problem solving. They are resistant to 'enculturation' (are unyielding to social pressure) and are creative, spontaneous and accept themselves and others. They have a freshness of appreciation and enjoy peak experiences more often than others (peak experiences include mystical experiences, exhilaration, appreciation, feelings of awe, and being at one with God and nature). Their motivating factors are aliveness, playfulness, unity, meaningfulness and the search for truth and self-sufficiency.

Aesthetic needs

This final set of needs includes the need for order, beauty and symmetry in art, music and literature and is part of the higher aspirations of human beings. This group of needs actually disproves the contention that lower needs must be satisfied before higher needs become important. History is littered with starving artists, poets and musicians who neglected their physiological needs to pursue this higher quest.

Metaneeds, metapathology and self-actualisation

Metaneeds or B-values are the evolutionary goals of self-actualisers, and failure to achieve them causes metapathology. These needs are truth (cynicism and mistrust), beauty (vulgarity), simplicity (confusion, bewilderment) and playfulness (grimness).

To become self-actualised, individuals must meet their esteem needs, first the esteem of others (that is, respect) and then internalised esteem (self-respect). Culture stifles, so they must also be able to overcome culture. Furthermore they must choose growth over safety and be free from what Maslow called the Jonah complex.

Towards the end of his life Maslow gave considerable thought to the mystery of evil. Based on his conversations with Frank Manuel he proposed the existence of a Jonah complex – an escape from greatness that is willed by the individual. It can be summarised as wilful failure on the part of individuals to develop their full potential and it touches at the heart of evil. Possession of this complex is the most important reason for failure to self-actualise. Many people are afraid of their own destiny and fear that maximising their potential will lead to situations with which they cannot cope.

There are a number of behavioural exercises to facilitate self-actualisation:

- Pay so much attention to the world that when you close your eyes you are able to describe everything around you.
- Make risky choices to expand your world, and learn from failures.
- Be more self-trusting.
- When in doubt, be truthful in order to simplify life.
- Acknowledge the need for discipline, and quickly satisfy the needs of life.
- Cultivate peak experiences by paying attention to the world and personal feelings.
- Abandon highly valued pathologies and psychological garbage because experiencing a great deal of pain does not denote sensitivity, it is merely foolish.

The importance of gratification

Maslow went on to formulate a complete theory of humans. In his view it was necessary to study healthy human beings, not just those who were frustrated, psychologically disturbed or sick. He was very interested in those whose lives were directed by higher needs. Such people were an important exception to his hierarchy of needs and he explained this with the concept of 'gratification'. He said that people with such values become martyrs as they will sacrifice everything for a particular value or ideal. They can be partly understood by what he called 'increased frustration tolerance through early gratification'. People who have satisfied their basic needs, especially in their earlier years, appear to develop considerable power to withstand the thwarting of their needs owing to their strong and healthy character structure. They can weather disagreement or opposition and fly in the face of public opinion, bearing witness to the truth at great personal cost. Those who have loved and been loved and who have had many deep friendships can withstand rejection, hatred or persecution.

Maslow felt that the most important gratifications come in the first two years of life, and those who have been made to feel secure in these years tend to stay secure in the face of adversity. There are no esteem, love and safety needs in a basically satisfied person. The only way in which a person might be said to have them is in the metaphysical sense that a sated person has hunger or a filled vessel has emptiness. If an individual wishes to discover what really motivates – not what has, will or might motivate – then a satisfied need is not a motivator. Maslow said that it should, for practical purposes, be regarded as not existing, as having vanished. He emphasised this point because it had been either contradicted or overlooked in every theory of motivation that he had come across. Healthy individuals are primarily motivated by the need to develop and actualise their full potential and capacity. If an individual has any other basic needs in an active, chronic sense, then that person is unhealthy. According to Maslow, self-actualisation involves not just an inner yearning but also a calling to service from the external, day-to-day world. Frankl echoed this when he wrote that 'we never self-actualize in a vacuum, but always in relation to people and circumstances around us' (quoted in Hoffman, 1989, p. 256).

Peak experiences

Maslow suggested that transcendent experiences occur universally and can be characterised by their content, being either theistic, supernatural or non-theistic. He said that each experience is as unique as the person experiencing it. However there are certain characteristics that are common to all peak experiences, regardless of their content and how they are interpreted and used. The term peak experiences encompasses the full spectrum of mystical states of consciousness. Maslow used this term because he wanted to secularise such experiences, defining them as natural and available without an organised religious context. He did not suggest that religious contexts are unimportant because he understood people's need for a framework of values to interpret and comprehend their experiences. However the framework of interpretation must encompass everyday life beyond the religious because peak experiences can be stimulated by non-religious settings and activities. According to Maslow (1970, p. 170), 'Religion becomes . . . a state of mind achievable in almost any activity of life, if this activity is raised to a suitable level of perfection.'

The prevalent idea in the field of psychology at the time of Maslow's study was that the inner mind could not be objectively studied because it was intangible. Maslow wanted to set up a framework that could be used both scientifically and personally to examine peak experiences with the help of a common language of terms, whereby the frequency of and variations between experiences could be measured and analysed. Individuals could use Maslow's terms to relate personal subjective experiences and make comparisons with those of others. This would facilitate the incorporation of mystical experiences into everyday language and culture.

In Maslow's opinion peak experiences are important because they are unifying, noetic and transcend the ego. They also provide a sense of purpose and a feeling of integration. They can be therapeutic because they promote free will, creativity, empathy, self-determination, personal growth, integration and fulfilment.

Work motivation

In 1962 Maslow was invited to visit Non Linear Systems (NLS), an electronics manufacturer whose owner and general manager had introduced a number of organisational innovations. Using Maslow's *Motivation and Personality* (1954) as a guidebook he had sought ways of making his employees happier and more productive. He had concluded that the workers would benefit from a sense of closure, from seeing a finished product they had made from scratch. Accordingly he had replaced his assembly lines with production teams of six or seven workers, each of whom had learned every stage of the production process for several products. They were allowed to engage in participatory management and decide the best way of producing their quota of products. Each team took total responsibilty for the assembly, inspection and packaging of the products. Scheduled breaks had been abandoned and breaks were now taken at a time convenient to the team. Each team had a private workroom, decorated according to their preferences.

NLS had also implemented the following innovations:

- Increased pay to 25 per cent above the San Diego average.
- Abolished time cards.
- Removed lateness or sickness penalties.
- Abolished salesmen's expense accounts.
- Given departments responsibility for their own financial records.
- Provided small-group sensitivity training for managers.
- Provided aptitude testing for those who wanted it.
- Introduced the post of vice-president for innovation.

As a result of all this the employees' morale and interest in their work had improved dramatically and staff turnover was a fraction of the national average, customer complaints had significantly reduced, sales and productivity had greatly increased and a radically democratic atmosphere now permeated the company.

While visiting NLS, Maslow was reminded of the concept of synergy, which had been originated by anthropologist Ruth Benedict in 1941. It originally referred to cultures in which cooperation was rewarded and seen as advantageous to everyone, but Maslow realised that it could also be applied to the business world.

He said of the owner of NLS, 'It's not so much foreign capital that is needed in most poor countries, it's entrepreneurs of this self-confident type' (quoted in Hoffman, 1989, p. 272).

Maslow's NLS notes, which were published as *Summer Notes on the Social Psychology of Industry and Management* (1962), strongly reflect Steiner's thesis that human motivation is brought about by self-determination among individuals who are free to choose their own workplace and work context by means of free negotiations between individuals.

Authoritarianism and the need for a value system

According to Maslow, self-actualising people have a democratic rather than an authoritarian outlook and he saw authoritarianism, prejudice, chronic boredom, anhedonia (lack of energy) and loss of purpose and meaning as real emotional illnesses. Writing at the height of the Cold War he said that the authoritarian character structure was 'the most important problem afflicting the human race'. In his view it was far worse than a medical illness and it was caused by the cultural malarrangements that were widespread even in the USA.

All people, including children, need a coherent value system, and the absence of such a system causes certain forms of psychological disorder. The fact that people crave and search for a coherent value system – with anything being better than nothing, however unsatisfying – helps to explain why authoritarianism becomes attractive when the values of society collapse.

The fourth force

Humanistic counselling was called the third force; Maslow brought in the fourth force or 'transpersonal psychology'. He liked to work with healthy, creative people and regarded psychoanalysis as overly concerned with disturbed and neurotic people, while behaviourist theory was too reductionist and mechanistic. His real interest was in higher human motivation. He and other humanistic psychologists such as Berne and Perls were influenced by existentialists such as Kierkegaard, Husserl, Sartre and Binswanger. These people did not subscribe to the idea that humans are the products of nature, heredity, nurture or the environment. Instead they believed that all individuals are responsible for their own destiny.

Conclusion

Maslow believed that psychology was far too concerned with neurosis and disturbance. He preferred to work with healthy, creative individuals. He also disapproved of behaviour theory because of its emphasis on reductionist and mechanistic theories. For Maslow there were more dimensions to human functioning than this. His real interest lay in higher human motivation and he was heavily influenced by philosophers and phenomenologists such as Binswanger, Husserl, Kierkegaard and Sartre. His theories have been of particular importance to the psychology of motivation in the workplace and the needs of employees beyond the reward of earning money.

Part Three
Existential counselling

☑ 10 Existential counselling

Introduction

The existential approach to counselling is above all philosophical. Its primary concerns are understanding the position of people in the world and determining what being alive means. When examining these questions existential counsellors adopt a receptive frame of mind, rather than employing a dogmatic approach that pigeon-holes clients into pre-established categories and interpretations. The main aim is to find the truth, using an open mind and an attitude of wonder.

This approach is underpinned by some 3000 years of philosophy. Throughout human history individuals have tried to make sense of human existence in general and their own personal situation in particular. This philosophical tradition can help us to understand any individual's position in relation to existential issues, but of greater importance are those philosophers whose work was or is directly intended to make sense of human existence. The philosophical movement of phenomenology and existential philosophy is of particular importance in that it was responsible for the generation of existential counselling or therapy. Among the most important existential philosophers were Kierkegaard, Nietzsche, Husserl, Heidegger and Sartre.

The Danish philosopher Søren Kierkegaard (1813–55) highlighted the anxiety, dread and despair – 'the sickness unto death' – of people estranged from their essential nature. He read theology but did not go on to take holy orders. He suffered from an ill-defined sense of guilt and chose to live as an obsessive bachelor. He rejected philosophical systems, saying that subjectivity is truth. He disliked Christian dogma and the supposed objectivity of science, regarding both as methods of avoiding the anxiety inherent in human existence. He was contemptuous of the way in which life was being lived around him. He wrote that truth could only be found by being, not from thinking, and that the element most lacking in people was the courage to live with passion and commitment from the inner depths of their being.

Friedrich Nietzsche (1844–1900) held a nihilistic picture of the world in which the basis of human self-affirmation was 'God is dead'. He considered that individuals are at their own mercy in their quest for a new, more intense reality. He developed a philosophy of freedom that involved breaking the chains of moral constraint and discovering one's own will. This would bring with it a new power to live. He insisted that individuals should not remain part of the herd but should stand apart and strive for a better destiny. This introduced the vital existential themes of freedom, choice, responsibility and courage.

Edmund Husserl's phenomenology provided the intellectual impetus for the existential movement. For Husserl (1859–1938) the natural sciences were based on the assumption that subject and object were separate. The result of such a dualistic approach was error, and thus a fresh approach was needed to investigate and understand the world. Assumptions and prejudices had to be abandoned so that the world could be seen afresh on the basis of intuition. Things needed to be described and understood, but not analysed and explained.

Martin Heidegger (1889–1976) applied Husserl's phenomenology to the understanding of the meaning of being. In *Being and Time* (1962) he examined the quest for being and analysed the concept of *Dasien*, the distinctively human mode of existence. He emphasised how poetry and deep philosophical thinking could provide greater insight into what it meant to be part of creation than scientific knowledge could. He was also an advocate of hermeneutics, a philosophical method of investigation and interpretation that seeks to explain how someone experiences something. It is interesting to compare this with the psychoanalytical approach, which provides a theoretical framework for individuals' experiences.

Jean-Paul Sartre (1905–80) was a Marxist philosopher, and like Nietzsche he wrote about a godless world. According to him, in the struggle against despair humans make the choices that create the essence of their existence, and as long as they live there can be no escape from the need to define themselves.

Two important religious philosophers, Buber and Tillich, also had an influence on existential counselling.

Martin Buber (1878–1965) was a Jewish theologian who saw human beings not as separate entities but as creatures of the 'in-between'. He proposed two types of in-between relationships: 'I–It' relationships, which involve functional relationships in which others are objects; and 'I–Thou' relationships, which involve mutual influence and full experiencing of each other.

Paul Tillich (1886–1965) was a Protestant Christian theologian whose book *The Courage to Be* (1952) looks at the human condition within a Christian framework. He saw courage as 'the ethical act in which man affirms his own being in spite of those elements which conflict with his essential self-affirmation' (ibid., p. 3).

For the interested reader there is a considerable body of literature on this subject, the most recent of which are based on Heidegger's work. There is a Germanic tradition and a French tradition. The Germanic tradition includes works by Jaspers, Tillich and Gadamer, and the French tradition includes works by Sartre, Camus, Ricoeur, Merleau Ponty and Levinas.

At the start of the twentieth century a number of therapists were inspired by phenomenology and the possibilities it offered for treating people. In this context it is worth mentioning the Swiss psychiatrist L. Binswanger, who was the first to apply existential insights to psychiatry. The translation of his work into English during the 1940s and 1950s, plus the emigration of Tillich and others to the USA, did much to popularise the use of existential ideas in counselling. Rollo May was also important in this, and his writing kept the existential influence going in the USA. This eventually led to the formulation of a specific form of therapy.

Existential philosophy has also influenced much of humanistic psychology, although the original meanings have usually been diluted and occasionally distorted.

In Europe the original existential concepts were combined with psychological insights, which led Boss to develop a method of existential analysis. Victor Frankl developed what he called logotherapy, which looks at the human search for meaning (see also Chapter 11 of this book). The ideas of Jean-Paul Sartre, Merleau Ponty and a number of practitioners have been important and influential in France, but no specific method of counselling has arisen from them.

What is existential counselling?

The word existence is derived from the Latin *existere*, meaning to stand out, to emerge. Existence involves the process of coming into being or becoming, and existential counselling is concerned with the science and processes of being, or ontology, which gets its name from *ontos*, the Greek word for being. The approach is aimed at enabling clients to affirm their existence or stand out, despite and within any prevailing constraints. It also looks beyond surface problems and helps clients to face the basic issues of their existence, including loneliness, despair, alienation, meaninglessness, anxiety and death, which cause what is called existence pain. To counteract this pain, freedom, love, creativity and responsibility are emphasised. In times gone by, individuals' existence was decided for them, but these days they have to create and define their own existence.

Modern existential counsellors

The approaches of Irvin Yalom and Rollo May are dealt with in this chapter, and the ideas of Viktor Frankl are examined in Chapter 11.

Irvin Yalom was born in 1931 in Washington DC to penniless Russian immigrants. During his childhood he hated his mother's 'vicious tongue' but he admired his father. He later recalled how black people attacked him for being white and white people attacked him for being Jewish. He received a BA degree from George Washington University in 1952, and an MA from Boston University in 1956. In the space of six years he worked as an intern at Mt Sinai Hospital in New York, a psychiatric resident at the Johns Hopkins Hospital in Baltimore and a consultant at the Patuxent Institution in Maryland, and served in the US army as a captain. In 1962 he became an instructor in psychiatry at the University of Stanford School of Medicine. In 1963 he was made assistant professor, then associate professor (1968) and professor (1973). He married in 1963 and has four children. He has published a number of scientific papers, and collaborated with his former therapist Rollo May on a chapter on existential counselling in *Current Psychotherapies* (May and Yalom, 1989). He retired from Stanford in 1993, but has continued his work as a psychotherapist and author.

Rollo May was born in Ohio in 1909. He was one of seven children and his father was a YMCA secretary. The family moved frequently, and relationships within it were not happy. May once described his mother as a 'bitch-kitty on wheels'. His older sister was a psychotic and spent some time in a mental institution. After gaining a BA in liberal arts from Oberlin College in 1930 he spent the next three years in Greece, teaching teenage boys and studying Greek civilisation. During one summer holiday he studied individual psychology with Alfred Adler in Vienna. He was awarded a BD by the Union Theological Seminary in 1938. It was there that he formed a friendship with Paul Tillich, who was to have a profound influence on his ideas. He received a PhD in clinical psychology from Teachers College at Columbia University in 1949. While studying for his doctorate he caught tuberculosis and was bedridden for two years in a sanitorium in up-state New York. It was during this time that he read and thought about the nature of anxiety, which eventually led to his book *The Meaning of Anxiety* (1977). In New York City he opened a private practice and wrote a number of books and articles. He was also an adjunct professor at the New School of Social Research and the University of New York, and worked as a training analyst and supervisor at the William Alanson White Institute. He then moved to San Francisco where he taught, wrote and saw clients. He married and divorced twice, and died in 1994.

The theoretical assumptions of existential counselling

Being and non-being

Human beings have the capacity for self-consciousness and can therefore choose their own being. Being, when used as a noun, means *potentia* or the source of potential. As the participle of a verb it means that someone is in the process of becoming something. Choices are continually made, but because of conformist and collectivist trends in society most people have to repress their sense of being and their choices are limited. The opposite of being is non-being or nothingness. In other words, because there is existence there is also the possibility of non-existence. Death is the best example of this. Those who confront non-being win a heightened sense of being that gives them greater awareness of themselves and others. A number of points should be made here:

- The human sense of being refers to the whole experience of existence, both conscious and unconscious.
- Individuals need to experience themselves in this world.
- They need to have a basic 'I am' experience, or 'Since I am, I have a right to be'.
- This 'I am' experience is the precondition for the solution to clients' problems.
- Being is threatened by anxiety, conformity, lack of self-awareness, destructive hostility and physical sickness.

There are four forms of 'Being in the world'. First, Umwelt is the 'world around' or the natural world. It includes animals as well as human beings and is accepted as real. It embraces biological needs, instincts and drives, daily and life cycles.

Second, Mitwelt is the 'with world' and is public and interpersonal, a world of human relationships. People influence each other in these relationships and the structure of meaning that develops. The bottom line of a relationship is that in the encounter both individuals are changed. How much individuals put into group relationships determines the meaning of such groups for them. The same is true of intimate relationships.

Third, Eigenwelt is our 'own world'. It is the private, intimate aspect of individuals and is unique to the human race. It is self-consciousness and self-awareness. It is formed from aspects of Mitwelt and an individual's culture; it is the individual in the environment. It means grasping the personal meaning of a thing or person, and owning our relationships to things and people. For example if someone says 'this scenery is awesome' it actually means 'For me, this scenery is awesome'.

Finally, Uberwelt is the abstract and spiritual; it is what makes human beings unique on Earth.

All these worlds are fluid and interact with one another.

Anxiety

May (1977, p. 205) defines anxiety as 'the threat to our existence or to values we identify with our existence'. Anxiety is part of the human condition, but threats can be used constructively as learning experiences during development. The sources of normal anxiety are vulnerability to nature, sickness and death, plus the need to become independent of parents and the consequences of this, such as crisis and tension. Individuals' reaction to normal anxiety should be proportionate to the objective threat being faced, there should be no repression, and it should be used to identify and confront the conditions that have brought it about.

The main function of existential counsellors is to help clients to come to terms with the normal anxieties that are an integral part of human existence.

Neurotic anxiety has the opposite characteristics to those of normal anxiety: it involves repression, it is a disproportionate reaction to an object threat, and it is destructive rather than constructive. Individuals react subjectively to objective threats in terms of their inner psychological conflicts and patterns. Repression and the masking of awareness makes them more vulnerable to threats because they lose access to vital information that would help them to identify and deal with these threats.

Guilt

Guilt, like anxiety, is a part of the human condition. There are three types of guilt.

First, normal guilt is caused by conscience and makes people aware of the ethical and unethical aspects of their behaviour. Second, neurotic guilt is caused by parental injunctions, social conventions and imagined offences against others. Finally, there are three types of existential or ontological guilt:

- The guilt that arises from failure to live up to one's potential. This is essentially a transgression against oneself and is associated with Eigenwelt.

- The guilt that arises from distortion of the reality of other people. This is associated with Mitwelt.
- Separation guilt, which relates to the whole of creation and involves Umwelt, Eigenwelt and Mitwelt.

Existential guilt is universal. Its roots are in self-awareness and it is inextricably linked to the concept of personal responsibility – the individual is the one who chooses or fails to choose. It does not arise from the contravention of parental rules and it is not a type of neurotic guilt, but it can become so. It can be constructive, in that if it is dealt with properly it leads to greater creativity, humility and sensitivity to other people.

Transcendence

The term transcendence derives from the Latin *transcendere*, to climb over and beyond. We talk and think in symbols, therefore we transcend time and space. Social relations can be transcended and we are capable of seeing ourselves as others see us. Moreover we can give consideration to the perceptions of others. The basis of freedom and responsibility is the ability to transcend immediate situations. This is part of the ontological or basic nature of human beings. Human existence is a process of emerging, which involves transcending the past and present to forge a future. All human beings are involved in this process unless they are hampered by anxiety, despair or illness.

The ultimate existential concerns

Death

Death is the fundamental source of anxiety. This can be neurotic, normal or existential. The fear of death can be conscious or unconscious but will probably be repressed. Nonetheless humans are preoccupied with death from an early age and denial-based defences are used to cope with the anxiety. Life and death, being and non-being are interdependent. The first existential conflict is between the desire to continue to live and recognition of death's inevitability. This is also called the conflict between fear of non-being and wishing to be.

Freedom

In Sartre's words we are 'condemned to freedom' (Sartre, 1956, p. 631) because our world is not well structured and has a groundlessness that precludes a secure existence. Freedom brings responsibility, for example for our actions, failure to act and so on. In essence we desire ground and structure but are faced with groundlessness and freedom.

Isolation

Individuals struggle between their awareness of fundamental isolation and their desire for contact, protection and to be part of a large whole. In Yalom's view existential isolation is a more fundamental isolation, it is 'separation from the world' (Yalom, 1980, p. 355). There are three forms of isolation:

- Interpersonal isolation: loneliness caused by psychopathology (mental disorder), lack of social skill, or simply by choice or necessity.
- Intrapersonal isolation: this occurs when individuals' awareness is blocked or they become dissociated from parts of themselves. By definition, this condition contains pathology.
- Existential isolation: there is an unbridgeable gap between ourselves and others in that we came into the world alone, we live here alone and we die alone.

Meaninglessness

A fundamental quest for humans is to find meaning in an indifferent world that has no meaning. We need purpose, significance and meaning in our lives. Accordingly we organise random stimuli into figure and ground, seeking pattern and meaning. Although human life may fit into some sort of cosmic pattern, we also need personal meaning in our lives on Earth. Loss of religious belief has accentuated this problem for more and more people.

Existential psychodynamics

This form of counselling and psychotherapy is centred on the problems of individuals' existence. There are two points to consider: (1) existential conflicts and anxieties stem from the inescapable givens of existence (death, freedom, isolation and meaninglessness – see above); and (2) existential counsellors and clients think deeply about ultimate existential concerns – they do not focus on everyday concerns.

It is interesting to compare this approach with Freudian psychodynamics. Psychodynamic conflict means there is a clash between opposing forces, and Freud saw this is as a conflict between the ego and instinctual sexual and aggressive drives. Deeper conflicts stem from infant psychosexual conflicts. Existential psychodynamics are not based on this archaeological or developmental model, where the earliest equates with the deepest. Rather it is the everyday and ultimate concerns that matter and have to be dealt with, as follows.

Death

Children can grasp the essence of death even though they may not understand it in intellectual terms. According to Yalom (1980) children have various mechanisms of denial, such as 'children do not die', 'I am special', 'death is temporary', 'there is an ultimate rescuer'. Some children are better than others at handling the major developmental task of coming to terms with death.

Exposure to death can be good if there are supportive adults, good genes and adequate ego resources. However it can be traumatic if the above factors are not available or the death in question is that of a of parent or sibling. A death in the family can exceed the coping resources of a child, and neurotic and psychotic patients are likely to have lost a parent.

Parents' approach to matters relating to death affects children's awareness and acceptance of death. More often than not children are protected from death by concerned adults who, if they would only admit it, also wish to protect themselves from the uncomfortable feelings that most people have about the matter – feelings that would be bound to emerge if they had to talk the issue through with a child. The issue is wrapped up in gentle religious imagery, fairy tales or pure evasion. In modern society we have lost the ability to face up to the question of death because the state has relieved us of much of the responsibility for it. So just as they do in relation to matters of sex, children satisfy their curiosity by obtaining information elsewhere.

Freedom

In recent times there has been an erosion of the religious systems and social mores that underpinned society for so long, and permissiveness has advanced at a rapid rate. Just a few decades ago people knew what they *had* to do. Now it is more a question of what they *want* to do. Many people, especially the young, are not equipped to cope with this challenge.

Isolation

Interpersonal isolation has been caused by the breakdown of centuries-old neighbourhoods and communities, the demolition of slum housing, the influx of outsiders, greater social mobilty and so on. In times gone by the corner shop, the local church or chapel, the family doctor and the local bobby underpinned people's sense of social cohesion. This is no longer the case and many people, especially the elderly, find this destabilising.

Meaninglessness

Religion once gave people's lives a meaning, a foundation. Nowadays most people either do not have a religious faith or do not attend traditional churches. Many have instead turned to house churches, cell churches, Christian fellowships or exotic religions such as Buddhism.

Another factor in loss of meaning is urbanisation, which has caused people to lose contact with nature and the seasonal cycles. Increasing numbers of people live in impersonal urban areas and no longer belong to or have a role in a local community. Many are also alienated from their work as it holds little interest for them.

In modern Western society the vast majority of people do not have to concern themselves with survival in the sense of finding food, water and shelter. The downside of this increased material security and the time it releases is that people have more time to contemplate the meaninglessness of their lives, especially when unemployment has destroyed the sense of identity that many people derive from their occupation. All this is exacerbated by concern about the state of the environment and the spread of weapons of mass destruction since the end of the Cold War.

Defence mechanisms

There are two types of defence mechanism: conventional defence mechanisms such as projection defend people against anxiety, while specific defence mechanisms defend people against each of the four ultimate concerns. Defence mechanisms may be reinforced when whole cultures collude in them, thus making them socially acceptable, and there may be an overlap between the various mechanisms. Although they provide safety these mechanisms restrict people's potential for growth and cause existential guilt.

Defences against anxiety about death

There are two major defence mechanisms for both adults and children:

- *Specialness*: although most individuals are conscious of being mortal with a finite lifespan, some have the irrational belief that they are inviolable or even immortal. Those without this defence mechanism may develop clinical syndromes such as a drive for power and control, workaholism, compulsive heroism, narcissism or ignoring increasing age. If death anxiety overcomes these defences, individuals may seek counselling.
- *Belief in an ultimate rescuer*: the belief that there is an omnipresent servant who will come to the rescue. Most people do not acknowledge this belief until the 'dominant other' psychologically withdraws, or the believer contracts a fatal illness.

Defences against anxiety about freedom

These include displacing responsibility onto others (including counsellors), avoiding autonomous behaviour, compulsiveness (for example in work, sex and leisure) and pathology in wishing, willing and deciding. These defences shield people from awareness of their responsibility for their own lives. According to Yalom (1980) we create our own selves, destinies, life predicaments, feelings and suffering.

Defences against anxiety about isolation

Here individuals use others as means of defence and do not relate to them in their own right. Defence mechanisms include the following:

- Affirmation: individuals need to be part of the consciousness of others and have their approval. They hide their inability to love under the guise of loving.
- Fusion: the individual fuses with another individual or a group.
- Compulsive sexuality: individuals have serial relationships that are mere caricatures of the real thing. Their partners are treated as objects.

Defences against anxiety about meaninglessness

There are two defences against meaninglessness:

- Nihilism: all sources of meaning that others find in their lives, for example service, are ridiculed or disparaged.

- Compulsive activity: the pursuit of money, power, leisure, status and recogntion in various combinations. In the case of 'crusadism', individuals pursue issues that will consume time and energy.

Existential counselling

In existential counselling clients are encouraged to experience their existence as real. Rather than a rigorous system, it is a way of viewing people. Clienthood is ubiquitous for the existential counsellor and clients are viewed in human rather than behavioural terms. There is great emphasis on an authentic counsellor–client relationship. Little time is spent digging up the client's past, rather the client's current circumstances and enveloping fears are all-important because in existential counselling the emphasis is on the depth of the clients' confrontations with ultimate concerns at that moment. Symptomatic 'cures' are a secondary goal.

The basic neurotic process has to do with repression of the ontological sense, involving the sense of being and the limiting of awareness and potential. Clients are helped to comprehend their inner conflicts in relation to the four ultimate concerns. Defence mechanisms are identified and their negative consequences are spotlighted. Counsellors helps their clients to develop other ways of dealing with anxiety, and they work on secondary anxiety by correcting restrictive ways of relating to the self and others. There is an eclectic use of approaches, but all must fit the existential framework. The decision to work on a conflict is made jointly by client and counsellor. Counselling is usually long term although short-term work can take place, with an emphasis on authenticity and responsibility.

The counsellor–client relationship

This relationship is between two real people on an individual basis. It should have presence, authenticity and commitment. The counsellor tries to understand the client's being, and does so as a real person rather than a reflector. This process consists of one existence communicating with another. The relationship is not viewed in terms of transference, and countertransference is also avoided. The elements of a good relationship are presence, caring, wisdom, touching clients at a profound level, extending oneself, being trustworthy, being interested, and the belief that the joint effort will be redemptive and healing.

Self-disclosure

Self-disclosure is very important in this sort of counselling because of the need for an authentic relationship. Self-disclosure serves to deepen the counsellor–client relationship. There are two types of self-disclosure: disclosure about personal struggles to come to terms with ultimate concerns of an existential nature; and the counsellor may have a process focus rather than a content focus.

Thoughts and feelings about the here and now are discussed to improve the relationship.

Counselling and death

When individuals gain increased awareness of death, perhaps because they or someone close is seriously ill, this can lead to a heightened appreciation of life. According to Yalom (1980, p. 202), anxiety about death is inversely proportional to satisfaction with life. Counsellors help their clients to come to terms with the prospect of death and to use it constructively. There are seven existential ways of increasing individuals' awareness of death.

1. *Giving permission.* Counsellors encourage their clients to discuss issues relating to death and refuse to collude with the clients' denial of death. Counsellors ensure that the counselling is kept superficial.

2. *Identifying defence mechanisms.* There is collaboration with the clients to identify their defence mechanisms. Persistence, tact and good timing are aimed at helping clients to recognise and abandon childish ways of regarding death.

3. *Working with dreams.* Unconscious themes appear without repression or strong editing, and these are related to existential conflicts.

4. *Working with reminders of finiteness.* A good example of this is working with the death of grandparents and parents, reminding us that ours will be the next generation to die. The death of children brings a realisation of people's powerlessness over the relentless inevitabilities of life. When an only child dies parents realise that they cannot achieve immortality by passing on genetic material through this child.

Illnesses such as cancer remind clients of their mortality. Transitions do the same, including the transition from childhood to adolescence to adulthood, entering a permanent relationship, children leaving home, divorce, entering middle age and contemplating growing old instead of growing up, and retirement. Reminders of the passage of time are physical signs (greying hair, deteriorating eyesight and so on), and birthdays and anniversaries.

5. *Aids to increasing the awareness of death.* These include death anxiety questionnaires, writing one's own obituary and fantasies about one's own funeral arrangements. There are two ways of getting clients to interact with the dying: (1) introducing someone with a terminal illness to an everyday counselling group; and (2) asking clients to observe a group of terminally ill people.

6. *Desensitising clients to death.* If clients are exposed again and again to the fear of death in a lessened form they become familiar with the fear and it therefore diminishes.

7. *Comprehending death anxieties.* The key point here is that childlike irrational fears lurk in the adult unconscious and must be brought into consciousness so that realistic assessment can take place. Therefore counsellors try to identify and break down anxieties associated with death. A distinction is made between the true helplessness caused by the inevitability of death and ancillary feelings of helplessness. The aim is to help clients to take control of those aspects of their lives that are possible to control. They are also helped to identity their

ancillary fears so that these can be confronted. Ancillary fears include loneliness, worries about loved ones, and painful death.

Counselling and freedom

Here the aim is for clients to take responsibility for their own lives. There are six techniques for increasing awareness and responsibility.

1. *Identifying defences and methods of responsibility avoidance.* When clients complain about their lot in life, counsellors ask how they brought it about. Clients are helped to understand the purpose of their behaviour, for example compulsiveness can be about avoiding responsibility for choices. When lonely clients criticise others their counsellor might challenge them by saying 'And you are lonely'. Counsellors also identify avoidance language, for example clients might say 'I can't' when they really mean 'I won't'.

2. *Identifying responsibility avoidance in the here and now.* This often crops up in the client–counsellor relationship and counsellors may challenge their clients' attempts to transfer onto them responsibility for what happens both inside and outside the counselling room. In such scenarios, counsellors work through client resistance by stating that if the clients knew what to do they would not be seeing a counsellor. Counsellors must be aware of their own feelings about their clients in order to discover how they elicit similar reactions from others. To illustrate this, a woman who habitually has relationships with abusive men may act towards a male counsellor in a way that in her usual relationships attracts the abuse she fears.

3. *Confronting realistic limitations.* The aims here are to change attitudes towards circumstances that cannot be changed, and to identify areas of the client's life that can be changed. To illustrate the latter point, clients with a terminal illness can be encouraged to be more assertive when seeking information from their doctors.

4. *Confronting existential guilt.* One of the purposes of anxiety is to act as a call to conscience. Guilt about failure to actualise potential is one source of anxiety. For example a man who indulges in compulsive sexual behaviour but is unable to be assertive in other aspects of his life is wasting his potential by limiting his life through compulsive sex. Identification of this leads to reduced compulsiveness and greater choice over life. There is a difference between feeling guilty about poor choices made in the past and refusal to make new choices. The point is that if clients perpetuate their past behaviour they will be unable to forgive themselves for their past choices.

5. *Releasing wishing.* Wishing comes before willing and clients need to be in touch with how they feel before they can wish. Thus counsellors explore the source and nature of their clients' blocks and the underlying feelings they try to own. All of this is facilitated by authentic relationships.

6. *Enabling decision making.* Decisions can be difficult if the alternatives are exclusive. Such decisions are boundary situations despite their basic groundlessness. The ability to make decisions is often hampered by the 'what if' situation: 'what if this fails and I lose everything?' Consequently a decision to

change may take a considerable time. The counsellors' role is to help their clients to see that every action is preceded by a decision, assist the examination of each 'what if' and its attendant feelings, assist the formation and evaluation of options for decisions, ensure that responsibility for decisions remains with their clients, encourage decisions that reinforce clients' acceptance of their own powers and resources, give the acceptance that is vital for clients to learn to trust their will and believe that it is their right to act, and ensure that the clients are aware of having this acceptance.

Examples of insights offered to will-stifled clients are 'I have the power to change', 'Only I can change my world', 'I must change to achieve what I really want' and 'There is no danger in change'.

Counselling and isolation

There are five ways of dealing with isolation.

1. *Confronting isolation.* Counsellors help their clients to realise that ultimately everyone is alone, recognise what can and cannot be obtained from relationships, experiment with periods of self-enforced isolation, increase their awareness of the terror of loneliness and increase their awareness of hidden resources and courage.

2. *Identifying defence mechanisms.* These mechanisms are used in the conflict between the need to belong and the fact of existential isolation. Examples of such mechanisms are compulsive sexuality, existing only in the eyes of others and fusion with others. Clients' awareness that these mechanisms are being used to protect them from existential anxiety can result in their doing something to rectify the problem.

3. *Identifying interpersonal pathology.* Here clients' methods of avoiding real relationships with others are identified and instruction is given in what Yalom called the ABC of the language of intimacy, for example how to own and express feelings. The following questions help this process:

- What specific distancing operations do you use?
- To what extent do you see others as objects to satisfy your wants and needs?
- How well can you love others?
- How good are you at listening?
- How good are you at revealing yourself?

4. *Using the client–counsellor relationship to reveal pathology.* Instead of clients transferring feelings and attitudes from past relationships onto them, existential counsellors use their relationship with their clients to highlight pathology that can distort the clients' current and future relationships.

5. *The healing relationship.* This is vital for the client for the following reasons. Existential counselling emphasises real relationships, and although counselling eventually ends the experience of intimacy may be permanent. This can be very affirming for clients because they are fully accepted by a person they respect, and who really knows them. All of the above help them to face existential isolation and accept that only they are responsible for their lives.

Counselling and meaninglessness

There are three ways in which existential counsellors work with clients whose lives lack meaning.

1. *Redefining the problem.* Clients tend to present their problem by saying either that life has no meaning or that they cannot find any meaning in it. Existentialism holds that people are meaning-giving not meaning-getting. Counsellors work on the basis that there is no inherent meaning in life so clients must create their own.

2. *Identifying anxiety defences.* An example of this is the extent to which people's pursuit of power, money, recognition or pleasure represents an escape from the existential concern of meaninglessness. Counsellors helps their clients to see that the consequence of such defences is a superficial existence that promotes the problems they are trying to avoid, whether consciously or unconsciously.

3. *Helping engagement in life.* Clients may be unable to find meaning in their relationships, work, leisure, religious worship and other pursuits. Therefore counsellors help their clients to analyse each area to identify obstacles that can be removed, thus enabling engagement in the stream of life (it is always assumed that clients have the desire to engage in life). It is necessary for counsellors to offer an authentic relationship in order to confirm their own engagement in the counselling process. Also explored are the clients' long-term goals, hopes, beliefs, ability to love and powers of creative expression.

Group counselling

Existential group counsellors try to show group members how their behaviour Is seen by others, Makes others feel, Creates the opinions that others have of them and Influences their opinions of themselves.

Groups consist of eight to ten people and work on issues relating to the ultimate concerns of death and meaninglessness. A good example of this is a group of people suffering from AIDS or cancer. 'Here-and-now' information is provided on members' methods of avoiding and assuming responsibility. Opportunities are provided to work on interpersonal distortions and maladaptive behaviours.

Qualities needed by effective counsellors

Existential counsellors need to be possessed of a good attitude and personality, experience in life, theoretical knowledge and professional training. However maturity is a real hallmark of the existential counsellor and this is manifest in the ability to see life from various perspectives.

There are a number of life experiences that prepare people for effective counselling. First, cross-cultural experiences develop the mind, put previous assumptions to the test and hence open up new perspectives on life and human existence. Second, caring for relatives or other dependants promotes the maturity that is essential to becoming a counsellor. Third, a varied experience of society is vital, including different areas of study, several jobs, contact with other social classes and experience of life outside the caring professions. Finally, personal experience of existential crises and the successful overcoming of these provides depth, maturity and insights into life.

With regard to theoretical knowledge, study of the leading branches of philosophy that have emerged over the centuries is of great use in this type of counselling. Knowledge of the history of psychology and psychoanalysis in all its forms is also important in that it provides an insight into the many facets of human nature and produces a truly broadminded person.

The training received by counsellors is eclectic but all-round, with the essentials of each technique being used in a consistent philosophical framework. There is much supervised clinical work with considerable analysis and self-reflection. Depth and perspective are more important than the number of hours spent in therapy.

Therapeutic style

Variability is the key feature of the existential approach and counsellors develop differing approaches that change as clients' needs change. However there are a number of common features. As far as possible, preconceptions and prejudices are put aside and the client's unique situation is consistently appreciated. Clients' dilemmas are taken seriously and simplistic diagnoses and solutions are avoided. Openness and wonder are the cornerstones of the existential philosophy of counselling, and appropriate humour is part of the authentic relationship. Normative theories are avoided and counsellors avoid steering their clients in a particular direction.

Counselling is non-directive but it has direction in that clients are helped to develop their own perspectives, philosophy and position in the world, with counsellors pointing out contradictions in or the implications of their clients' perspectives. A didactic approach is followed only if a client has overlooked some aspect of the problem, in which case the missing element is put forward for consideration, but even then the counsellor never does the client's work for him or her. Clients' approach to life is revealed in attempts to evade the task being tackled. This is reflected upon, as is the relationship between client and counsellor. Counselling takes place as a dialogue and varies in pace according to whether complicated ideas are being explored, in which case things move slowly, or emotions are being explored, in which case there is greater speed. The two parties operate as a team because existential counselling deals with human issues that are of much relevance to the counsellor as they are to the client.

Therapeutic strategies and techniques

Rather than using specific techniques and strategies, in existential counselling a philosophical method of enquiry is followed that includes a combination of the following.

1. *An open mind.* By assuming an open-minded, naive stance to facilitate the uncovering of issues, new perspectives on the world can be formed.

2. *Assumptions.* People take their assumptions about the world for granted and therefore are normally unaware of them. What they have to say is mostly based on these assumptions, so by clarifying them new insights can be gained into clients' problems.

3. *Themes.* Themes emerge from the confused statements of clients, and counsellors listen out for unspoken links. When the counsellors are sure of these the clients are informed.

4. *Meanings.* Clients may hide behind the words they use, masking the real significance of what they mean. Counsellors question the superficial meaning of what the clients have said and ask them to reconsider what it is they want to say. This can produce a new awareness.

5. *Developing a naive or open attitude.* Counsellors approach their clients with an open mind as this can foster a sense of exploration and discovery and give clients a new world view.

6. *Vicious circles.* Many clients set themselves low goals and standards and become caught up in a vicious circle of doom and failure. Counsellors work with their clients to break such circles.

7. *Facing limitations.* Clients are helped to identify the limitations of the human condition.

8. *Consequences.* Clients are asked to weigh up the consequences of choices they have made, both past and present. By considering the implications of their actions they become aware of limitations as well as possibilities.

9. *Dreams.* Dreams are messages from the dreamers to themselves and reveal their attitudes towards the various aspects of existence. This is also true of the stories and fantasies told by clients, as each is a snapshot of the way in which they react to the world.

10. *Paradoxes.* These aid clients' quest for authenticity as they may be inclined to side-step the fundamental dilemmas of life and death and adopt a form of self-affirmation that amounts to misinformed egocentricity. The search for truth depends on clients' awareness of their capacity for certainty and doubt, success and failure, freedom and necessity, and life and death.

11. *Personal world view.* All of life's problems, tasks and dimensions are explored by client and counsellor in the light of information revealed by the client.

12. *Questions.* Questions are asked as little as possible and clients' world views are examined in an observation-oriented manner. Deductions are only made when there is enough evidence to draw a conclusion. When questions are asked they do not suggest a conclusion or imply right or wrong as counsellors want to uncover the inclinations and opinions of their clients.

13. *Talents.* Clients' preoccupation with personal problems may have led to suppression of their talents and abilities, so counsellors draw attention back to them. Practical talents of the client can be used as similes or metaphors for greater understanding.

14. *Beliefs.* Therapists uncover belief in a spirit of complete respect. Moreover values are not be challenged by an alternative set of values. The aim is to uncover the client's conscience and an inner source of truth, rather than to foster conformity by challenging deeply held values.

15. *Recollection.* Clients tend to have a fixed view of their past. Therapists treat memories as flexible and open to interpretation, and clients are helped to reinterpret their past in new ways. This allows them to see that their view of the past influences their future. If they look at it in a different way they can open up new frontiers for themselves. Clients come to see that they are the ultimate controllers of the meaning of their past, present and future. The aim is to make living an art rather than a duty.

16. *Emotions.* Each emotion has an important message for therapy. Shame, hope and envy show up desired values that are missing. Love, pride and joy show a sense of ownership of what is valued. Sorrow and fear arise from giving up and losing what truly mattered. Anger and jealousy are reactions to a threat to something that is valued.

17. *Enquiry into meaning.* What makes the world meaningful for the client? Examination of this question is aimed at helping clients to find motivation and purpose, and to abandon misleading and irrelevant motivations.

18. *The fourfold world.* This model of the four dimensions of existence makes it possible to examine clients' accounts of their preoccupations with the different levels of existence, and to identify priorities, imbalances and impasses.

19. *Existential guilt.* This can be hidden beneath anxiety, depression, guilt and even self-confidence. It involves a sense of being in debt to life, and clients' belief that they owe it to themselves to do or not to do something.

20. *Anxiety.* This shows awareness of life's inevitable limitations, and of death. Sensitivity may be dulled to avoid life's challenges or clients may find ways of disguising them; some are simply overwhelmed. Clients are guided towards coming to terms with this.

The process of change

The aim is for clients to come to terms with life's ups and downs and all its attendant contradictions. The client will find a way forward when they face up to reality. Another aim is for clients to stop deluding themselves that they are not responsible for what is taking place in their lives, and to cease making excessive demands on life. They are often in a rush, thinking that they can hurry life and extract rewards from it with minimal effort.

If personal distress is measured against the yardstick of the human condition, it provides a better ideological foundation for assessing personal hopes and fears, and some relief from worrying preoccupations as clients take these more in their stride. They also become more adept at and steadfast in dealing with failure, loss, personal inadequacy and ultimately death. They accept that life is a series of transformations with both losses and gains. The aim is not to fight or speed up change, but to tune into it. Clients learn to monitor their own attitudes, actions and moods because they are empowered to do their own thinking. In so doing they learn to contemplate, to rediscover recreation, and above all to feel alright about relating to themselves.

The change process is born in the counselling room, but it is accomplished between sessions and after counselling has concluded because change is a never-ending process. Existentialism emphasises that this is part of life's condition and hence there should never be complacency or self-satisfaction. Rather continued change can be seen as a sign of successful engagement with life. Therapy ends when the client feels able to take up the challenge of life once more, so the contract may last anywhere between six months and two years, or, because there are no criteria for healing in existential counselling, it could end up being an endless process.

In summary, change is about having the courage to change those things which can be changed, accepting those things which cannot be changed, and knowing the difference between the two. It is also about coming to terms with the givens, having the courage to tackle uncertainties and discovering what matters enough to be committed to it, to live for it, and perhaps even die for it.

Conclusion

The emphasis that existential counselling places on self-reflection and under-standing results in certain limitations. For example clients who find it hard to trust others tend to go for existential counselling because they feel they are not surrendering control. To overcome this limitation it is necessary for counsellors to help their clients to use their self-reliance for positive ends, rather than fight it or simply leave it unchallenged. Further more existential counselling is often seen as merely intellectual, so some clients choose this approach because they are seeking help that will not tap into their feelings, intuition or senses; indeed some counsellors do concentrate on the cognitive aspects of their clients' problems. In truth a good counsellor will accommodate all these levels of experience because only an openness to all the facts of being will yield complete self-understanding.

Existential counselling is not helpful to those who wish to relieve specific symptoms because there is no emphasis on the illness–health dimension. Thus clients who hope to regress and use the counsellor as a substitute parent will be disappointed because this is not on offer. Instead clients are provided with systematic support in coming to terms with the truth. In fact clients relate more to themselves than to the counsellor.

It naturally follows that existential counsellors must be wise and have a high degree of maturity, experience of life and training so that their understanding of the human condition will be wide-ranging and profound.

▚ ▐ ▐ Logotherapy: Victor Frankl

Viktor Frankl was born in 1905 in Vienna to Jewish parents. He corresponded with Freud while still at school, and at Freud's invitation he published his first article in 1924 in the *International Journal of Psychoanalysis*. He was influenced by Freud and Adler, but reacted against some of their ideas. Existential philosophers such as Heidegger, Jaspers and Scheler were a further influence. Frankl's search for meaning in his early years resulted in the genesis of logotherapy. The term logotherapy was coined by him in the 1920s, but in the 1930s he used the word *Existenzanalyse* (existential analysis) as an alternative. In 1928 he founded the Youth Advisement Centres in Vienna, which he headed until 1938. He received an MD from Vienna University in 1930 and then worked at the Neuropsychiatric University Clinic until 1938. Between 1938 and 1942 he was first a specialist in neurology and psychiatry and then head of the Neurological Department at the Jewish Hospital in Vienna. From 1942–45 he was incarcerated in the Auschwitz and Dachau concentration camps, where he was able to observe human nature *in extremis*. Some prisoners were spiritually deepened by their experiences in the camps and rose to the challenge of finding meaning in their lives. In 1946 Frankl became head of the Department of Neurology at the Poliklinik Hospital in Vienna, and in 1947 he became assistant professor of psychiatry and neurology at Vienna University, becoming full professor in 1955. He has held many other posts and has written over 30 books.

Introduction

Logotherapy gets its name from the Greek *logos*, which can be translated as both 'meaning' and 'spirit'. Human beings have a need to seek meaning in their lives, and logotherapy helps clients with this quest. As Nietzsche said, 'He who has a *why* to live for can bear almost any *how*' (Frankl, 1963, p. 121). Frankl himself said, 'I have seen the meaning of my life in helping others to see in their lives a meaning' (Frankl, 1988, p. 160).

Logotherapy is sometimes called the third Viennese school of psychotherapy, the other two being Freud's psychoanalysis and Adler's individual psychology. They differ in that psychoanalysis focuses on the will for *pleasure*, individual psychology focuses on the will for *power* and logotherapy focuses on the will for *meaning*. Pleasure and power though are by-products of the will for meaning. What people need is not a tensionless state but the tension of striving for a meaning worthy of them, so it can be said that the will for meaning is not concerned with reducing tension or rationalising instinctual drives.

Theoretical assumptions

Life is transitory in nature and full of potential and possibilities. We have to recognise these possibilities and constantly decide which to actualise and which to pass by.

As human beings we have freedom of will. We are the only animal with the ability to be self-detached and to reflect on and judge the choices we make. The important thing is not our character, instincts and drives, but the stance we take in relation to them. We are free to shape our characters and we are responsible for what we make of ourselves. When we rise above the bodily and psychic dimensions of our existence we enter a new dimension called the 'noological' dimension. In this dimension are three distinctly human functions: conscientiousness, instance reflection and the capacity to make the self into an object.

The will for meaning is our fundamental motivational force and throughout our lives we are faced with the need to find meaning. We need something to live for, so we encounter other people and search for meanings to fulfil. Meaning sets the pace for being, and our existence is compromised if we do not live in terms of transcendence towards something beyond ourselves. People can only actualise themselves to the extent that they fulfil meaning, because self-actualisation is, according to Frankl, only a side-effect of the will for meaning.

Consciousness and unconsciousness

The search for meaning involves both conscious activity and getting in touch with the unconscious layers of the self. Logotherapy focuses on our spiritual existence because we are essentially spiritual beings. It should be emphasised that 'spirit' is not used here in the religious sense of the word. Our spiritual phenomena can be conscious or unconscious; consciousness implying awareness. One of the purposes of logotherapy is to increase clients' consciousness of the spiritual self. It is vital for people to be conscious of their responsibility for discovering and acting in relation to the unique meaning of their lives in the various situations of their lives.

The spiritual unconscious

All humans have an existential and personal spiritual core around which their somatic (bodily), spiritual and psychic features are individualised and integrated. The deep centre, the basis of human existence, is ultimately unconscious, though the border between conscious and unconscious is fluid. There is a distinction between the spiritual and the instinctual unconscious. While Freud regarded the unconscious as a well of repressed instincts, depth psychology follows clients into the depths of their spirit rather than focusing on this repressed material.

There is a difficulty in that the self is basically unreflectable: 'Existence exists in action rather than reflection' as Frankl (1975, p. 130) put it.

The religious unconscious

When dreams are existentially analysed, repressed and unconscious religiousness is uncovered. The religious unconscious, or unconscious religiousness, is in the spiritual unconscious, and even in atheists religiousness is latent.

Human beings have always stood in an intentional relation to transcendence, even if only on an unconscious level. There are two points to consider here: the human relation to God is hidden, and God is hidden. Although people are responsible *for* themselves, they are not responsible *before* themselves. Rather than being an instinctual factor, the religious unconscious is an existential agent.

In Jung's view, unconscious religiousness comes from an impersonal reservoir of images shared by humankind. Frankl, by comparison, says that it stems from the personal centre of each human being. The existentiality of religiousness has to be spontaneous, and if it is to be genuine it has to unfold at its own pace. We commit ourselves to religiousness by choosing to be religious, and it is worth remembering that repression of religiousness, as with the other facets of the unconscious, causes neuroses, or as Frankl (1975, p. 70) put it: 'once the angel in us is repressed, he turns into a demon'.

Conscience

Conscience has its origins in the spiritual unconscious and is highly individual compared with other instincts. It intuitively reveals the possibility of meaning being actualised in any given situation. Conscience can be described as the 'ethical instinct' and has a transcendent quality. Conscience discloses the transcendence of the spiritual unconscious because it is the voice of transcendence and is itself transcendent; as Frankl put it, a trans-human agent sounds through it.

Freedom and conscience can be defined as 'from what' and 'to what'. The latter is a response to conscience and it requires us to have a dialogue rather than a monologue with it as something other than ourselves. Only then can we be the servants of our conscience.

Meaning

The meaning of life

As human beings we are different, responsible and conscious, and responsibility is the cornerstone of human existence. Freedom as human beings means the freedom to accept responsibility; it is what we *are*, not what we *have* (and can therefore lose). Because we are not determined or preconditioned, and have so many potentialities we can decide what we want to be, and it is such decisions that mobilise the potential within us to achieve it. According to Frankl (1955, p. 85) we can never 'escape the mandate to choose among possibilities'. We have to take account of the restrictions of society, biology and psychology, and we can either shape, conquer or submit to them.

Many people ignore their past as a source of meaning in their lives, but identifying sources of meaning in the past can help provide meaning in the present.

The meaning of death and destiny

Death belongs to life and gives it meaning. Responsibility is born of our finiteness – if we were immortal we would probably put things off indefinitely. So every moment of our lives we must recognise the full weight of responsibility we bear.

Destiny is also vital to the meaning of life. Destiny can be defined as those circumstances we cannot control, so freedom has to be seen in the context of destiny. Nonetheless we have an inner freedom to defy our destiny.

Self-transcendence

Self-transcendence is a basic characteristic of human existence. We transcend ourselves by encountering another person lovingly and/or by fulfilling a meaning. The basic human need is to search for meaning rather than search for the self, as only when we achieve meaning can we achieve identity. A major problem with humans is that they can become too focused on themselves – it is when they forget themselves that the self-transcendent quality of human life is most apparent.

For Frankl the chief lesson of the concentration camps is that survival is pointless, meaningless and impossible unless life points to something beyond itself. Those who do not find meaning by transcending themselves suffer from neurotic problems that reflect problems in self-transcendence. The two main factors in failure to transcend are hyperintention (paying excessive attention to fulfilling one's desires) and hyperreflection (excessive self-reflection).

Self-transcendence can be attained by finding meaning in three ways: by doing a deed, by suffering and by experiencing a value. In turn, finding meaning depends on creative values (what we give to life), experiential values (what we take from life) and attitudinal values (the stance we adopt towards something we cannot overcome, such as terminal cancer).

Meaning in work

Work is important because we bring our own unique human qualities to our occupations; it is one of the ways in which we can reach out beyond ourselves to reach others. All work affords this opportunity, although some jobs are so mundane that creative fulfilment can only be found in leisure pursuits. Many people try to escape the emptiness of their existence by burying themselves in their work, but the meaning of life is not to be found just in job satisfaction.

Unemployed people can suffer from a lack of creative meaning. Unemployment neurosis is an existential position that manifests itself in depression and apathy, but it can be combated by finding ways of being active and involved.

Meaning in love

In logotherapy love is not seen as a secondary phenomenon to sex (which is how psychoanalysis views it) and sex is not seen as a form of love in itself, although it can be an expression of mature love. In Frankl's view, love is not the best and certainly not the only way to find meaning in life.

Love as a form of self-transcendence means relating to other people as spiritual beings and comprehending the inner core of their personality. The spiritual core of a person so loved can move individuals to the depths of their spiritual being. Love has a permanence because the spiritual core of the loved person is irreplaceable and unique. Furthermore it outlasts death because the essence of the unique being of the loved person has a timeless quality and can never die. Love is synonymous with monogamy because its object is identified with what the other person 'is' and not seeing the other as a possession; it also precludes jealousy. It means seeing the inherent potential of the people we love and helping them to achieve it.

Love is not infatuation as this seldom lasts, or sex drive as this vanishes as soon as it is gratified.

Meaning in suffering

Attitudinal values are inherent in the attitudes we display in circumstances we cannot change (for example Frankl's incarceration in concentration camps, or enduring a terminal illness). Attitudinal values can turn the tragic facets of existence into something creative and positive; even the 'tragic triad' of guilt, pain and death can be included in this. People should take attitudinal values on board only when it is clear they cannot escape their fate, but then the opportunity is provided to actualise the highest value and fulfil the deepest meaning, that is, the meaning of suffering. We have choices over our response to suffering, and life can have meaning right to the end if we face the cause of our suffering with courage.

Suprameaning or the ultimate meaning of suffering and life

We do not have the ability to comprehend the ultimate meaning of human suffering, and we are unable to break through the dimensional differences between the human and divine worlds. Suprameaning cannot be grasped by intellect; it can only be experienced through faith. Here logotherapy contrasts with secular existentialist philosophy in that our task as humans is not to endure life's meaninglessness, it is to bear our inability to grasp life's ultimate meaningfulness in a rational manner.

Trust in God precedes the ability to have faith in life's ultimate meaning. God is silent, not dead. The modern trend is to move away from an emphasis on the differences between the various denominations rather than away from religion itself. According to Frankl there is a move towards a profoundly personalised religion in which individuals speak to God in their own way.

The existential vacuum

Frankl uses the term existential in three ways: to refer to existence itself, to refer to the meaning of existence, and to refer to the striving to discover meaning in personal existence. The existential vacuum is experienced as an inner void and has three causes. First, unlike animals we are not programmed by instincts and drives that determine what we do. Second, values, traditions and conventions no longer dictate what we should do. Sometimes people do not know what they want to do and therefore take refuge in one of two stances: conformism (doing what others do) or totalitarianism (doing what others want them to do). The final cause is the problem of reductionism, whereby people are not deciding agents but an amalgam of instincts, drives, defence mechanisms, conditioning and reaction formation.

Existential frustration

This is caused by frustration of the will for meaning and its main characteristics are boredom and apathy. Worry about the meaning of life is a form of spiritual distress, not a disease or a neurosis. Unhappiness about the meaninglessness of life can be a sign of intellectual sincerity and honesty.

Noogenic neurosis

This occurs when the existential vacuum leads to clinical symptomatology (the complex of symptoms of a disease). It is caused by a spiritual problem or a moral or ethical conflict, for example a conflict between the superego and what Frankl calls the 'true conscience'. Existential frustration is a vital ingredient of noogenic neurosis, the root of the problem lying in spiritual conflicts that arise from an aspiration for meaningful existence and the thwarting of the will for meaning. Hence noogenic neurosis has a spiritual and an instinctual dimension.

Frankl's 'mass neurotic triad'

This term covers the three main effects of humankind's neuroticisation by the existential vacuum, which goes beyond meaninglessness and noogenic neurosis. These effects are:

- Depression: suicide is on the increase, especially among the young, and is caused by existential frustration.
- Addiction: individuals with little purpose in life are more likely to take refuge in drugs and alcohol than those with greater purpose.
- Aggression: this can thrive when individuals are trapped in emptiness and meaninglessness. The same applies to sexual libido.

Meaninglessness

Meaninglessness is acquired through learning, it is part of the human response to life and can be valuable as a growth experience if worked through in the right way.

The problem is that many people grow up in cultures and societies in which it is much more difficult to find meaning than it was in the past. There are three main reasons for this: traditional values have eroded, thus maintaining the existential vacuum; there is tendency towards reductionism and the belief that individuals are determined rather than determining; and the young have difficulty finding an educator, role model or exemplar who has been successful in finding meaning.

Meaninglessness is maintained by the following:

- Avoidance of responsibility: this includes conformism, totalitarianism and the neurotic triad of depression, addiction and aggression.
- Repression: the repression of spirituality and religiousness divorces people from their spiritual centres, which are the deepest sources of their sense of meaning. By repressing the will for meaning they shackle their perception of the existence of meaning.
- Lack of self-transcendence prevents happiness and fulfilment as these are the result of self-transcendence or forgetting oneself.
- The neuroticisation of humanity: it is difficult to get help from others in one's search for meaning because the problems and symptoms of meaning-lessness are so widespread. This contributes to and maintains the inner vacuum.

Counselling

Dealing with the existential vacuum

Counselling takes place in the context of a caring, committed, 'I–thou' relationship where the uniqueness of each client is respected. This relationship provides a safe foundation for clients to progress towards finding their own meanings. Therapy does not become too individualised, and the therapist acts as a responsibility educator.

During diagnosis clients work on issues of meaning. Covert signs of an existential vacuum include boredom and apathy. Overt signs include the client saying that his or her life has no meaning. Clients are assured that existential despair is not a neurosis or a superficiality, rather it is presented as an achieve-ment and an indication of intellectual depth.

There are three ways of increasing existential awareness, all of which focus on the importance of responsibility and the finiteness of life. The first involves explaining that finiteness does not rob life of meaning; on the contrary it gives existence a meaning. The second is the offering of maxims: 'Live as if you were living for the second time and had acted as wrongly the first time as you are about to act now' (Frankl, 1955, p. 75). The third is the use of similes. Clients are asked to imagine that their life is a series of moving pictures that are currently being filmed. Life's clock cannot be turned back, so clients are told that the pictures cannot be cut or changed in retrospect. Clients are sculptors with a limited time span to complete their works of art, but, they do not know when the deadline is.

Finding meaning

Meaning is an individual matter so counsellors individualise and improvise. There is no preaching, teaching or issuing of moral exhortations. The aim is to expand clients' field of vision so that every facet of meaning and values is apparent to them. There are eight methods of focusing on meaning, as follows.

1. *Taking responsibility for meaning*. Clients are responsible for finding meaning in the specific situations of their unique existence; in fact life is an assignment. Life never ceases to have meaning under any circumstances. If clients are religious it is emphasised that they are responsible to God as taskmaster, as well as being responsible for fulfilling their own life's tasks.

2. *Listening to personal conscience*. Meaning cannot be given, it must be discovered, and it is conscience that guides the search. It is counsellors' job to provide existential examples of their commitment to the search.

3. *Asking clients about meanings*. This focuses on meaning in relationships and suffering. Clients are asked about creative achievements they could strive for.

4. *Widening horizons in respect of sources of meaning*. If clients want to find a job that would give meaning to their life through fulfilment, their counsellor helps them to see that their attitude towards the performance of the job also offers the possibility of fulfilment. Likewise meaning can be found in other spheres, such as private life, voluntary work and so on.

5. *Socratic questioning*. When one of Frankl's clients told him that she was worried by the transitory nature of life he asked her to name someone whose achievements she admired. She named her doctor, and Frankl used a sequence of questions that enabled her to see that even though her doctor had died the meaningfulness of his life remained (Frankl, 1988).

6. *Logodrama*. This can be used in counselling groups and it is aimed at helping clients to see that adversity can give life meaning. In one of Frankl's groups there was a woman who had lost one of her two sons and the other was paralysed. He asked another woman in the group to imagine that she was old and to look back on a life that had brought no children but was full of success in terms of wealth and fame. She concluded that her life had been pointless. He then asked the woman with the paralysed son to do the same with her life. She concluded that in giving her son a fuller life than might have been expected she had achieved a life full of meaning (Frankl, 1963).

7. *Offering meanings*. An elderly man was stricken with grief for his dead wife. Frankl got him to see that he had spared her the same ordeal by surviving her, and that the price was his own suffering and mourning (Frankl, 1963, pp. 178–9).

8. *Analysing dreams*. Dreams are useful in bringing spiritual phenomena into consciousness. In religious logotherapy this process brings the religious unconscious into consciousness, the client's religiousness having been re-pressed because of what Frankl called 'the intimate quality inherent in genuine religiousness'.

Psychogenic neurosis

There are two therapies for psychogenic neurosis, both of which are based on the qualities of self-detachment and self-transcendence.

Paradoxical intention

This is used for short-term treatment of obsessive-compulsiveness and phobias. Anticipatory anxiety is targeted in the case of phobias in which clients react to events with the fear that they will recur. This reaction causes hyperintention or excessive attention, preventing the clients from achieving what they desire. In other words, anticipatory anxiety causes those things which the clients fear.

The clients are encouraged to focus on whatever it is that they fear, and humour is used so that by laughing at their neuroses they can increase their sense of detachment.

The fear experienced by obsessive-compulsive neurotics is fear of themselves – they are afraid of the possible consequences of their strange thoughts. The more they fight their thoughts the worse the symptoms become, hence the counsellor employs paradoxical intention to help them to stop struggling with their obsessions so that they will decrease and ultimately vanish. An example related by Frankl is of a woman with a counting compulsion and an obsession with checking that her dresser drawers were tidy and locked. She was encouraged to leave the dresser untidy and say to herself that it should be as untidy as possible. After two days the counting problem ended, and after four days she no longer needed to check the dresser. When the obsessive-compulsive urges returned she was able to ignore them or make a joke out of them (Frankl, 1955, p. 143).

Dereflection

This is used to combat excessive attention or hyperreflection by helping clients to ignore their symptoms. Frankl gives an example of a woman who compulsively observed her swallowing as she feared the food would go down the wrong way. She was dereflected by saying 'I don't need to watch my swallowing, because I don't really need to swallow, for actually I don't swallow, but rather *it* does' (ibid., p. 235).

Somatogenic psychoses

Frankl coined the expression 'medical ministry' for his method of working with cases where a somatic (of the body) cause could not be removed. When tackling psychoses and deep-rooted depression, logotherapy works with the non-diseased part of clients to find meaning in the stance they take towards their suffering. People with psychoses retain a measure of freedom, and importantly their inner core remains unaffected. Clients who believe that their suffering has no meaning can become very demoralised as a result. Frankl (1988, p. 131) relates the story of a schizophrenic youth who had been in an institution for two and a half years and was having doubts about his religious faith, but nonetheless blamed God for his condition. Frankl suggested that perhaps God wanted him to face his confinement in the institution. The youth said that was why he still believed in God, and that it was possible that God wanted him to recover. Frankl said that God did want this and that his spiritual level should be higher than before he became ill. The youth's condition improved and he found meaning not only despite but also because of his psychosis.

Part Four

Cognitive therapy and
behavioural counselling

■ ▽ 12 Cognitive therapy: Aaron Beck

Aaron Beck was born on 18 July 1921 in Providence, Rhode Island. He was the fourth son of Russian Jewish immigrants. At the age of seven he had a near fatal illness that made his mother even more overprotective than she already was. One of her sons had failed to survive and her daughter had died in the influenza epidemic of 1919. Aaron developed many phobias and anxieties while growing up, including fear of surgery, abandonment, heights, suffocation and public speaking. At his high school graduation he was top of his class and he went on to major in English and political science at Brown University. He gained an MD at Yale University School of Medicine but went into psychiatry as there was a shortage of psychiatric residents, completing a six months' rotation. He decided to remain in psychiatry and from 1950–52 was a fellow in psychiatry at the Austen Riggs Center in Stockbridge, Massachusetts. The American Board of Psychiatry and Neurology certified him in psychiatry in 1953, and in 1958 he graduated from the Philadelphia Psychoanalytic Institute. His work between 1960 and 1963 led to the development of cognitive therapy.

What is cognitive therapy?

According to the principles of cognitive therapy the way in which people interpret their experiences determines how they feel and act. Consequently cognitive counselling takes an information processing approach to the client. Because clients learn incorrect processing and interpreting habits during their cognitive development, counselling is aimed at helping them to correct erroneous thinking habits and distortions and to learn more realistic ways of processing information.

Theoretical assumptions

Schemas

Schemas are the cognitive structures that organise experience and behaviour. Beliefs and rules are the contents of schemas and therefore determine the content of the thinking affect and behaviour. Schemas are stable cognitive patterns and they influence how we select and synthesise data through our beliefs. They are similar to Kelly's 'personal constructs' and can be specific or general. Individuals can have competing schemas, and experiences are evaluated and categorised through a matrix of schemas. Schemas contain anything from inanimate objects to personal relationships. They can be adaptive or maladaptive, but they are not pathological by definition.

There are five categories of schema:

- Cognitive: these deal with abstracting, interpreting, recalling and evaluating the self and other people.
- Affective: these are responsible for generating feelings.
- Motivational: these are concerned with wishes and desires.
- Instrumental: these prepare people for action.
- Control: this category involves self-monitoring and inhibiting, modifying and directing actions.

The system of interlocking schemas is responsible for the process between receiving a stimulus and responding to it. Incoming data is selected, evaluated and a relevant strategy is formed. For example a danger stimulus triggers a danger schema, which processes the information. The cognitive schema interprets this information and decides whether the danger is real. If it is the affective schema is activated by a feeling of anxiety. This in turn activates the motivational schema, which impels the individual to escape. Next the action or instrumental schema is activated, telling the individual to run. Finally the control schema directs or inhibits the action of running away.

Schemas have structural qualities such as flexibility, breadth and relative prominence in an individual's cognitive organisation. They range from latent to hypervalent according to how much energy is devoted to them; if a schema is hypervalent it is prepotent (greater in power or force) and easily triggered. Psychopathology arises from the activation of inappropriate schemas, that inhibit or even crowd out more appropriate schemas.

Information processing is shaped by the fundamental beliefs embedded in our schemas. Because of our schemas we all have a unique set of sensitivities and vulnerabilities that incline us towards psychological distress. Our personal schemas and beliefs influence the way in which we process data about ourselves, and this is done incorrectly if we have dysfunctional schemas and beliefs.

Automatic thoughts

These reflect schema contents or deeper beliefs and assumptions, but are not as available as voluntary thoughts in human awareness and are not as deeply located as beliefs and schemas. Self-evaluation and self-instruction are derived from self-schemas, which are deeper structures. In psychopatholgy or dysfunctioning, some automatic thoughts lead people off course. This is characterised by biases in information processing. Depression is characterised by negative self-image and a negative view of experience and the future. Anxiety reflects fear of psychological and physical danger.

Automatic thoughts are part of an individual's internal monologue and can take the form of images, words or both. They are very rapid and normally take place on the edge of awareness. They precede emotions, feelings and inhibitions, and recur despite our attempts to block them. They are plausible and we assume they are accurate. They can be linked with more subtle thoughts that underly our more obvious thoughts. Finally, they affect facial expression, tone of voice and gestures.

Primal and higher level cognitive processing

Human beings have primal cognitive processes that mediate normal and pathological reactions. The thinking associated with primary processing is primitive; situations are seen in global and crude ways. Higher level processes test reality and correct the primal conceptualisations; such corrective functions become impaired in psychopathology and can become psychiatric disorders.

Cognitive distortions include the following:

- Arbitrary inference: coming to a specific conclusion when the evidence contradicts it, or when there is no evidence.
- Selective abstraction: focusing on an out-of-context detail at the expense of more relevant information.
- Personalisation: relating external events to oneself without adequate evidence.
- Magnification and minimisation: evaluating events as much more or much less than they really are, resulting in serious distortion of the facts.
- Overgeneralisation: using a few isolated incidents to form a general rule, which is then used out of context, in too broad a sense and in unrelated situations.
- Dichotomous, absolutistic thinking: polarised, black-and-white thinking that puts all experiences into one of two opposite categories.
- Biased explanations: partners make negative attributions about each other when their relationship is going through a bad patch. They consider there to be a wicked motive behind what they regard as the offensive actions of their partner.
- Tunnel vision: believing whatever fits our state of mind when in reality it is only a part of a wider situation.
- Mind reading: this is divided into two errors: 'I know what he is thinking' and 'he should know what I think'.
- Negative labelling: the product of biased explanations, where partners label each other's actions in a critical way. This causes them to react to the labels allotted to each other.
- Subjective reasoning: if an emotion is felt strongly enough it must be justifiable.

Cognition is related to emotion in the following way. The basic cognitive themes contain four basic emotions:

- Sadness is felt when individuals fail to reach a positive goal, experience loss of status or someone close, or fail to realise their expectations. It is common for people in this situation to withdraw their energy and commitment from the cause of their disappointment.

- Joy is felt when we experience a gain, such as achieving a cherished aim. It can also result from expressions of affection.
- Anxiety can be caused by a threat or a perceived threat. It can lead to withdrawal or appeasement as it focuses attention on physical danger and emotional vulnerabilty.
- Anger can be caused by the offensive qualities of a threat and may lead to counterattack and/or aggressive self-defence.

These emotions are linked to the mobilisation and maintenance of basic cognitive structures and strategies by their attachment to individuals' pleasure and pain centres. If successful, activities aimed at survival and reproduction are pleasurable, but they are painful if they fail. Anxiety serves to lessen the chance of self-defeating and dangerous activities. Behaviours that promote survival and bonding are encouraged by expecting and experiencing pleasure.

There is continuity between normal emotions and behaviours and those found in psychiatric disorders, the latter being exaggerations of normal adaptive processes. Depression is intensification of the normal reactions to failure, loss and deprivation, that is, sadness and withdrawal. Mania is manifest as excessive euphoria and goal-directed activities, while anxiety disorders are marked by awful anxiety and self-defeating avoidance behaviours caused by the increased sense of vulnerability that arises when threats and dangers approach.

The human cognitive structures and schemas associated with depression, personality disorders and anxiety disorders have developed during the evolution of the human species. A great deal of animal behaviour is preprogrammed, and the underlying processes are visible in their overt behaviour. It is possible that some aspects of normal and abnormal behaviour in humans can be explained by animal analogies. The study of depression, for example, could be helped by observing higher primate behaviour.

The evolution of strategies

Strategies are programmed behaviours that serve biological goals. As with all other species, human survival strategies have evolved over time through the process of natural selection. The problem is that in recent millennia these automatic strategies have not evolved as quickly as humans have changed their environment, and some strategies are unsuited to the sort of society we live in today. The four primal survival strategies are fight, flight, freeze and faint.

According to Beck the strategies that accompany personality disorders could be inherited from our prehistoric ancestors (Beck *et al.*, 1990, p. 4). Circumstances dictate whether a strategy is adaptive or maladaptive, and those associated with personality disorders are maladaptive exaggerations of normal ones. For example avoidant personality disorder reflects a fear of being injured or hurt so an avoidance strategy is employed, and dependent personality disorder reflects a belief in personal helplessness and a fear of abandonment, so an attachment strategy is employed.

Genetic variations influence the vulnerability of individuals to different sorts of distress. In the case of depression a key factor is neurochemical abnormality.

Temperamental and behavioural differences that are relatively stable are probably present at birth; it is life's experiences that strengthen or weaken these innate tendencies. For example a shy child may grow up to be a confident adult due to the quality of its interactions with others. There may also be mutual reinforcement, for example an individual with an innate need for care may elicit a response from others with an innate need to provide care.

Vulnerability

Cognitive therapists look at many factors when seeking the cause of a psychological dysfunction. These factors can be grouped under four headings – evolutionary or genetic, biological, environmental and developmental – and include the following:

- Physical problems such as hyperthyroidism.
- Developmental traumas that cause specific vulnerabilities, for example the loss of a parent in childhood may lead to depression in adult life.
- Inadequate personal experiences that lead to a lack of coping mechanisms, for example parents may fail to teach their children how to cope with rejection.
- Inadequate cognitive patterns with inappropriate values and goals, and assumptions learnt from significant others.
- External stress, for example loss of a partner or physical danger.
- Insidious external stress, for example the unabating disapproval of significant others.

Childhood traumas

Specific affect-laden childhood incidents may create dysfunctional underlying beliefs, for example:

- A little boy whose pet died when he was away on a trip now believes that something bad will happen to those who matter to him if he is away from them.
- A man dreads Christmas because when he was young his father had a heart attack during the Christmas holidays.
- A little girl whose father left home for ever after a row with her mother believes that if she makes others angry they will leave her.

Social learning

While Beck agrees with social learning theory he stresses that every person has a unique learning history, and that our ways of attaching meanings to earlier events are quite idiosyncratic (Beck and Weishaar, 1989).

Among the many reasons for the development of personality disorders is the reinforcement of strategies by parents and other key figures. An example is someone with a dependent personality whose clinging and help-seeking strategies are not only rewarded but also reinforced by his or her being discouraged from striving after self-sufficiency. Other important reasons are identification with other family members; negative life experiences that intensify a predisposition, for example negative experiences could cause a shy child to become an avoidant adult; and modelling, for example rules on what should and should not be done in a marriage may be based on what parents did in theirs.

Negative treatment in childhood

Consistently negative treatment of children can have an adverse effect on their self-esteem and this makes them vulnerable to psychological distress in later years. Another danger is that parents or other significant others may engage in abusive behaviour that children replicate and inflict on others at a later date.

Inadequate coping, self-assertion and communication skills

An important factor in anxious people's assessment of a threatening situation is their ability to cope with it. A good example is bullying: those who develop coping skills for dealing with bullies feel less anxious about them.

Non-assertive people tend to be more vulnerable to depression for two reasons: the actions of others undermine their self-esteem, and they disparage themselves for their inability to be self-assertive.

Marriages may run into trouble if the following communication skills are inadequate: diplomacy and tact, giving listening signals, not interrupting, asking questions skilfully and tuning in to the partner's mood.

Depression and anxiety

When a cognitive shift takes place, energy is diverted fom the normal, higher level of cognitive processing to processing by pathological primal schemas. Energy is used to activate and inhibit unconscious patterns. This happens in panic attacks, depression and general anxiety disorders when the panic mode, depressive mode and danger mode are energised in that order.

Modes reflect the way in which a schema is expressed. For example when the depressed mode is activated, hopelessness and self-blame cognitions predominate. There is usually a balance between modes, so if one is active for a long time the opposing mode will be activated. For example the anxiety mode may be activated to counterbalance hostility. In psychopathological disorder the dominant mode is prevented from being turned off. This causes systematically biased interpretations of dangerous events in anxiety disorder and negative events in depression.

According to the continuity hypothesis, depression, anxiety and personality disorders are exaggerated mechanisms of normal functioning. People can develop dysfunctional schemas, automatic thoughts, rules and behaviours without them getting out of hand, but if their vital interests are threatened a cognitive shift is triggered. Cognitive errors from dysfunctional schemas include overestimating the chance of a threat, overestimating the magnitude of a threat, catastrophising (magnifying) negative consequences, underestimating one's personal capacity to deal with a threat and taking insufficient note of the available support factors, for example people who could help.

Psychopathology is initially caused by a major life crisis, but as time passes it can be triggered by more minor stressors. For example the first attack of recurring depression may be caused by a severe life stressor such as divorce, but later episodes may be triggered by less personally relevant stressors such as hearing of a sister's divorce, the latter taking on exaggerated meaning owing to the previous experience.

Two types of people are prone to depression. First, sociotropic (socially dependent) people value closeness and sharing. Their cognitive vulnerability is caused by rejection, disrupted relationships and social deprivation. The disruption of any close relationship can activate the schema of irreversible loss implanted by an earlier experience. Second, autonomous people value independent achievement, solitude and mobility. Vulnerability is activated by failure, defeat, enforced conformity and immobilisation.

There are three main causes of anxiety disorders: increased demands, for example as a result of promotion, the birth of a child and so on; added threats in one or more areas of life, for example a hostile new superior at work; and reversals and stressful events such as failing an exam or a marriage failure can cause anxiety about career prospects or loss of status as a family man.

Some individuals readily accept their dysfunctional beliefs during depression and anxiety because their information processing is based on dysfunctional schemas. It is also permeated with automatic thoughts full of cognitive errors. Cognitive errors hamper people's ability to reality test their thought processes, and as a result they think in rigid, stereotypical terms. They are unable to detect the difference between fact and inference. They do not see their thought content as a series of testable hypotheses. Instead they jump to conclusions based on inadequate evidence and regard these conclusions as facts. They do not incorporate feedback that could clarify their perceptions and thoughts, so instead of the information processing system being open for the assessment of new data it remains closed.

Other relevant factors are significant others who provide negative experiences, model inefficient thinking and behaviour, and fail to provide them with enough opportunities to learn coping skills; external stressors such as antisocial neighbours or a hostile superior at work; and reciprocal interactions where anxious or depressed people trigger negative behaviour in others because they shun company and this leads to them being criticised or rejected.

Cognitive models of depression

Beck developed his basic model of depression into six separate but overlapping models: the cross-sectional, structural, stressor-vulnerability, reciprocal-interaction, psychobiological and evolutionary models. Key concepts include the following.

Cognitive triad

In Beck's view depression is a cognitive state as well as mood. It activates three major cognitive patterns called the cognitive triad: (1) individuals' negative views of themselves, for example that they are helpless, unlovable, worthless and incapable of attaining happiness; (2) individuals' negative views of their present and past experience of the world – their world presents massive obstacles to the achievement of goals and is too demanding for them; and (3) individuals' negative view of their future, which offers no prospect of improvement and is seen as hopeless, resulting in an urge to commit suicide. Such hopelessness causes the symptoms of depression, including motivational symptoms such as paralysis of the will, behavioural symptoms such as inertia, and physical symptoms such as fatigue.

Predisposing schemas

These are formed early in life. Depression can be triggered by incidences of loss that are similar to those embedded in the schema. There can be differences between the events that trigger depression in sociotropic and autonomous individuals. A series of traumatic episodes can also cause depression, and as the depression worsens the depressive schemas may become so hypervalent that individuals cannot regard their negative thoughts objectively and become totally preoccupied with them. Related to depressed individuals' schemas are absolute beliefs such as 'I can't do anything right', 'I'm useless' and so on.

Cognitive deficits and distortions

Hypervalent depressive schemas and beliefs hamper normal cognitive processing and impair the following: long-term memory, perception, recall, inferences, reality-test interpretation of events, and problem solving. As dysfunctional schemas gain momentum, so too does the occurrence of systematic cognitive errors such as selective abstraction and arbitrary inference. It is from these underlying schemas and beliefs that dysfunctional automatic thoughts evolve. The characteristics of depressive thinking are:

- Devaluation of the self for falling short of personal standards.
- Emphasis on the negative aspects of life's events.
- Generalisation of specific deficiencies into pervasive, lasting deficiencies.
- Self-attribution of responsibility for problems in all situations.
- The belief that problems cannot be removed or diminished.

The cognitive model of anxiety disorders

People with anxiety maximise the likelihood of harm and minimise their ability to deal with it. Anxiety is a strategic response to threat, and the main theme in anxiety disorders is danger. The normal evolutionary survival mechanism of anxiety becomes a disorder when it malfunctions and becomes exaggerated.

Beck makes a distinction between primary and secondary appraisal. Primary appraisal takes place when a potentially harmful situation arises and involves appraisal of the physical or psychological threats the situation poses. Secondary appraisal involves assessment of the nature of the threats and the available personal resources to deal with them.

Dysfunctional schemas and beliefs, like depression, may predispose individuals to anxiety. Dysfunctional beliefs can be caused by threats, stresses and new demands interacting with previous problems.

Distressed relationships

What attracts a couple to each other in the first place is rarely enough to keep the relationship going. The relationship may be blighted by poor communication skills or unfulfilled expectations of the relationship and each other as expectations in marriage are less flexible than in uncommitted relationships. Much behaviour in marriage has idiosyncratic, symbolic meanings attached to it, hinging on symbols of love or rejection, security or insecurity.

This can release powerful emotions and reduce the partners' ability to reality test their own interpretations, thoughts, feelings and actions and those of their partner. The partners' reaction to their 'invisible reality' is based not on what actually happens but on expectations, fears and internal states, and the triggering of dysfunctional schemas can lead to a negative cognitive set about the other partner. Voluntary and automatic thinking results in cognitive errors and the emphasis shifts to what is wrong in the relationship rather than what is going well. Their thoughts about each other tend to be in black and white terms and negative labels are applied, such as selfish, inconsiderate and so on, and then they react to these labels. This can lead to a tendency to believe that these are permanent traits. They may also misinterpret and misunderstand the words and actions of each other, and attribute each other with malicious and undesirable motives. They may refuse to check the accuracy of illogical conclusions and negative explanations. Furthermore partners send each other barbed comments designed to hurt and anger. This leads to them feeling wronged, getting angry as a result and wanting to fight back. Hostility is part of the primeval fight or flight instinct, but the urge to fight can destroy a relationship because it increases the perceived threat, which in turn causes partners to be rigid and inaccurate in their way of thinking. This may prevent remedial work on the relationship.

Psychopathological disorders can affect relationships in the following ways:

- Partners abandon altruism in favour of egocentric behaviour and attitudes.
- One or both develop a negative cognitive set about the other.
- The latter involves biased expectations, observations and conclusions.
- Everything the other partner thinks, feels and does is subjected to negative interpretation.
- If one or both have low self-esteem they can become biased against themselves, which will cause them to come to unjustified negative conclusions about how their partner sees them.

There are many beliefs, often expressed in the form of automatic thoughts, that weaken the will to address a distressed relationships. There are four main groupings:

- Beliefs about change: 'nothing can be done to improve the relationship'; 'my partner does not have the ability to change'; 'the situation can only deteriorate further'.

- Self-justifying beliefs: 'my behaviour is normal'; 'my thoughts feel right'; 'my partner has hurt me so deserves to be hurt too'.
- Reciprocity arguments: 'I refuse to make an effort unless my partner does too'; 'it is unfair that I have to do all the work'; 'my partner has hurt me so must make up for it'.
- The partner is to blame: 'my partner is impossible'; 'I had no problems until I married my partner'; 'my partner has no interest in improving our relationship'.

Personality disorders

These partly reflect evolutionary strategies that are ill-suited to modern society. Each disorder is determined by genetic predisposition and learning background and is characterised by a basic belief and an overt strategy to deal with it:

- Obsessive-compulsive disorder. Basic belief: 'mistakes are bad. I mustn't make mistakes'. Strategy: perfectionism.
- Schizoid disorder. Belief: 'I need plenty of space'. Strategy: isolation.
- Dependent personality disorder. Belief: 'I am helpless'. Strategy: attachment.
- Paranoid disorder. Belief: 'People are potential opponents'. Strategy: wariness.
- Avoidant disorder. Belief: 'I might get injured'. Strategy: avoidance.
- Narcissistic disorder. Belief: 'I am brilliant'. Strategy: self-aggrandisement.
- Passive aggressive disorder. Belief: 'I could be put upon'. Strategy: resistance.
- Histrionic disorder. Belief: 'I need to impress'. Strategy: dramatics.
- Antisocial disorder. Belief: 'Other people are there to be defeated'. Strategy: attack.

Each disorder involves an overdeveloped and an underdeveloped strategy, for example in dependent personality disorder attachment is overdeveloped and independence is underdeveloped. There is also a cognitive shift in that energy is diverted from normal cognitive processing into the various schemas that make up the disorder, and in the process more adaptive schemas are inhibited.

Cognitive therapy

Cognitive therapy, in contrast with other forms of psychotherapy, is problem-oriented. The main goal is to help clients to solve the problems they have highlighted for change. Therapy aims to re-energise the reality-testing system to deal with dysfunctional interpretations. Clients are taught to correct erroneous cognitive processing and to strengthen assumptions that permit them to cope. In short the process is a learning exercise aimed first at symptom relief and ultimately at the removal of systematic biases in clients' thought patterns. Behavioural skills are also important. Examples commonly include assertion skills for shy people and communication skills for distressed relationships.

There are five learning processes:

- Monitoring negative automatic thoughts.
- Recognising the connections between cognition, affect and behaviour.

- Examining and reality testing evidence for and against distorted automatic thoughts.
- Substituting more realistic interpretations for biased cognitions.
- Identifying and changing any beliefs that cause clients to distort their experiences.

Cognitive therapy focuses on removing the symptoms of disorders by means of counselling alone or in tandem with medication, and reducing the possibility of relapse when treatment has ended. Towards this end clients are encouraged to be more compliant about taking medication prescribed for them. Other focuses are the psychosocial difficulties that have either been caused by or preceded the problem in question, such as low self-esteem or marital difficulties, and the schemas (underlying psychological beliefs) that are causing the dysfunctional behaviour and psychopathology

Cognitive therapy works best with people who are able to focus on their automatic thoughts and are capable of self-help. It is not recommended for people with a diminished reality-testing ability, such as those suffering from delusions or hallucinations, or people with impaired reasoning ability and memory capacity as a result of, for example, organic brain syndromes.

Treatment is highly structured and short term: for anxiety disorders there are 5–20 45-minute sessions, and for depression there are 15–20 sessions over 12 weeks. Counselling is reduced gradually and clients have booster sessions a month or two after ending the regular contract. Personality disorders take longer to treat and can take a year or more.

Defining the problem

New clients undergo a three-hour induction process that includes a clinical interview and psychological tests. The interview is aimed at identifying the factors behind the clients' problems, their prominent symptoms, level of functioning and the expectations they have of counselling. It also provides an opportunity to establish the client–counsellor relationship. The psychological tests include the Beck depression inventory, the anxiety checklist and the dysfunctional attitudes scale.

During the functional analysis questions are asked about the components of the problem, how the is problem manifested, the situations that make it occur, how often the problem happens, how intense it gets, how long it lasts and the nature of its consequences.

Cognitive analysis identifies the images and thoughts experienced by clients when their emotions are aroused, the extent to which they are in control of their images and thoughts, and the likelihood of a feared problem happening.

Working in the sessions

Clients are taught to monitor their feelings, thoughts and behaviour, and to identify how they are interconnected. They are also asked to record their automatic thoughts in times of distress.

In order to establish the treatment priorities, lists are drawn up of behaviours, pervasive problems and specific symptoms. The priority given depends on the severity of the symptoms, the severity of clients' distress and how entrenched a particular problem is. Counsellors take each problem in turn and select a suitable cognitive and behavioural therapy. They explain to the clients their rationale for choosing particular methods, and client feedback on techniques is sought.

When drawing up a personalised treatment plan during the case conceptualisation stage it is important to comprehend the cognitive profile of the clients' disorders and their unique beliefs. Counsellors form hypotheses about their clients' idiosyncratic dysfunctional beliefs, core schemas, specific vulnerabilities and the stresses that interact with these vulnerabilities to produce the clients' symptoms. The hypotheses are modified as new information emerges and this is discussed with the clients. Counsellors may use a flip chart or blackboard to show the clients how their beliefs have led to misinterpretation.

With regard to beliefs, Beck gives an example of a man with a narcissistic personality disorder who directed violent outbursts at his partner for continually nagging him about not doing chores. His beliefs incorporated a 'should' – she should show him more respect – and a 'must' – he must control the behaviour of others. He had a conditional belief that people would take advantage of him if he gave them a chance, and a fear that he would be put upon, caused by the core schema 'I am a wimp'. The formulation had a similar analysis of his partner's beliefs, which sprang from her core schema, 'I am a helpless baby' (Beck et al., 1990).

The roles of the counsellor

The counsellor–client relationship

The counsellor–client relationship is a vital vehicle for improvement. Counsellors aim to understand their clients as individuals, and to create an emotional atmosphere with non-judgemental acceptance and genuine warmth. Counsellors use language that their clients can understand so that the counselling process will not be a mystery to them. Respect is important, so counsellors explain their rationale for both the overall approach and the techniques used.

Responsibility for treatment is shared by discussing the case conceptualisation and jointly setting goals and session agendas. Clients are encouraged to give feedback on the counsellors' suggestions and their behaviour. Counsellors monitor transference and encourage the clients to express their reactions to them. Transference helps to spotlight automatic thoughts and interpersonal distortions so that they can be worked on. Closer and warmer relationships can usually be forged with clients with a personality disorder than with clients suffering from acute disorders such as anxiety and depression. Nonetheless there can be a problem of non-collaboration with all clients.

Collaborative empiricism: coinvestigation with clients

Clients are active partners in the counselling process. Hypotheses on the clients' cognitions are developed by the counsellors in order to identify cognitive errors and the clients' underlying beliefs. The clients are then asked to discuss whether or not these hypotheses fit the facts. The aims here are to get the clients to see their thoughts as personal constructs of reality, and to teach them how to evaluate their validity.

Socratic dialogue: the counsellor as questioner

Questions comprise the greatest proportion of the counsellors' verbal communication. They reflect the empirical orientation of the cognitive approach and are preferred to disputation and indoctrination. Their immediate purpose is to transform the clients' closed belief systems into open systems. Counsellors may ask awareness-raising questions such as 'What's going through your mind at this moment?' Socratic questioning helps clients to evaluate and expand the way in which they think, and this is aided by being conducted in an emotional atmosphere of acceptance and warmth.

In specific terms, questions are meant to help clients realise what their thoughts are, examine their thoughts for cognitive distortions, substitute more balanced thoughts and develop new thought patterns. Typical questions are 'What is the logic?', 'What can you gain?', 'What have you got to lose?', 'What can you learn from this experience?' and 'What's the worst thing that can happen?' Typical questions asked by clients to question the validity of their thoughts are 'What evidence is there to support my interpretation?', 'What evidence is there against my interpretation?', 'Does it logically follow that a person's actions have the motive I have attributed to them?' and 'What is the alternative explanation of this behaviour?'

Guided discovery: the counsellor as guide

Clients develop their skill in using and assessing information and probabilities to gain a more realistic perspective. Counsellors do not engage in indoctrination, disputation or cajoling. The process of guided discovery includes assisting clients to discover themes that pervade their automatic thoughts and beliefs, and to link these beliefs to comparable experiences in the past in order to piece together the history of the beliefs. Guided discovery is also used when counsellors act as guides to help clients in reality testing to find errors in logic by experimenting with different behaviours.

Cognitive techniques

Bringing out and identifying automatic thoughts

There are six main methods of achieving this.

1. *Providing a rationale.* Counsellors provide a rationale for examining the connections between how clients feel, think and act. They may bring in the concept of automatic thoughts and provide examples of how feelings are influenced by underlying perceptions. For example someone's reaction to a creaking noise in the night might depend on whether its perceived cause is a

draught moving a door or an intruder moving through the house. Counsellors may inform their clients that a major tenet of cognitive therapy is that they are having difficulty reality testing the validity of their interpretations.

2. *Questioning.* Counsellors question their clients about automatic thoughts generated during upsetting incidents. If the clients have difficulty remembering these thoughts, then role play and imagery will be employed. Clients are carefully observed during questioning for signs of affect that will reveal avenues for further questioning.

3. *Using a blackboard or flipchart.* Seeing their initial thoughts in writing can prompt clients to disclose less obvious and more disturbing thoughts.

4. *Homework: self-monitoring of thoughts.* Clients may be asked to complete a daily log of automatic thoughts, in which they record situations that lead to negative emotions, the emotions felt and their degree on a scale of 0–100, and any automatic thoughts and their belief in these thoughts on a scale of 0–100. Wrist counters are used by some clients to record automatic thoughts as soon as they occur.

5. *Encouraging clients to engage in feared activities.* During the counselling sessions clients are encouraged to engage in anxiety-provoking activities. Examples include writing letters or making phone calls they have been avoiding. The counsellors then ask them what is going through their mind. The same technique is used in real life situations, such as going to crowded places and then talking about what they think and what it feels like there and then.

6. *Focusing on imagery.* An excellent way of accessing automatic thoughts is to gather information on imagery. Clinical observations have shown that although individual differences exist, many people who visualise scenes respond to them as though they were real.

Reality testing and correcting automatic thoughts

There are nine main ways of doing this.

1. *Socratic questioning.* By means of questioning, clients are led to challenge the validity of their thinking and to discover that there is a range of alternatives from which to choose an interpretation that best fits the facts.

2. *Identifying cognitive errors.* Clients learn about magnification, arbitrary inference and other common cognitive errors. They are challenged to recognise errors in their thinking during the counselling sessions and as homework. In a three-column table the clients describe (1) the scenarios that provoke negative emotions, (2) their automatic thoughts and (3) the types of error in these thoughts.

3. *Reattribution.* Automatic thoughts and underlying beliefs are tested by considering alternative ways of assigning responsibility. The degree of responsibility clients feel for negative events and feared outcomes are rated on a scale of 0–100. Counsellors loosen up their clients by offering and evaluating alternative explanations.

4. *Decatastrophising.* The basic question here is, 'So what if it happens?' Areas covered include the probability of an event and its severity, the clients' coping capacity and support factors, and the clients' ability to accept and deal with the worst possible outcomes.

5. *Decentring*. Clients are helped to challenge their belief that everyone is focusing on them and instead to evaluate what others are actually doing. They are also encouraged to observe how often they really attend to others. This reveals the limitations of their observations and allows them to see that the observations made by others are probably the same.

6. *Redefining*. This involves defining problems in terms of what the client can do about them. For example people who feel uncared for and lonely could redefine this problem by deciding that they themselves need to be more caring and to reach out to others.

7. *Rational responses*. Clients are taught to formulate rational responses to their automatic thoughts. Through questioning, clients learn to use their inner monologue positively instead of against themselves. For example a woman might be angry because her husband goes out to sell insurance during the evening instead of staying at home. A rational response would be that unfortunately this is part of the job because many of his clients are at work all day, and therefore the only time he can deal with them is after they arrive home in the evening.

8. *Imagery techniques*. These include helping clients to achieve more realistic perspectives through the repeated visualisation of fantasies, exaggerating their images, for example of harming others, and imagining they are in the future looking back on their present situation.

9. *Daily recording of rational responses*. In their daily log of automatic thoughts, clients rerate their belief in their automatic thoughts on a scale of 0–100, and specify their subsequent emotions and rate these on a scale of 0–100.

Identifying underlying beliefs

Underlying beliefs are more difficult to assess than automatic thoughts but are revealed by themes in clients' automatic thoughts, coping strategies, behaviour and personal histories. Clients normally find it difficult to put their beliefs into words, so the counsellor presents them with hypotheses to accept or reject. If a hypothesis is rejected, counsellor and client work together to develop a more accurate description of the belief.

Modifying underlying beliefs

This involves five processes.

1. *Socratic questioning*. Examples of questions are 'Does this belief appear reasonable?', 'Can you examine the evidence for it?', and 'What are the advantages and disadvantages of holding on to this belief?'

2. *Cognitive experiments*. These are used to test the validity of clients' beliefs. For example a woman might be afraid to make a mental commitment to her partner for fear that he might prove untrustworthy. Her underlying belief is that she must not put herself in a vulnerable position. This distorted thinking creates distance in the relationship. A suitable experiment would be to test the hypothesis that if she gave total commitment to the relationship and looked for positive rather than negative things she would feel more secure.

3. *Imagery*. The use of imagery helps clients to relive traumatic events and to restructure the experiences and beliefs that have resulted from them.

4. *Reliving childhood memories*. This is vital when dealing with chronic personality disorders as it helps clients to review and release their underlying beliefs. Pathogenic developmental situations are recreated through role playing and role reversal, which enable clients to modify or even restructure the beliefs formed as a result of these situations.

5. *Reshaping beliefs*. Clients with a strong feeling of inadequacy and rejection may be driven to be the best at everything they do. This could be reshaped or modified to acceptance that it is rewarding to be highly successful, but lesser success is also rewarding and has nothing to do with adequacy or inadequacy.

Behavioural techniques

Behavioural techniques form the basis of later cognitive work, although in couple counselling the emphasis is on changing behaviour first because this is easier than changing thinking patterns. Moreover partners may reward each other for positive changes in behaviour.

Some techniques are used in the early stages to provide symptom relief and improve motivation. For example depressed clients may be persuaded to carry out small tasks in order to counteract their withdrawal, involve them in constructive activities and make them aware of the possibility of deriving satisfaction from activities they previously found pleasurable. However it should be noted that depressed clients, unlike normal people, might not change their negative thought processes even if they change their behaviour.

Other techniques are designed to help clients to reality test their automatic thoughts and beliefs, to help them face up to feared activities, and to train them in specific behavioural skills, as follows.

1. *Activity scheduling*. Depressives tend to reduce their level of activity and spend considerable time pondering negative thoughts. The activity schedule is an hour-by-hour timetable of what each client should do. It is explained in detail and a clear rationale is given. The schedule enables clients to realise that they can control their time. It is also an experiment to see whether certain activities will improve the clients' mood. The emphasis is on which activities the clients are willing to engage in rather than on how much they can accomplish, so a client may spend an hour on gardening at a set time each day rather than try to do the whole garden in one go. Time is set aside each evening to draw up the plan for the following day. An important aspect of this work is to monitor the thoughts and feelings that accompany it.

2. *Rating mastery and pleasure*. Clients rate each activity on a scale of 0–10 according to the degree of mastery achieved and the amount of pleasure derived from it. Such ratings give depressed clients an insight into which activities reduce their dysphoria (dysphoria is a state of mind that is characterised by anxiety, depression and restlessness).

3. *Rehearsing behaviour and role-playing.* This is aimed at developing the skills required for specific social situations. Demonstrations and video feedback are utilised, and clients are rehearsed in a number of responses.

4. *Behavioural experiments.* These are designed to elicit information that contradicts clients' automatic thoughts, underlying beliefs and faulty predictions, especially during the later stages of counselling. For example a young man who wanted to cancel a date because he was afraid he would not know what to say was encouraged to treat this as an experimental hypothesis when on the date. In his case the hypothesis was disproved, but even if clients are unsuccessful the experiment is still valuable because it provides vital information on what is blocking their activities.

5. *Graded tasks.* These are used to challenge all or nothing thinking, for example clients may think they have succeeded in everything they have set themselves, or failed completely. Counsellors set easy homework tasks at first, followed by increasingly difficult ones. Clients frequently fail because they try too much too soon, so hierarchies of feared and difficult situations are drawn up to tackle progressively and at a pace the clients can cope with.

6. *Diversion techniques.* These are intended to divert clients from negative thoughts and emotions and include socialising and physical activities.

7. *Homework.* The purpose of homework is to reduce the time spent in counselling and to promote development of the cognitive and behavioural skills that will be required when counselling is terminated. Homework includes self-monitoring, engaging in activities that enable reality testing of underlying beliefs and automatic thoughts, practising procedures to deal with specific situations, and engaging in activities aimed at developing cognitive skills, including highlighting cognitive errors, making rational responses and reshaping beliefs.

8. *Relaxation.* This helps clients with anxiety-related problems. It is taught during the sessions and/or an instruction tape is taken home. Techniques include breath control, graded muscle relaxation, meditation and the visualisation of pleasant scenes. The purpose of relaxation is to provide a coping technique to reduce anxiety, to promote self-awareness and the monitoring of bodily states, to provide a feeling of mastery over symptoms and to provide a coping mechanism to help with the execution of behavioural experiments.

Other techniques are role play as a cognitive change technique, and cognitive and behavioural rehearsals for difficult homework. Behavioural techniques based on skills training methods are used when clients have practical problems, for example assertiveness training or social skills training may be provided to clients with inadequate interpersonal skills.

Assessment of progress

Progress in indicated by relief from symptoms, a change in thinking inside and outside counselling, changes in reported and observed behaviour, homework performance, ability to reality test and ability to modify and/or abandon distorted interpretations.

The termination of counselling

This is established at the beginning of counselling because the cognitive approach is short term and structured. Termination takes place gradually, with weekly sessions being reduced to fortnightly ones before final termination. Booster sessions are held one and two months after the termination of counselling.

Preventing relapses

Clients are taught self-help skills to reality test their interpretations, and the homework assignments set during counselling have the added purpose of preparing them to manage without their counsellors once the contract is ended. Furthermore, clients are helped to anticipate and develop strategies for handling any problems that may occur in the future, and the booster sessions encourage the use and maintenance of their improved information-processing abilities.

Conclusion

The limitations of this approach are much the same as for any other form of psychotherapy. For example talking therapies cannot be used with people with a severe mental illness, especially if they are beset by delusions and hallucinations. An important construct is motivation to change, but this may not be assessable until therapy is in progress. Other clients may find the emphasis on homework and self-help a limitation. When treating depression, clients who are able to endorse ideas about self-control will benefit from this approach, otherwise medication will be more suitable. It is also easier to use this approach if difficulties can be defined as problems. A great advantage of cognitive therapy is that it is embedded in scientific method, so it is now being used to treat a growing range of disorders.

☑ 13 Behavioural theory

Behavioural theory is both an overall theory and an experimentally based attempt to describe the principles and laws by which human behaviour is learned. The main emphasis is on the large part played by chance environmental emergencies in the acquisition and continuation of certain forms of behaviour. In its most basic form the behavioural model states that human actions derive from two main factors: biological forces such as hunger and sex drive, and the learning history of the individual. Although concepts such as mind and free will are not recognised a growing distinction is made between stimulus-response approaches and approaches that allow for cognitive mediating variables. The former is more deterministic than the latter.

The behavioural model, being a set of experimentally developed principles of learning, allows greater precision in the examination of observable (rather than intrapsychic) human behaviour than do the psychoanalytic, humanistic and existential models. However, much of the related research has been performed on animals such as cats, dogs and pigeons, and therefore a question has to be raised about the extent to which the findings of laboratory experiments on animals can be extended to human beings in their natural settings. Despite this proviso, behaviourists have made an important and distinctive contribution to counselling theory. This chapter considers the work of Pavlov, Watson, Skinner, Wolpe and Eysenck.

Pavlov: classical conditioning

Ivan Pavlov (1849–1936) was a Russian physiologist who investigated the activities of digestive glands by studying how external stimuli could be made to affect reflex actions such as salivation in dogs. At the age of 50 he began to investigate the functioning of the cerebral cortex of canines. He spent the rest of his life on this and eventually accumulated a large staff. His research activities were very extensive, but he is best remembered for discovering the conditioned reflex.

Reflexes

Reflexes are the inherent or automatic response to internal and external stimuli. The nervous reactions of animals depend on stimuli that are either excitatory or inhibitory. In Pavlov's words, there are 'regular causal connections between certain definite external stimuli acting on the organism and its necessary reflex action'. However reflexes alone are insufficient to guarantee the survival of an animal. Specialised interaction between the animal and its environment is mediated by the cerebrum, which reacts to signals from 'innumerable stimuli of interchangeable signification' (Pavlov, 1927, p. 16).

Conditioned reflexes

Pavlov's book *Conditioned Reflexes* (1927) is subtitled *An investigation of the physiological activity of the cerebral cortex*. In it he explains the precautions he took when constructing a laboratory that would exclude, as far as possible, stimuli that were beyond his control. The dogs involved in his experiments were given an operation that enabled the extent of their reflex salivation to be recorded. The operation involved transferring a saliva duct from the mucous membrane in the mouth to the outside skin. When food is placed directly in a dog's mouth salivation commences after a couple of seconds. This reflex results from the presence of food in the dog's mouth, as opposed to the sight of food or the association of food with a stimulus, in that the physical and chemical properties of food stimulate the receptors in the membrane of the mouth and tongue.

During Pavlov's experiment a dog was placed on a stand in one section of a double chamber; the experimenter occupied the other section. A conditioned or learnt reflex was secured by repeatedly linking the sound of a stimulus (a metronome) to the provision of food. Eventually, in the absence of food the dog's salivary glands remained inactive as normal, but nine seconds after it heard the sound of the metronome; 11 drops of saliva were secreted in 45 seconds. In addition the dog vigorously licked its lips and turned to face the direction from which its food normally arrived.

Salivation at the sound of a metronome is a learnt reflex and a response to a signal sent to the cerebral cortex. Automatic reflexes do not involve learning or signalisation. When signalisation is involved, the definition of reflexes as causal connections between external stimuli and their reflex actions still applies. The difference lies in the fact that the reflex reaction to signals depends on more variables than those involved in unconditioned reflexes.

In another experiment on the same dog stimulation was not followed by the presentation of food. The metronome was activated for 30 seconds and this was repeated every two minutes. Over successive trials there was a lengthening of the latency period before secretion and a reduction in the amount of saliva produced. Such weakening of a reflex response to a conditioned stimulus is called the extinction of conditioned reflexes. If the experiment had been continued the conditioned reflex would have disappeared completely.

The learning of a conditioned response is known as classical or respondent conditioning. Pavlov and his colleagues went on to explore other related areas such as conditioned inhibition and the generalisation of stimuli.

Watson and conditioned behaviourism

John Watson (1878–1958) is regarded as the founder of behaviourism. For him 'the subject matter of human psychology is the behaviour of the human being' (Watson, 1931, p. 2). Behaviourists see psychology as an experimental branch of the natural sciences and its purpose as predicting and controlling behaviour.

In Watson's time there were two dominant fields of American psychological thinking. First, 'old psychology' was introspective or subjective psychology and included concepts such as consciousness and introspection. Second, behaviourism was a new and objective psychology that rejected the concepts of 'old' psychology because the investigation of animal behaviour required no reference to consciousness and the same applied to human beings as they were on the same behavioural plane.

Stimuli, responses and conditioning

Humans and other animals adjust to their environment by means of hereditary and habit equipment. Humans have evolved sense organs, such as eyes, skin and viscera, that are sensitive to numerous types of stimuli in the external environment (and in the internal environment due to tissue changes in the body), and because of conditioning people respond to an ever-increasing variety of stimuli. Responses can be overt or implicit, learned or unlearned. Unlearned responses are those things we do automatically, such as breathing more heavily and sweating when exercising, while conditioning and habit formation produce learned responses. 'Instinct' has little meaning in behavioural psychology because, according to behaviourists, everything attributable to instinct is actually the result of training or conditioning, and can thus be classified as learned behaviour.

Watsonian behaviourists consider that all psychological problems and their solutions can be schematised in terms of stimuli and responses. Often a stimulus can be predicted if the response is given, and a response can be predicted from a given stimulus. Unconditioned stimuli prompt particular responses from birth, such as closing the eyes or looking away from a bright light, but most responses are conditioned or learned, for example a small child might learn either to fear spiders or to be interested in them.

Humans are born with a variety of structures that, subject to individual variations, compel them to react to stimuli in certain ways. For example babies respond with heartbeat, breathing and sneezing, which in behavioural psychology are classified as unlearned behaviour. Short-lived unlearned behaviours include suckling and unlearned grasping. Unlearned behaviours are conditioned soon after birth and include circulation and respiration.

Watson coined the term 'activity stream' to describe the ceaseless stream of activity that starts at conception and becomes more complex with age. Likewise unlearned action systems begin with unlearned responses that become more complex as a result of conditioning. For example unlearned vocal responses become the conditioned action system that we call 'talking'.

Determinism and habit formation

According to Watson a healthy child can be trained from birth to become any type of person at all – artist, doctor, beggar or thief. Hence it can be said that Watsonian behaviourists are strictly determinist. The view that abilities, talents, temperament and mental constitution are inherited characteristics is not accepted because they depend on training. It is probable that habit formation starts at the embryonic stage and rapidly accelerates after birth. Babies are helpless at birth but then develop three habit systems (visceral or emotional, manual, and laryngeal or verbal) that distinguish human beings from the rest of the animal world. Examples of dominant habit systems are the ability to talk (laryngeal) and shyness (visceral).

Emotional conditioning

There are three types of unlearned emotional reactions or responses to stimuli, namely fear, rage and love. For example a loud noise stimulates a fear response. Many of the phobias in psychopathology are seen as direct or transferred conditioned reactions that can be traced back to infancy or childhood. This view is based on an experiment conducted by Watson and Raynor (1920) on Little Albert, an 11-month-old boy.

During the first stage of the experiment they set out to condition an emotional response of fear by making an unpleasant sound (a loud noise produced by striking a bar) when the child was touching a white rat. After a while the rat was presented without the noise but Albert still displayed the fear responses of crying and crawling away.

During the second stage Watson and Raynor demonstrated that the conditioned fear response was transferable to other furry animals (a rabbit and a dog) and objects such as cotton wool and a fur coat. Thirty-one days later the conditioned fear response (rat) and transferred fear responses (rabbit and fur coat) were still present, but in a less intense form. This experiment provided an initial understanding of how emotional reactions are conditioned.

Watson advocated behaviouristic freedom uninhibited by the customs and conventions that shackle the individual because they are not founded on a clear comprehension of behavioural principles. His vision was of a world where people could talk and act freely without clashing with group standards.

Thinking and memory

Thinking refers to all habitual, subvocal word behaviour and is the same as talking to oneself. Language development is the conditioning of verbal responses to unlearned vocal sounds. Sometimes the subvocal use of words can be become an automatic habit. On other occasions, when dealing with a new situation, human thinking can be like the trial and error behaviour of a rat in a maze. When subjects are asked to think aloud it is possible to see how they have solved a problem by word behaviour. Words are manipulated to form new verbal creations such as poems. In behavioural theory there is no such thing as personal meaning.

Memory is the retention of verbal habits. If, after a lapse of time, someone re-encounters a stimulus they engage in the habitual thinking learnt when the stimulus was first encountered.

Personality

Watson (1931, p. 274) defines personality as 'The sum of activities that can be discovered by actual observation of behaviour over a long enough time to give reliable information. In other words, personality is the end product of our habit systems.'

Studying personality involves taking a cross-section of the habit systems in the activity stream at a given age. Watson felt that most judgements of personality are superficial because they are arrived at without a proper study of the individual in question, resulting in serious injury to that individual. Watson judged personality by studying the individual's education chart, achievement chart, spare time and recreation record, emotional make-up in the practical situations of daily life, and responses to psychological tests.

The concept of mind is not considered by behavioural therapists when considering mental disorders. Diagnosis is based on the analysis of behaviour as personality problems are viewed as behavioural disturbances and habit conflicts that can be cured by unconditioning and conditioning.

Operant behaviourism

According to Skinner (1971) no response can be predicted or controlled; only the probability of a similar response happening in the future can be predicted. 'Operant' behaviour operates on the environment to produce a response or consequence. Skinner used operant as an adjective, as in operant behaviour, and as a noun, indicating the behaviour defined by a given consequence.

Contingencies of reinforcement

The environment is essential in forming and maintaining behaviour as the latter not only operates on the environment to produce consequences, it is also controlled by or contingent on the consequences produced by the environment. Three elements must be specified in any adequate description of the interaction between an organism and its environment:

- The occasion on which a response occurs.
- The response itself.
- The reinforcing consequences.

The interrelationship between these three elements makes up what are called 'the contingencies of reinforcement'. For example in an experiment with pigeons the 'occasion' of the response will be (1) any stimuli in the experimental space, such as light or sound; (2) the apparatus used in the experiment, such as a disc the pigeon can peck; and (3) any special stimulating devices used prior to the response. Pecking the disc might be the response; the reinforcing consequence might be the food provided when the pigeon is hungry.

Positive and negative reinforcement

Both positive and negative reinforcement increase the probability of a response. Positive reinforcement includes the presentation of food, water or sexual contact; negative reinforcement is the removal of, for example, an electric shock or a bright light. The difference between positive and negative reinforcement depends on whether it is the presence or absence of the reinforcer that increases the probability of response. Withdrawing a positive reinforcer has the same effect as presenting a negative reinforcer.

Primary and conditioned reinforcers

According to Skinner, all reinforcers derive their power from evolutionary selection and it is human nature to be reinforced in particular ways by certain things. For example there is survival value in food (a positive reinforcer) and escaping from danger (a negative reinforcer). A small part of behaviour is governed by reinforcers of biological significance such as food, water and sexual contact. These are called primary unconditioned reinforcers. However most behaviour is a response to reinforcers associated with or conditioned to primary reinforcers. For example if a light is turned on each time food is given, eventually the light becomes a conditioned reinforcer and can be used to condition an operant. Conditioned reinforcers are broadened or generalised when they are paired with two or more primary reinforcers. This is important because a generalised conditioned reinforcer, for example money, attention, approval or affection, is attached to many states of deprivation rather than just one, such as hunger. There is more likely to be response with this kind of reinforcer.

Schedules of reinforcement

A great many features of the shaping and maintenance of behaviour can only be explained by examining the properties of schedules of reinforcement. Non-intermittent schedules of reinforcement include continuous reinforcement of every response emitted, and extinction, where no responses are reinforced. Intermittent schedules of reinforcement include the following:

- Fixed interval: here the first response is reinforced after a fixed time and this is followed by another fixed interval.
- Fixed ratio: every nth response is reinforced. 'Ratio' means the ratio between response and reinforcement.
- Variable interval: reinforcements are scheduled into a random group of intervals with a given mean and lying between arbitrary values.
- Variable ratio: reinforcements are scheduled into a random series of ratios with a given mean and lying between arbitrary values.

- Multiple: one schedule of reinforcement is used for one stimulus and a different schedule is used for another stimulus. For example when a key in a pigeon's box is red there is a fixed interval; when the key is green there is a variable interval.
- Differential reinforcement of rate of response: here the rate of response is reinforced only if it follows the previous response after a given time, such as three minutes, or before the end of a given interval, such as half a second.

Maintenance, extinction and reinforcement by successive approximation

Learning is not equivalent to operant conditioning: learning is the acquisition of behaviour; while operant conditioning is the acquisition of behaviour plus its maintenance, so behaviour continues to have consequences or reinforcements. If these do not appear then extinction occurs. For example if the action of a pigeon pecking a plate has been reinforced by the consequence of food but this ceases to happen, then the frequency of the action will decline. Similarly people are less inclined to behave in a way that produces rewarding consequences if the reinforcement ends. Schedules of reinforcement are relevant to extinction, for example intermittent reinforcement may generate greater resistance to extinction than continuous reinforcement. 'Operant strength' is the probability of a given response. Low operant strength that has resulted from extinction often needs treatment.

It is possible to shape behaviour by reinforcing successive approximations to the desired response. For example in one experiment a pigeon was taught to use its beak to swipe a wooden ball down an alley and knock down toy tenpins. Completion of the full action was to be reinforced by food, but the pigeon did not respond. The decision was taken to reinforce even the weakest response and then to reinforce those responses which came closest to the full action. Within minutes the pigeon was striking the ball properly.

Stimulus discrimination and control

Operant behaviour occurs through important connections with the environment. For example in an experiment where neck-stretching behaviour is reinforced by a pigeon only when a signal light is on, the stimulus (the signal light) is the occasion, the response is stretching the neck and the reinforcement is food. The process causing the response to the light is called discrimination. Put another way, the response can be said to be under the control of a discrimination, that is, it is under stimulus control.

It is possible to increase or decrease the occurrence of responses by presenting or removing the discriminative stimulus once the operant discrimination has been conditioned. An example of the effect of stimulus control on humans is an effective display of goods in a shop increasing purchasing behaviour. An effect of induction or generalisation is created when the reinforcing effect of one stimulus spreads to other stimuli. An example of generalisation is reacting to someone in a similar way as we react to a person we know because he or she remind us of that person.

The self

The 'self' is an assemblage of behaviours appropriate to a particular group of reinforcement contingencies. It is developed by an environmental history of reinforcement, and maintained or extinguished by current contingencies of reinforcement. Thinking can be explained in terms of contingencies of reinforcement. Environmental contingencies determine how people perceive and know. The environment also shapes consciousness or awareness, which is a social product.

The traditional view of behavioural causation holds that people are autonomous agents who are responsible for their own lives, while the scientific view holds that they are members of a species that has been shaped by the evolutionary struggle for survival, their behaviour being controlled by their environment.

Self-control

To carry out a functional analysis of behaviour it is necessary to identify the independent variables involved in behaviour and behavioural control. People manipulate events in their environment to control their own behaviour. There are two interrelated responses in self-control. First, the controlling response acts on the environment to change the probability of the controlled (or second) response occurring. For example individuals may walk away (a controlling response) to control their anger response. Second, desirable behaviours are more likely to take place if certain stimuli are present. For example proximity to the necessary tools and materials can act as a stimulus to complete a DIY task.

Reciprocal inhibition

Extinction: conditioned, reactive and reciprocal inhibitions

According to Wolpe (1958) partial recovery of the response known as spontaneous recovery happens if a stimulus is not applied for a while. Spontaneous recovery's partial nature shows that two elements are involved in the inhibition of response during extinction:

- Reaction inhibition: this describes an inhibited state dissipating with time.
- Negative conditioning: this leads to a permanent reduction in the probability of a response occurring.

Each time an organism responds to a stimulus a fatigue effect follows, and this serves to inhibit a closely following repeat of the same response. The stimulus is closely connected with the drive reduction associated with the ending of the activity and to some extent becomes conditioned to the inhibition of the response to which it was joined. This means that when the stimulus appears again the response decreases in strength, even when sufficient time has passed for the reactive inhibition effects to dissipate. If the response is a reinforced one the positive effects will supplant the development of conditioned inhibition. In short, inhibition is developed during extinction through traces of the the conditioned stimulus being simultaneous with reactive inhibition of the conditioned response.

According to Wolpe (1958), by allowing new habits to develop in the same situation as old habits the latter may disappear. The term 'reciprocal inhibition' covers all situations in which the drawing out of one response causes a reduction in the strength of a simultaneous response. For example a response that is antagonistic to anxiety can be made to occur in the presence of an anxiety-evoking stimulus so that there is complete or partial suppression of the anxiety responses, the bond between the stimulus and the anxiety responses will be weakened. Wolpe also proposed that if the conditioned response is inhibited by an incompatible response, this causes drive reduction and considerable inhibition of the original response.

Neurotic fears and habits

Neurotic behaviour is the result of a persistent, unadaptive habit acquired by learning. A habit is a set of responses that is consistently triggered by the same circumstances. People can have habits of emotion, thought and movement, all of which are hindered by anxiety. Neurotic habits almost always involve anxiety, this being the autonomic response to harmful stimulation ('fear' and 'anxiety' are interchangeable in this context). The general measure of the severity of a neurosis is the degree of unadaptive anxiety.

Neurotic fears can be autonomically conditioned by single or multiple events that evoke intense fear. For example it someone is injured in a road accident caused by a driver jumping the traffic lights at a junction, the injured person may henceforth be afraid of vehicles approaching such junctions. A multiple-event example is the social fear of 'doing the wrong thing'. This very common problem is conditioned by constant chastisement by parents who criticise almost everything their children do. Fear can also be conditioned by misinformation, for example that masturbation is injurious to health.

Eysenck's incubation theory

Eysenck's four sources of neurotic anxiety responses

First, a fear may be innate; that is, it is present before the stimulus is first encountered. Second, 'preparedness' means that certain fears are highly 'prepared' to be learned by people. Here the fear is weak but is easily conditioned when the stimulus is first encountered. Innate fears, and those to which the concept of preparedness applies, lie in the evolutionary development of the species. Third, fears can be learned through modelling (imitation). Fourth, classical conditioning (also known as Pavlovian conditioning) is the most important way of learning fear responses. The main unconditioned stimulus causing fear responses is frustration or 'frustrative non-reward', not pain or Watson's three stimuli (loud noises, loss of support, and physical constraint). Such frustration can have physiological and behavioural consequences that are identical to pain.

Eysenck's biological theory of personality states that introverts condition more easily than extroverts, making them more prone to developing neurotic fear responses.

Extinction and incubation

Eysenck hoped to prompt the collection of clinical and research data when he first put forward his incubation theory of neurosis. He knew that it ventured well beyond proven fact, and was largely derived from experiments with animals.

A conditional stimulus (CS) only presentation nearly always provokes a decrease in the strength of a conditioned reflex (CR), but it can also cause an increase. The two possible consequences of CS-only presentation are extinction of the CR, which takes place when the decrease exceeds the increasing tendencies, or enhancement (incubation) of the anxiety/fear response, which happens when the increase exceeds the decreasing tendencies. There are two classes of CR: those which have drive properties and lead to enhancement, and those which do not and lead to extinction. An example of CR leading to extinction when the CS alone is presented is salivation by a dog, because salivation is not the cause of the hunger drive. Conversely, CS-induced enhancement is produced if rats are given a shock after a CS-only presentation.

To summarise:

- Fear/anxiety is a response with drive properties, that is, it is resistant to extinction and is enhanced by presentation of the CS.
- The initial position is that the unconditional stimulus (UCS) produces fear/anxiety but the CS does not.
- If the UCS is paired with the CS, after conditioning the presentation of the CS alone produces a fear/anxiety CR. This is identical to the CR.
- The CR's drive properties make it the equivalent of the UCR in functional terms, and this reinforces the CS-only presentation.
- So when a CR such as fear/anxiety has drive properties, the presentation of the CS causes incubation (enhancement) of the CR.
- There arises a positive feedback cycle in which the fear/anxiety associated with the CS-only presentation is established. This is a painful event in itself, and the stimulus associated with the CS through classical conditioning produces more fear. This process is responsible for the development and continuation of neurotic responses.

Incubation allows the CR to surpass the UCR. It may also be the reason for the slow development of neurotic responses with few exposures to CS-only presentations over a period of time. There is evidence to suggest that the duration of the CS-only presentation is important, with short presentations favouring the incubation of fear/anxiety reactions. There is not so much evidence that a strong UCS presentation, as opposed to a weak one, does so. Stable extroverts more readily extinguish than the other extroversion-neuroticism groupings. Neurotic introverts show most evidence of incubation.

■ Ⅳ **14** Behavioural counselling practice

Behavioural counselling is based mainly on the theoretical principles described in Chapter 13, although counsellors do not have to have to limit themselves to methods deriving from these and are at liberty to use other methods that have been proved effective. Counselling also depends on whether learning based on classical and operant conditioning are paramount, or whether cognitive change is emphasised too.

Counselling goals

Krumboltz (1966) sets out three principles for establishing the goals of counselling:

- Each goal should be stated differently for each client.
- The goals need not conform to the counsellor's values, but they should at least be compatible.
- The degree to which the goals are eventually attained needs to be observable.

Goals are sometimes interrelated, but they are not always scientifically based because there are a great many influences on the client's choice of goal, and on the methods used by individual counsellors. Clients' goals include the following:

- Overcoming deficits in behavioural repertoires.
- Strengthening adaptive behaviours.
- Diminishing or eradicating maladaptive behaviour.
- Conquering debilitating anxiety reactions.
- Gaining the ability to relax.
- Acquiring a capacity for self-assertion.
- Acquiring good social skills.
- Gaining competence at sexual functioning.
- Gaining self-control.

Behavioural assessment

The starting point of counselling is to assess the behavioural objectives of treatment so that an appropriate method can be chosen. A good behavioural assessment will allow the counsellor to identify which stimuli are causing the responses being considered for treatment, while an inadequate assessment could result in the wrong approach being used for the wrong problem. The chosen method is re-evaluated after the initial sessions, based on how effective the counselling has been so far.

The SRC assessment

Here S = the stimulus of situational antecedents, R = the response variables and C = the consequences or consequent variables. SRC analysis is aimed at identifying the key variables that control clients' behaviour. These may be masked, such as when a person exhibits aggression as a result of a failing marriage. SRC analysis is used when clients claim to be feeling depressed, tense or without friends.

Behavioural analysis strives for high specificity. For example when analysing a response, details of its frequency, generality, duration and strength are collected. Assessments can take place inside and outside counselling interviews, and clients can conduct self-assessments in addition to or as part of the counsellor's assessment. Counsellor empathy is important in that it is instrumental in developing a rapport, it helps clients with self-closure and it ensures that counsellors accurately hear their clients' revelations.

Basic client information is collected, such as age, sex, marital status and occupation. In the early stages clients are encouraged to describe their problems in their own words. Linked with this is the objective of providing basic clarification of the goals of the initial behavioural assessment. Counsellors ask specific questions during the SRC analysis. To identify the personal and situational variables that are perpetuating the clients' problems, questions beginning with how, when, where and what are used; 'why' questions are avoided if possible. There are differences between behavioural counsellors in terms of the extent to which they collect historical material on the presenting problems brought by their clients and how these problems have been learned. Such information can include aspects of family life, education, career development, sexual history and social relationships. Case has to be taken to ensure that strong counsellor direction and questioning do not make clients feel threatened and deter them from entering new areas of investigation.

Clients' verbal and non-verbal behaviour may also be important facets of the initial assessment. Socially inadequate clients may reveal part of their problems during this interview, and emerging problems are explored as the assessment proceeds. Assessment is made of clients' motivation for change, environmental influences that are likely to help or hinder change, and clients' expectations of the chance of change. Counsellors take note of things that clients find reinforcing, such as praise and attention, because these aid behavioural change.

Other sources of assessment data

The following sources of information help to determine the goals of counselling, and to assess progress and the counselling outcome.

1. *Medical information.* If there is any suspicion that a client's problem has a physiological cause a medical examination must be carried out. The behavioural

assessment cannot be completed until a report is received, and further consultation with the doctor may be necessary.

2. *Records of previous psychological treatment.* Information can be gained on clients' concerns and the likely outcome of counselling strategies from records of previous psychological and psychiatric treatment. There may be consultation with the psychologists and psychiatrists concerned.

3. *Self-report questionnaires.* These concentrate on overt behaviour, emotions and clients' perception of their environment. The most commonly used questionnaires investigate the types of situation that make clients anxious. For example Wolpe's fear inventory (1982) asks clients to indicate on a scale of one to five how disturbed they feel in 87 situations, including being in the presence of angry people, people in authority, on airplanes and in darkness. Another questionnaire is Alberti and Emmons' (1990) assertiveness inventory, which contains items such as 'Do you speak out or protest when someone takes your place in line?' MacPhillamy and Lewisohn's (1971) pleasant events schedule examines rewarding events, activities and experiences and helps to identify potential and actual reinforcers that can be used in tandem with counselling.

4. *Client self-monitoring.* Clients fill in daily diary sheets that aid investigation of the SRC elements of the behaviour being monitored. This continues for a week, or as long as needed to glean the necessary information. Examples of monitoring sheets are provided by Sharpe and Lewis (1976). These cover a wide range of behaviours and are based on a 'What would you like to have done' format.

5. *Direct observation in natural settings.* Sometimes counsellors accompany their clients to an outside setting in order to observe their behaviour. For example they may go to a pub or a football match in order to assess how the clients function in such places. They discuss their behaviour and emotions as they take place, or as soon after as possible. It should be noted that clients may well behave differently when the counsellor is present because, for example, they feel more confident and secure. This is beneficial in itself in that the clients grow in confidence and may eventually take the risk of going to such places alone.

6. *Indirect observation in natural settings.* This involves collecting information from significant people who interact with clients in their day-to-day lives, including parents, teachers and spouses. It is important to ascertain the extent to which the reported behaviours are representative of clients' behaviour in particular situations, and to be alert to the danger of observer bias. Clients may well change their behaviour if they are aware of being observed, but secrecy raises the ethical consideration of observing clients without their knowledge and permission. On occasion valid indirect observations in natural settings can be made through behaviour monitoring codes, and by making frequency counts of various behavioural categories.

7. *Direct observation in simulated settings.* One such method is role play, in which clients enact with their counsellor examples of their normal behaviour, and perhaps a variety of other roles in the same situation. This can help pupils and students who find it difficult to converse with their parents. The same is true for marital partners struggling with a breakdown in communication. Another method is observation from behind a one-way mirror to assess how clients interact with a particular group.

Research on behavioural assessment

Swan and MacDonald (1978) carried out a national survey to identify the top ten assessment procedures used by behavioural therapists in the US. They found that the procedure used varied according to the stage of counselling reached. The results were as follows:

- Client interview: 89 per cent.
- Client self-monitoring: 51 per cent.
- Interview with client's significant others: 49 per cent.
- Direct observation of target behaviours: 40 per cent.
- Information from other professionals: 34 per cent.
- Role playing: 34 per cent.
- Self-report measures: 27 per cent.
- Demographic questionnaires: 20 per cent.
- Personality inventories: 20 per cent.
- Projective tests: 19 per cent.

On the basis of research evidence Kazdin (1993) concludes that the collection of systematic information during counselling does not eliminate bias because behavioural counselling, like all other counselling, sometimes intersperses subjectivity with objectivity. Even so he feels that systematic information does more to improve the care of clients than impressionistic evaluations of the progress of therapy.

Goal specification

The behavioural analysis facilitates the selection and specification of therapy goals, which involves the following: describing what the problems are, describing how they have arisen and defining what is maintaining them. These help form the hypothesis to be tested during counselling and allow precise specification of the variables in need of modification. These can be situational antecedents, or the component parts of the problem behaviour and the associated reinforcers.

Counselling goals are usually called target behaviours. Many counsellors specify anxiety reduction goals as well. Decisions have to be made about how to define goals so that counsellors and clients can assess whether or not clients change.

Clearly defined goals help counsellors to select the right methods to achieve them. Goals are defined in consultation with the client, whose cooperation is also sought when choosing a counselling strategy. When clients have more than one area of concern a list of priorities is drawn up. An important factor in this is the extent to which the problem behaviour is preventing the client from leading a satisfactory life.

Continuous assessment and monitoring are essential to determine whether the goals are being reached or whether they should be revised. Changes in a client's circumstances, for example a new job or a change in marital status, may require a change of goals and consequently a different counselling method.

The client–counsellor relationship

Behavioural counsellors often form a warm and empathic relationship with their clients. Little attention used to be paid to the client–counsellor relationship, but for the following reasons it is now viewed as a vital part of the treatment process:

- Client and counsellor need to agree on the goals to be achieved.
- Targets need to be mutually set and amended at regular intervals.
- A good relationship reduces the likelihood of drop-out, especially in the early stages of counselling when client discomfort is at its worst.
- It improves client cooperation and therefore facilitates a good outcome.

It is sometimes mistakenly believed that to be a counsellor in this field requires specialist expertise and expert theoretical knowledge. At one time behavioural therapy was the province of psychologists and doctors, but now nurses and other mental health professionals are working as counsellors.

The amount of counsellor input varies from client to client. Some need a lot of guidance and coaching, including modelling, pacing and encouraging, while others need only basic assessment and instructions. Change is brought about by the systematic application of intervention techniques, so it is a doing as well as a talking process. Discrete behaviours are analysed as long as they can be specified in quantifiable terms and techniques that have been empirically validated can be applied to them. Counsellors need to be directive because setting targets and pacing the rate of therapy are vital elements of the process.

Principal methods of behavioural treatment

Relaxation

There are seven relaxation techniques, as follows.

1. *Progressive muscular relaxation.* The counsellor's office should be restfully decorated, have dimmed lighting and be free from distracting noises. Clients are taught to relax on mattresses or reclining chairs. The aim is to reduce tension and irritability and enable clients to get to sleep at night within a set time. Clients need to understand the relevance of the procedures used to solve their problems because they involve a lot of time and effort. The counsellor explains that as a lot of tension is learned, it can be unlearned with training and practice. Clients come to see relaxation as a coping skill that is relevant to ordinary life, and that practice and homework are important.

Each cycle of the tension–relaxation exercise consists of five stages:

- Focus attention on a particular muscle group.
- Tense the muscle group.
- Hold this tension for 5–7 seconds.
- Release the tension.
- Relax the muscle group.

This exercise is first demonstrated by the counsellor, and then the client is asked to do the same. Counsellors take their clients through each muscle group, which will be demonstrated by the counsellors if necessary. Having learned the procedure, clients are instructed to keep their eyes closed during relaxation practice. Upon completion of a cycle the clients are asked if they have relaxed completely. If not, they raise the index finger of the hand nearest the counsellor. So that genuine relaxation can take place, counsellors encourage their clients to share any feelings of tension. The clients' body posture and breathing is observed to check their degree of relaxation, and if a client continually fails to relax a muscle group the muscle group strategy may be changed. Complete relaxation should not be expected immediately.

Towards the end of the session clients may be asked to summarise their relaxation experience and there will be an investigation of any intrusive thoughts or worries that may be affecting them. At the termination of the session the counsellor counts from five to one, whereupon the clients are asked to 'wake up', as though they had been peacefully sleeping. There may be an enjoyment period of a few minutes, during which the clients dwell on their pleasant state of relaxation.

At the end of the initial session the importance of practising muscular relaxation may be further emphasised. Clients are given relaxation homework to practice once or twice a day for 15 minutes. They are also asked if they are likely to have a problem finding somewhere quiet enough to practice, and if so they are helped to devise a strategy to overcome this and any similar problems. The clients should be given a log to monitor their homework because this makes it more likely they will persevere.

2. *Brief muscular relaxation procedures.* These are introduced once the full muscular relaxation procedure has been learned and mastered, the object being to achieve deep relaxation with less time and effort. Brief muscular relaxation procedures consist of simultaneous or sequential tension–relaxation cycles. Such skills are useful outside the counselling sessions as well.

3. *Verbal relaxation procedures.* These involve the counsellor instructing the client or the client mentally self-instructing. The latter is useful when the client is in public situations such as a meeting where the tensing of muscle groups would not be appropriate. Verbal procedures are a useful self-help strategy in stressful situations. Example one: focus on the tension in a muscle group and follow the relaxation procedure. Attention should be directed at letting go and allowing the tension to leave the body. Example two: count from one to ten, pause after every second digit and focus attention on the tension around particular muscle groups. Clients can practice these procedures for homework.

4. *Mental relaxation.* This is used in conjunction with other relaxation procedures and after going through a muscular relaxation procedure. It involves visualising a peaceful scene such as lying in a boat that is drifting slowly along a stream on a sunny day.

5. *Differential relaxation.* This involves tensing the muscles needed to carry out a particular physical activity and relaxing all other muscles. Muscular or verbal procedures are used to achieve the appropriate tension in the designated muscle groups and eradicate tension in the other groups.

6. *Conditioned relaxation.* Here clients associate a cue word such as 'relaxing' or 'mellow' with a deeply relaxed state achieved by progressive muscular relaxation. The cue word is then used to overcome anxiety in stressful situations.

7. *Relaxed lifestyle.* An important consideration here is whether or not a client's lifestyle is sufficiently relaxed. There are a number of simple precautions that can be used as goals for clients and should be included in their behavioural assessments. These include:

- Not having excessive commitments.
- Allowing sufficient time to get to work in order to allay fear of being late.
- Taking proper holidays.
- Keeping fit.
- Having hobbies and recreations.

Systematic desensitisation

This has three elements:

- Training in deep muscular relaxation.
- The construction of hierarchies of anxiety-evoking stimuli.
- Asking the client to imagine items from the anxiety-evoking hierarchies.

Relaxation is a vital part of this approach and is employed when behavioural assessments show that clients have specific anxieties or phobias, as opposed to just general tension.

In the hierarchy of anxiety-producing stimuli the latter are ranked according to how much anxiety they cause. There are four main considerations when constructing such hierarchies.

First, suitable themes have to be identified for classifying the stimuli. These are unearthed in the behavioural assessment process, and typically concern such issues as examinations, public speaking and relationships with the opposite sex.

Second, the concept of a subjective scale of anxiety or fear is explained to the client. A common way of classifying the ability of a hierarchy item to produce anxiety is to rate it on a scale of zero (no anxiety at all) to 100.

Third, relevant hierarchy items have to be generated around each theme. Situations need to be specifically and graphically described because clients will be asked to imagine these items. The counsellor explains the best way for items to be formulated. There are a number of sources of hierarchy items:

- Data from behavioural assessments.
- Questionnaires.
- Self-monitoring homework assignments.
- Suggestions from counsellor and client.

Finally, items from a particular theme are ordered into a hierarchy by rating them on a subjective anxiety scale. If necessary hierarchies can be modified as the counselling process moves on. Items can be written on cards to assist the ordering. Generally speaking, gaps on the subjective anxiety scale of more than ten units should be avoided. If these occur, time is spent by counsellor and client on identifying one or more intervening items.

It is assumed that when clients are relaxed they can imagine scenes as though they are real life situations. It is very important to check whether a client might become anxious about an image before considering this procedure. Clients' imagination capacity is tested by asking them, when they are not relaxed, to imagine a scenario that causes them real anxiety. The process is aided by getting the clients to put into words what they see in these situations, and by the counsellor offering a fuller description of these scenes.

The desensitisation sessions start with the client being verbally relaxed by the counsellor. Next the counsellor presents scenarios such as 'I want you to imagine you are sitting at your desk revising for your exams. There are still some weeks to go, and you are thinking about what is to come.' The counsellor starts with the least anxiety-provoking scene in the hierarchy and clients raise their index finger if they feel any anxiety. If there is no anxiety, after five to ten seconds they are asked to stop imagining the scene and return to a state of pleasant relaxation. After 30–50 seconds they are asked to imagine the same scene again. If there is no anxiety the scene is withdrawn, they relax once more, and then move on to the next item in the hierarchy. If they do raise a finger to indicate anxiety the scene is withdrawn at once, and deeper relaxation is encouraged before further presentations. If a scene causes repeated anxiety a less anxiety-provoking item is chosen from the hierarchy. Once a low-rating item has ceased to cause anxiety all the other items in the hierarchy are moved down the rating by ten points, that is, the 100-point item becomes a 90-point item and so on.

More than one hierarchy may be used during desensitisation work, which is part of a longer process that focuses on other problems utilising other methods. Records are kept of all scene presentations and their outcomes.

There are three variations of systematic desensitisation.

1. *In vivo or real life desensitisation.* This method is used when clients have difficulty imagining scenes and/or the hierarchy is suitable for real life presentations. Relaxation may be used as part of the *in vivo* process, for example clients who fear speaking in public are relaxed at the start of the session. They then deliver a short talk over a number of sessions before an increasingly large audience, who also ask increasingly difficult questions.

2. *Group desensitisation.* Here the counsellor works with groups of people who have the same anxiety. A good example is students facing their final exams. It involves constructing a standard hierarchy rather than individual ones. The hierarchy is compiled from items collected beforehand or from members of the group who are already undergoing counselling. The group works through the hierarchy, and new scenes are not attempted until all the members have eliminated their anxiety about the current scene.

3. *Cassette-recorded desensitisation.* Cassettes can be used for the relaxation training part of systematic desensitisation, imagination training and presenting hierarchy scenes at home. Up to five homework items can be placed on a cassette, and it is assumed that all the items will generate only a small amount of anxiety or that clients will not move on to more anxiety-causing items until they

are comfortable with the earlier ones. If clients become tense they turn off the cassette and relax for a while before continuing.

Behaviour rehearsal

Client deficits in areas such as self-assertion and interpersonal skills such as active listening, self-disclosing and providing feedback are revealed during the behavioural assessment.

One approach to rectifying these problems is behaviour rehearsal, which employs dramatic enactments or role playing of appropriate responses to replace the clients' maladaptive responses. The counsellor shapes the clients' behaviour in certain situations, by means of modelling, coaching, constructing hierarchies of more difficult tasks and specific cognitive interventions.

Behaviour rehearsal consists of five stages:

- Assessment and analysis of areas that are causing difficulties for the client.
- Motivating the client to take part in behavioural rehearsal.
- Defining suitable behaviour for a given situation (this is a joint client–counsellor exercise).
- Using role-play to give the client practice in appropriate responses, with the counsellor playing the part of the other person in the interaction.
- Using rehearsed behaviour in real life situations, the counsellor giving praise and reinforcement when this is successful.

Assertive training

According to Wolpe (1982, p.118) 'assertive behaviour is the appropriate expression of any emotion other than anxiety toward another person'. The neurotic fears of almost all clients inhibit them from normal behaviours, so assertive training is aimed at weakening clients' fears and changing how they speak and act. Clients need to be encouraged to express any legitimate emotion inherent in their problems because this enables them to deal with the fears that prevent its expression. Each time they are successful the fear habit is weakened.

Various types of behaviour are addressed in assertiveness training:

- Oppositional behaviour: standing up for personal rights.
- Affectionate behaviour: communicating affectionate feelings when appropriate. This is important because the expression of positive as well as negative feelings is part of assertive behaviour.
- Non-assertive behaviour: inhibited behaviour in which people are self-denying and passive.
- Aggressive behaviour: self-enhancement at the expense of others.
- Assertive behaviour: positive self-enhancement that also enhances the other party in an interaction.

Assertiveness training has five stages. The first stage consists of a behavioural assessment and often includes an assertiveness questionnaire. This establishes whether there is a need for assertiveness training in general or just in specific areas.

During the second stage clients are prepared by the counsellor for the behaviour rehearsal method. It may be necessary to examine the client's religious or philosophical beliefs as these may be promoting self-effacement. Some Christians, for example, deny their own needs and feelings, which has the effect of diminishing their effectiveness as people and as followers of Christ.

The third stage involves client and counsellor working together to decide on appropriate behaviour for given situations, for example making a complaint, requesting a pay rise or asking someone out on a date. This involves generating and considering alternative responses. Clients may also be asked to observe models of behaviour that are suitable for imitation. Clients' personal style must figure in the development of assertiveness so that their new behaviour will feel natural. Added to this, timing is vital because clients will not achieve success in their assertiveness tasks if they are not ready. For this reason a hierarchy of progressively difficult tasks is drawn up.

In the fourth stage assertive behaviour is rehearsed. This includes verbal behaviour, voice inflection, tone and volume, eye contact, gestures, facial expressions, body posture and fluency and timing. Rehearsal also involves preparing for the likely consequences (both positive and negative) of assertive behaviour.

The final stage consists of real life enactments. Homework tasks are set and between-session attempts at assertive behaviour are monitored. The adequacy of the new behaviour is indicated by feedback, which also shows where improvements can be made. Clients are made aware of the consequences of their assertiveness, and if the consequences are negative the appropriateness of the new behaviour is reviewed.

Reinforcement techniques

Reinforcement techniques are designed to modify behaviour by altering its consequences, so they reflect operant rather than classical conditioning principles. Both positive and negative reinforcement strengthen the likelihood of a response from the client. With positive reinforcement something is added to a situation, and with negative reinforcement something is taken away. The aim of punishment or the presentation of a negative state of affairs is to weaken the probability of a maladaptive behaviour taking place. Extinction aims to diminish the likelihood of a response by withdrawing customary reinforcers. Systematic reinforcement requires the identification of what is reinforcing individual clients.

Identifying reinforcers

These are five ways of identifying what reinforces clients:

- Ask them.
- Ask others about them.

- Listen attentively to what they say in interviews.
- Observe what they do in interviews.
- Get them to observe and monitor themselves outside interviews.

There are a number of self-report questionnaires to assess reinforcers. Cautela's (1967) reinforcement survey schedule assists the identification of reinforcement stimuli and their relative reinforcing values. The emphasis is on highlighting stimuli that are suitable for creating adaptive responses. The four major sections of the schedule deal with reinforcers that are presentable in conventional settings, reinforcers that are presentable only through imagination or facsimile, situational contexts the client would like to be in, and a frequency count of daily behaviours and thoughts.

MacPhillamy and Lewinsohn's (1971) 'pleasant events schedule' lists 320 events and activities that have been deemed to be pleasant. Each item is rated according to a five-point scale of pleasantness by the subject. Lewinsohn and Graf (1973) have produced a shortened version of this. It contains 49 items associated with improved mood for a large number of people. These fall into three categories:

- Social interactional items.
- Items that are incompatible with depression.
- Activities that prompt feelings of competence and adequacy.

Reinforcement programmes

In applied settings positive reinforcement is the main way of changing behaviour. Positive reinforcement programmes are used to increase desirable behaviour and reduce undesirable behaviour by reinforcing alternative behaviour. Counsellors design positive reinforcement programmes alone or with the help of clients' significant others. According to Hosford (1969) four elements are needed in a counselling programme that carries out operant procedures. First, reinforcement should be strong enough to motivate clients to persevere with desired behaviours. Second, reinforcement must be systematically applied. Third, there must be a clear contingency between demonstrating the desired behaviour and the application of the desired behaviour. Finally, counsellors must elicit any behaviour they wish to reinforce. Once a behaviour is elicited there must be immediate reinforcement or the differential effect will be lost. Continuous reinforcement serves to establish behaviours initially, but intermittent reinforcement can be used thereafter because resistance to extinction is greater if fewer responses are reinforced.

Counselling as reinforcement

Here the counsellor's role is to control interviews by giving out reinforcers. Put another way, the counsellor is an influencer or social reinforcer who manipulates and shapes the client's behaviour. At the same time counsellors need to be aware that clients may be reinforcing their own maladaptive interview behaviours.

Praise, eye contact, warmth, empathy, genuineness and attention by the counsellor can reinforce the client. Counsellors are far more effective if they have a high degree of empathy, genuineness and non-possessive warmth. If counsellors are weak in these attributes they will have a negative effect on their clients.

The above 'Therapeutic conditions' are important because they reinforce clients' human relations, self-explanatory behaviour, (behaviour that is obviously understood), positive self-concepts and self-evaluations.

Overt reinforcement

During the behaviour rehearsal stage of assertiveness training, clients behaviour is shaped by reinforcement until it is likely to succeed in real life. Moreover counsellors reinforce the successful achievement of assertive goals by making positive comments.

Direct, indirect and substitute reinforcement

Reinforcement can be directly administered by means of actual reinforcers or indirectly with tokens that are exchangeable for reinforcers. The process of reinforcement is aided by clients seeing others being rewarded for desired behaviours, for example sweets can be used to reinforce desired behaviours in a remedial reading class.

Token reinforcement programmes must have clear rules of exchange, with a defined number of tokens being required to procure back-up reinforcers. This method is used with delinquents, children and hospital patients. Token reinforcement has improved classroom results in primary and secondary schools and resulted in a significant fall in disruptive behaviour. The removal of token reinforcement leads to the extinction of desired behaviours.

It may be necessary to procure the cooperation of and to train significant others in the clients' environment as part of the token reinforcement programme. Such figures include parents and teachers, who may be inadvertently reinforcing the very behaviours they are trying to eliminate.

Generalisation needs to be planned, not depended on as an incidental consequence of the use of tokens. Teaching behaviours that will continue to be reinforced after training is one way of strengthening resistance to extinction.

Substitute reinforcement, for example praise, can be phased in to replace token reinforcement. Elderly people in institutions can be socially rewarded with increased attention for incorrect behaviours such as dependency and helplessness, while independent behaviours are not rewarded. The latter behaviours can be increased by means of a positive reinforcement programme. Clients can use self-reinforcement to maintain behavioural gains, the provision of reinforcers being dependent on the successful performance of desired behaviours.

Reinforcement by punishment

Punishment procedures to reduce the frequency of a behaviour are used in conjunction with positive reinforcement of alternative desirable behaviours. There are three punishment procedures.

1. *Aversive events.* These reduce the probability of a behaviour being repeated and include threats, anger and hitting people.

2. *Time-out.* This is frequently used with disruptive children, who are removed from situations in which they normally receive reinforcement. For example an attention-seeking child in a classroom may be receiving reinforcement in the form of attention by the teacher and his or her peers. However if the child is made to leave the room this reinforcement is no longer available. Adequate warning should be given that the time-out procedure will be triggered by an undesirable behaviour. If this goes unheeded, time-out should be applied in a systematic and unemotional way. Time-out usually lasts for 5–20 minutes, but for very young children 1–5 minutes is normally enough.

3. *Response costs.* Here undesired behaviours trigger deductions from the client's collection of reinforcers.

Helping clients to obtain reinforcement

Assisting clients to increase the number and scope of reinforcers available to them is a vital part of treatment. It involves finding activities and situations that can deliver the required reinforcements. A low rate of positive reinforcement is an important factor in depressive behaviours, so improvement is aided by an increase in positive reinforcement.

Lewinsohn and Libet (1972) describe a study based on the 160 items in the 'pleasant events schedule'. The items regarded by each subject as most pleasant were organised into an activity schedule for that person. For 30 consecutive days the subjects reported on the activities they had taken part in that day. There was found to be a significant correlation between mood and pleasant activities, but with large variations between the 30 participants. According to Lewinsohn and Libet, activity schedules are a valuable aid in assessing which activities are potentially reinforcing, showing clients that they have a low rate of behaviours that bring positive reinforcement, goal setting and monitoring behavioural change.

In a similar study by Turner *et al.* (1979) moderately depressed college students were successfully helped by means of activity schedules, with pleasant activities being increased over their usual level. Likewise Zeiss *et al.* (1979) report that depressed outpatients were helped by activity schedules that increased the frequency of pleasant activities.

According to the above authors such treatment reduces depression by increasing clients' feeling of self-worth in that the self-help skills they are taught enable positive reinforcement by their own skilfulness. Training helps clients to:

- Study their own behaviour.
- Set goals for themselves.
- Identify suitable reinforcers.
- Plan graded steps to achieve their goals.
- Gain the confidence to complete tasks.
- Build up the necessary skills to start a self-management programme.

Self-observation

Self-observation boosts clients' motivation and clarifies their goals. While the effects of self-observation are often short-lived it is important at the beginning, during and after a self-reinforcement programme: at the start of the programme it establishes the baseline and increases self-awareness; during the course of the programme it serves as a progress check; and after the programme it is important to maintaining gains. It can be expanded to include observation of the internal and external cues that precede actions, and the consequences of these actions. Counsellors provide the necessary training and check the clients' progress. Counsellors also teach clients to collect quantitative data with the help of charts, tally sheets, wrist counters and pocket counters.

Stimulus control

Clients can use two general strategies to influence their actions:

- They can attempt to modify their environment in order to control their target actions before executing them (stimulus control).
- They can reward themselves for actions that achieve a goal.

Stimulus control involves modifying or removing environmental stimuli or cues that are associated with maladaptive responses and forming new cues that are associated with adaptive responses. For example in weight reduction programmes the environment is modified to control food intake by keeping food out of sight and reach. Fridges can be fitted with time locks and only enough food is kept as can be eaten in a short time. The client also avoids contact with people who overeat.

Positive self-reinforcement

Clients are helped to draw up a programme to reinforce themselves when they achieve a goal. Self-reinforcement can be external or internal. External reinforcement involves self-administration of new reinforcers that are outside the everyday life of the client, or denial of a pleasant everyday experience until a desired action is accomplished. Internal reinforcers include self-congratulatory statements when a target is achieved, for example 'Brilliant !'

When planning a self-reinforcement programme it is important to identify suitable rewards. A positive self-reinforcer should be relevant to the target behaviour, such as buying clothes that will only fit the client when a weight reduction has been achieved. The tasks should be graded according to degree of difficulty so that clients reward themselves for accomplishing progressively more difficult tasks. The connections between achievement and reinforcement must be clear, so clients draw up personal contracts that specify the relationship between positive self-reinforcement and the desired actions. Bilateral contracts between client and counsellor may be entered into during transitional phases in the programme in order to build up the client's self-help skills. Opportunities to improve confidence and skills are also provided by education, recreation, religion and self-help literature.

Self-punishment, covert sensitisation and aversion

Self-punishment can be administered by clients when they fail to reach a target, for example slimmers may give an amount of money to charity if they fail to reduce their calory count and/or gain weight.

Covert sensitisation involves imagining aversive consequences such as being physically sick if something on a list of forbidden foods is eaten.

Aversion therapy increases the level of clients' distress. It involves inflicting an aversive punishment for undesirable behaviour, for example an electric shock. Such methods are normally used in clinical settings rather than in regular counselling.

Flooding or implosive therapy

Stampfl, the founder of this approach, saw his clients' symptoms as conditioned fear reactions and/or conditioned anger reactions acquired from past experiences that involved punishment, frustration and pain.

Counsellors gather information during preliminary interviews and then present a series of scenes for the client to imagine, each one getting progressively nearer to what it is that the client finds disturbing. The aim is to get as near as possible to the original conditioning event. According to Stampfl (1975), repetition of such scenes reduces their ability to cause anxiety, and eventually extinction is achieved. He found the psychodynamic emphasis on toilet training, aggression and infantile sexuality useful since many conditioning events originate from that stage of clients' lives. The purpose of the strategy is for clients to confront and beat their nightmares.

A current flooding technique is to expose clients continuously to a strong fear stimulus (real or imaginary) until the anxiety diminishes. This can take between ten minutes and an hour, and can be so traumatising that the client gives up. Although this has been successful with a variety of phobias, Wolpe claims that desensitisation is a better treatment in most cases, especially as it is less stressful (Wolpe and Wolpe, 1988).

Conclusion

This approach is useful for perhaps 25 per cent of neurotic clients and 10 per cent of adult psychiatric patients. One problem with exposure is the discomfort the client must suffer in defeating the problem. Some 25 per cent of clients refuse treatment or abandon it soon after its commencement. Of those who persevere, most will make considerable gains, but few lose all traces of anxiety or rituals in the face of provoking stimuli. A minority are unsuccessful despite compliance, though they are also generally resistant to other approaches, including antidepressants. Although behavioural counselling emphasises external cues, increasing attention is being paid to internal cues, and the exposure principle can be applied to anxiety disorders that lack external triggering factors.

☒ 15 Social cognitive theory: Albert Bandura

Albert Bandura was born in 1925 in Alberta, Canada. He graduated in psychology from the University of British Columbia in 1949 and received a doctorate in clinical psychology from Iowa University in 1952. He served a post-doctoral internship at Wichita Guidance Center before joining Stanford University in California as an instructor. He became a full professor in 1964 and in 1974 was awarded a chair, the David Starr Jordan Professorship of Social Science in Psychology. In the same year he became president of the American Psychological Association.

Introduction

Knowledge of social and cognitive processes are vital to the understanding of emotions, motivation and action. Social cognitive theory affirms both society's contribution to how people think and act, and the importance of cognitive processes to emotions, motivation and actions.

Bandura's particular contributions were his detailed challenge of Skinner's views on how reinforcement principles work, his ideas on observational learning, which aided comprehension of how clients learn both helpful and harmful ways of thinking and behaving, and his elaboration of cognitive processes such as self-regulation.

Theoretical assumptions

Human nature

Human beings have to learn behaviour, because apart from basic reflexes they are not born with sets of behaviours. Biological factors limit the learning process, for example physical development is governed by genes and hormones, which also influence behavioural potentialities. Faculties such as speech have a basic natural endowment that is developed through learning. It is often more useful to analyse the determinants of behaviour than to try to establish how much behaviour is learned or natural for the simple reason that physiological and experiential influences are difficult to separate. Within biological limits, we have immense potential to be shaped by varying experiences into various forms. The social cognitive approach avoids reductionism and makes a distinction between biological and psychological laws, that is, the reduction of psychology to biology and then to chemistry, physics and so on is avoided. The emphasis on psychology aids the development of belief systems and personal competencies. This cannot be done by merely concentrating on the neurophysical processes involved. The key question is how the cerebral processes are activated to produce the new cognitive events that characterise personal agency.

Human cognitive capabilities

There are five cognitive capabilities.

1. *Symbolising capability*. Humans can convert experiences into symbols and then process these symbols. They can also conceptualise ideas that transcend sensory experience. The ability to symbolise does not imply rationality because quality of thinking depends on the quality of information available, and on the individual's thinking skills.

2. *Forethought capability*. Most human behaviour is controlled by forethought rather than being a response to the environment. Individuals anticipate the consequences of their actions and then set goals. Forethought entails reflection, but it is not the product of previous consequences.

3. *Vicarious capability*. Nearly all of human learning derives from observing the behaviour of others and the consequences of that behaviour, rather than by direct experience. Vicarious learning is important because it reduces the time needed to learn skills. Some skills could not be learnt without modelling because they are so complex. A good example of this is the development of language skills.

4. *Self-regulatory capability*. Individuals develop internal standards that enable them to evaluate behaviour. Such evaluation influences their subsequent behaviour.

5. *Self-reflective capability*. Reflective self-consciousness is a distinctly human capability and it enables individuals to evaluate their thought processes and analyse their experiences. Judgement of one's ability to deal with different realities is the most comm type of thought used in self-reflection.

Human agency

Human agency is the ability to self-direct by controlling personal thought processes, motivation and action. There are three ways of conceptualising human agency:

- Autonomous agency is where individuals are completely independent agents.
- Mechanical agency rests on environmental determinants.
- Emergent interactive agency is the model used in social cognitive theory, as discussed below.

Emergent interactive agency is based on a tripartite reciprocal model in which there is interaction between three factors that operate independently as determinants of one another. The three factors are behaviour, cognitive and personal factors, and environmental influences.

Influences vary in selective strength and do not act simultaneously. Human behaviour is the result of interaction between external events and personal determinants. The latter include genetic endowment, reflective thought, acquired competencies and self-initiative. Human beings are free because they have the ability to exercise self-initiative and determine their actions.

Learning

There are two main modes of learning: observational learning and enactive learning.

Observational learning

Most behaviour and cognitive skills are learned by observing models. This instructs us in the rules and skills of behaviour and inhibits or disinhibits existing behaviour. Modelling facilitates responses and serves as prompts and cues to perform behaviour already in our repertoire. It also elicits emotional arousal – we perceive and behave differently in states of heightened arousal. Finally, it shapes our images of social realities by its portrayal of human relations and the activities pursued.

The power of modelling derives from its ability to influence the processing of information that takes place during learning. There are four main processes in observational learning, as follows.

1. *Attentional processes.* People must accurately perceive the modelled behaviour if they are to learn from modelling. There are two sets of attentional variables:

- Set one – characteristics of the modelling stimuli: availability, personal attractiveness, distinctiveness, functional value.
- Set two – observer characteristics: arousal capacity, perceptual habits, sensory capacities, past reinforcements.

2. *Retention processes.* Modelling has to be remembered if it is to be effective. Retention methods include the coding of modelled events into easily usable verbal symbols, the imaginal storing of information, mental rehearsal of the modelled behaviour and practice in carrying it out. Material is more likely to be remembered if it is meaningful to observers and builds on their experience. Retention is aided by cognitive skills and structures.

3. *Production processes.* Symbolic representations of modelled behaviour are eventually translated into effective action. Accurate cognitive representations of modelled behaviours are needed to compare sensory feedback from enactments. An effective way of feeding back when observers show performance deficits is corrective modelling.

Variables that influence the reproduction of modelled behaviour by observers include their physical capacities, whether their response repertoire has the necessary complement of responses, and their ability to make corrective adjustments when trying a new behaviour.

4. *Motivational processes.* Individuals are not motivated to enact everything they learn in that anticipation of positive or negative consequences can determine which facets of modelled behaviour are observed or ignored. Modelled

behaviour is adopted if it brings external rewards, if it is internally positively valued and if it has been seen to bring rewards to the model.

Modelling thought processes

Thinking skills can also be learned by observing models, but covert thought processes tend not to be conveyed by modelled actions – that is, if a model solves a problem cognitively the observer may see the resulting actions but remain unaware of the thought processes behind them. To remedy this, models verbalise what they are thinking when they take part in problem solving. Observers' cognitive skills improve most when models demonstrate both actions and thought processes. There are advantages to be gained from combining verbal and non-verbal modelling, including the ability of non-verbal modelling to gain and hold attention and the possibility of overt behaviour giving added meaning to cognitive processes. Observers' cognitive skills are more likely to improve with models that demonstrate actions and thought processes rather than actions alone.

The role of reinforcement

Observational learning does not have to have extrinsic reward. Learning comes through cognitive processing during modelling, before observers perform any responses.

According to Skinner's (1957) operant conditioning model, observational learning takes place when responses corresponding to the actions of the model are reinforced. Divergent responses are either unrewarded or punished. The behaviour of others becomes a stimulus for matching responses. This explanation has the following shortcomings:

- Observers may not perform the behaviour in the same setting as that in which it was modelled.
- The modelled behaviour may take place a considerable time later.
- Neither the model nor the observer may be reinforced.
- The operant model does not explain how new response structures are acquired through observation.

In observational learning facilitative rewards are provided, so the observer's attention is increased by the expectation of the reward to be had from using a modelled behaviour. Rewards can also motivate them to symbolise and rehearse modelled activities.

Enactive learning

Enactive learning involves learning from experience and it takes place everywhere. There is a distinction between knowledge and skill – individuals frequently have to go beyond knowledge structures in order to develop competent actions. To achieve this they need to have accurate conceptions of the necessary skills against which to match their attempts to perform these skills. Enactment translates knowledge into skilled action, and information gleaned from enactments can be used to adjust the spacial and temporal features of performance so that the closest possible match is achieved between what individuals do and their cognitive conception of skilled performance.

The functions of response consequences

Social cognitive theory regards learning through response consequences as a mainly cognitive process. People experience the consequences of their actions, both positive and negative, through enactments. They also notice the effects of their responses. Reinforcement strengthens a tendency to respond by changing the informational and motivational cognitive variables. Behaviour is mobilised and strengthened if the response consequences are highly valued. Put another way, contrary to the mechanistic view, behaviour is determined by consequences through intervening thoughts. The use of the term 'reinforcement' can be misleading since it can be interpreted as synonymous with automatic responding, and 'strengthening' responses might not be applicable in those cases where it may not be possible to strengthen further. Regulation of behaviour is preferable to reinforcement.

The efficiency of enactive learning

Learning is most efficient when consequences follow actions immediately, regularly and without confusing occurrences, but it becomes difficult when the same consequences do not follow the same actions. Learning from enactive experiences does not ensure the development of the best ways of acting as it tends to develop adequate skills rather than the best or most effective ones. This is because individuals will accept a solution if they deem it adequate, rather than try to find a better one. Competencies that are lacking can be developed by verbal instruction on the types of behaviour that are most useful and practical. Individuals can be physically guided when enacting behaviours. They can also participate in graduated modelling procedures.

Forethought and predictive knowledge

Anticipation and evaluation of the likely consequences of actions are necessary for effective functioning. Consequences shape beliefs and expectations rather than form stimulus–response connections. Stimuli and cues gain predictive value via their connections with response consequences. Individuals tend to pay close attention to those parts of their environment that predict consequences and ignore those that do not. For example a child's behaviour tends to be more aggressive in the presence of a lenient parent than a strict one. Foresightful action is made possible by knowledge of response consequences and their predictive value. Information that can be used for prediction comes from three sources:

- Enactive information comes from direct experience of response consequences.
- Symbolic information comes from explanations of the particular circumstances in which positive and negative response consequences occur.
- Vicarious information comes from noting the response consequences experienced by others.

Regular confirmation from direct experiences is needed to maintain the predictive value of cues, be these verbal or symbolic. Accurate predictive judgements require attention, a good memory and integrative cognitive skills. Environmental cues with predictive relevance have to be isolated and the relevant factors formed into rules of action. The establishment of predictive rules is helped by information on conditions that lead to certain consequences. If events are misread, predictive accuracy declines. Examples include overestimating the adequacy of knowledge and misjudging threats.

Motivators

External motivators

External consequences are influential motivators of behaviour. There are two broad classes of motivators: biologically based motivators such as physical pain and physical deprivation, and cognitive motivators. The latter operate in two main ways. The first involve people's personal values and the standards and self-evaluations that result from these. The second involve future outcomes in the form of material incentives (for example food), sensory incentives (new pleasant/unpleasant sensations), social incentives (approval/disapproval), token incentives (money, good marks at school), activity incentives (the chance to engage in preferred activities) and status and power incentives.

Vicarious motivators

The knowledge we gain from observing others' response consequences enables us, through our symbolic capability, to regulate our actions. Observed outcomes are similar to directly experienced outcomes in that they can alter behaviour. Furthermore the value of external incentives can be changed by observed outcomes. For example if individuals receive less praise than others for a similar performance they feel less rewarded than would have been the case if they had not observed the others being praised. Nonetheless, if observers see the behaviour of others being rewarded they are likely to behave in a similar way. In fact rewarded modelling is better than unrewarded modelling in promoting certain patterns of behaviour. Punished behaviour diminishes the prospect of observers behaving in like fashion, although constructive alternatives are a more effective way of preventing undesirable behaviour.

There are several mechanisms that mediate the results of observing others' response consequences:

- The information function: observation of others provides information on the types of action that are likely to have positive or negative consequences.
- The motivation function: as a result of the above, expectation is aroused in observers that they will experience similar consequences if they carry out similar actions.
- The emotional arousal function: observation of others provides information on behaviour that causes pleasure or unhappiness.

- The valuational function: observation of others' reactions to their own behaviour, based on their personal standards, can alter the observer's values and standards of behaviour.

It should be noted that many dysfunctional fears and avoidance behaviours arise mainly or in part from unpleasant vicarious experiences.

Self-regulatory motivators

Much human activity is directed not towards immediate reward but towards future gains or even losses. Guides and motivators are created for actions that lead to future attainment. Our symbolising and self-reactive capabilities allow us to form internal standards of behaviour that provide a benchmark for self-evaluation. Such internal standards can become self-incentives. There are three subprocesses in the self-regulation of behaviour.

1. *Self observation*. This fulfils the function of providing the information needed to set realistic performance standards and evaluate behaviour. However as people's mood states, attention levels and self-conceptions can negatively affect accuracy, self-observation can be unreliable.

With regard to measuring behaviour, there are a number of evaluation dimensions on which behaviour can be measured. For example writing can be measured by quantity, quality and originality; social behaviour can be measured in terms of sociability or deviance. Such dimensions vary according to the activity in question. People can set themselves progressive goals for advancement and improvement if they observe their performance closely. This self-monitoring may evoke self-reactive influences and cannot be easily separated from other subprocesses of self-regulation.

2. *Judgement*. Mere observation of personal behaviour is not enough if something is to be done about it. It is also necessary to judge whether the behaviour in question is positive or negative. An important facet of the judgement subfunction is the development of personal standards. There are three main social influences on the development of personal standards:

- Direct tuition.
- The evaluative reactions of others to one's behaviour.
- Personal standards modelled by others.

There are two points to note here. First, if a particular behaviour has value to individuals they are more likely to make a performance judgement than if it is insignificant to them. Second, the judgement of personal behaviour depends in no small measure on the reasons for a satisfactory performance, and individuals' achievements will elicit more pride if they are the result of their own ability and efforts.

3. *Self-reaction*. The combination of judgemental skills and personal standards permit a self-reactive influence over personal behaviour. People tend to engage in activities that create positive self-reactions and avoid any that will cause negative ones. It is through the motivational function that personal standards affect behaviour because people work hard to reach an appropriate level. In a number of areas personal standards are quite stable, but when cultivating skills

and pursuing achievements, as soon as earlier challenges are met people raise their standards. Tangible self-motivators such as recreational activities, free time and relaxation breaks are important in that they can be made contingent on performance attainments. For many people self-incentives provide better motivation than external incentives. Unduly high standards can lead to dysfunctional self-evaluative systems, which in turn can create a feeling of worthlessness, leading to depression.

Influences on behaviour

The fact that human beings have the ability to influence their behaviour through self-produced consequences gives them a capacity for self-direction. There are two types of incentive in the self-regulation of behaviour: conditional or short-term incentives that provide direction for courses of action, and longer-term incentives to keep to internal standards. Incentives include:

- Personal benefits such as gains arising from the improvement of skills or the control of aversive behaviour aimed at avoiding discomfort.
- The receipt of social awards or observing others receive social rewards.
- Observing others master tasks through the maintenance of personal standards.
- Negative sanctions such as adverse criticism for lowering performance standards.
- Particular environmental contexts may support the maintenance of personal standards, for example a high value may be put on performance standards.
- Self-criticism and other types of self-inflicted punishment help people to keep to personal standards by providing an incentive to discontinue negative cognitions and lessen the negative reactions of other people.

Self-efficacy and goals

Efficacy is the power or capacity to produce a desired effect; the ability to achieve results. Self-efficacy is central to human agency and is more than knowing what to do. For a skilled performance, people need the necessary skills and the efficacy to use them. Perceived self-efficacy is defined as 'judgement of one's capability to accomplish a certain level of performance' (Bandura, 1986, p. 391). Outcome expectations relate to judgements about the probable consequence of such a performance. For example the judgement that one can pass an exam with honours is an efficacy judgement, but the anticipated social recognition this will give rise to is an outcome expectation. Outcomes are the consequences of acts, not the acts themselves.

Efficacy expectations have three important dimensions:

- Magnitude: the magnitude or degree of difficulty of the task in question can cause efficacy expectations to vary; for example performance expectations will be higher for easy tasks than for difficult ones.
- Generality: here we are looking at the degree of generalisation of mastery expectations beyond the specific treatment situation.
- Strength: perseverance with personal mastery tasks despite discouraging experiences.

Efficacy beliefs have an important bearing on how people operate. For example deciding what to do is affected by conceptions of personal efficacy. Perceived efficacy has the effect of encouraging engagement in activities, while perceived inefficacy can lead to avoidance of experiences that are potentially enriching. Any extreme misjudgement of efficacy is dysfunctional. The most functional efficacy judgements are those which slightly exceed what is possible at any given moment.

Efficacy beliefs influence how much effort to use, how long one should persevere when there are difficulties and setbacks, and how one feels and thinks. When attempting a difficult task, strong efficacy belief strengthens resilience. People who believe they are inefficacious in coping with environmental demands will also exaggerate personal deficiencies, become disheartened and give up more easily. People with a strong sense of efficacy, on the other hand, are likely to persevere with a challenge even if they are temporarily demoralised by a setback. They are also likely to redouble their efforts when their performance is inadequate. Resiliency is a key factor in activities where staying power is needed.

Perceived efficacy aids development of the skills necessary to tackle complex tasks, while perceived inefficacy hampers their development. Perceived efficacy is affected by lack of incentives and performance constraints. For example a person may have the appropriate skills but lack the incentive to utilise them, or may not have access to the necessary financial or other material resources.

Accurate efficacy beliefs can be a problem for cognitive skills because it is often the case that what is needed is not easily observable. Finally, efficacy beliefs may be inaccurate due to flawed cognitive activities.

Sources of self-efficacy information

Enactive attainment

The most important source of self-efficacy information is personal experience of success because it raises efficacy expectations – failure lowers them. Once enhanced, efficacy beliefs have a tendency to generalise to situations that resemble those which led to the beliefs being enhanced in the first place.

Vicarious experience

Efficacy expectations can be changed by noting the positive and negative consequences of other people's behaviour. However efficacy expectations that result from modelling tend to be weaker than those which arise from successful task performance. There are two important things to note here. First, inferences are made by observers from modelled successes and failures. If observers see others succeed as a result of persistent effort they will gain greater belief in their own capabilities. Observing failure has the opposite effect. Second, the importance of competent models is that they transmit knowledge and the observer learns effective skills and strategies for dealing with environmental demands. The development of these enhanced skills increases perceived self-efficacy.

Verbal persuasion

Persuasion is probably most useful when it encourages people to make an effort to succeed. This also leads to their efficacy beliefs being boosted. Conversely the fostering of unrealistic efficacy beliefs that are uncorroborated by success may be counterproductive.

Physiological state

There are three ways in which efficacy beliefs are affected by people's physiological state. First, when people are in a state of anxiety their emotional arousal or physiological state can have a negative effect on their efficacy expectations. A state of high arousal normally debilitates performance, and lowered expectations of efficacy are partly based on lowered performance. Efficacy beliefs and performance are enhanced by approaches that diminish debilitating emotional arousal in response to subjective threats. Cognitively generated arousal is positively influenced by perceived self-efficacy in controlling thoughts. When the range and degree of aversive cognitions can be restrained the perceived efficacy or inefficacy to control personal thoughts has a strong correlation with levels of anxiety.

Second, people's judgement of their personal efficacy is influenced by their mood states. Perceived efficacy is boosted by a positive mood and lowered by a depressed mood. Third, when activities depend on strength and stamina, people judge their fatigue and pain as an indication of weak physical efficacy.

Efficacy information

Information is cognitively processed if it comes from an enactive, persuasive, physiological or vicarious source. There is a distinction between information deriving from environmental events and information chosen, weighted and integrated with self-efficacy judgements. There are two distinct processes in the cognitive processing of efficacy information: first efficacy-relevant information is selected, and then the information is weighted and integrated.

Enactive information

There is not a simple relationship between quality of performance and perceived self-efficacy in that even a good performance may not be sufficient to improve self-efficacy. The difficulty of the task, the amount of effort made and the amount of external aid received are three important factors in the extent to which performance contributes to self-efficacy.

Vicarious information

Similar models or models slightly higher in ability provide the most accurate comparative information.

Persuasive information

The effect of this is related to the confidence of recipients in the view of their persuaders.

Physiological information

Physiological information is cognitively processed. The foremost considerations here are the sources and level of arousal, and how performance is affected by past experiences.

Social cognitive counselling

The purpose of goals

Personal agency works through two cognitively based sources of motivation: forethought and goal setting, with self-evaluation of personal behaviour. People motivate themselves by setting performance levels or standards that cause disequilibrium, and then they struggle to achieve them. Feedback control results in adjustments to secure the desired results. Goals define the conditions for satisfaction with performance, and therefore act as motivators.

Goals play a vital part in the development of self-efficacy by providing benchmarks against which to judge personal capabilities. Progressively difficult short-term goals are really useful in this context because they act as incentives for action. In addition, when they are achieved they provide efficacy information and the confidence to persevere. Goals are lowered when people perceive inefficacy, which has the effect of diminishing their dissatisfaction with below par performances.

Participant modelling

Participant modelling revolves around the performance of feared tasks. Success in this is the main springboard for psychological change.

The counsellor repeatedly models feared activities to show the client that it is possible to perform them without the feared consequences taking place. Joint performance with the counsellor allows the client to take part in activities that are too frightening to tackle alone. The counsellor uses hierarchies of increasingly difficult tasks.

Response induction aids or protective conditions may be introduced by counsellors to diminish the client's fear. For example when dealing with a snake phobia this could involve securely holding a snake by its head and tail and wearing protective gloves. The counsellor gradually withdraws the performance supports to the point where the client can cope without any assistance. The client may have a period of self-directed performance during which he or she interacts with the feared object alone. At first the counsellor may stay in the room, but later withdraws to observe through a one-way mirror. The underlying rationale is that perceived self-efficacy is best promoted by independent achievement as this convinces clients that their success is due to their mastery of the feared situation.

Other uses of social cognitive theory

Career counselling and development

Using the four sources of efficacy information, career counsellors can design more effective interventions for individuals and groups of both sexes. Self-efficacy beliefs are extremely useful in looking at how willing women are to consider occupations traditionally seen as male preserves. They are also important in assessing career entry behaviour and academic performance.

Educational settings

To improve motivation and academic achievement counsellors try to develop perceived self-efficacy in teachers, students, parents and faculties. Counsellors can work with individuals or groups, or as consultants. Guided mastery is the main method of developing cognitive competencies and it resembles the participant modelling approach mentioned above. Steps include the use of cognitive modelling and instructive aids to teach the necessary knowledge and skills in graded phases. This includes instruction in when and how to use the cognitive strategies to solve a wide range of problems. Counsellors can help teachers to design and put into operation curricula that develop the perceived self-efficacy of students even when the counsellors have neither the knowledge nor the time to teach instructional content.

Health settings

Self-management approaches based on social cognitive theory can be established by counsellors to help people develop and maintain habits that will promote good health.

Conclusion

This approach is important in its recognition of the social contribution to how people think and behave and the importance of cognitive processes to emotions, motivation and actions. Bandura is a diligent researcher and studier of others' research. From his labours he has provided an invaluable challenge to the theories of Skinner. Furthermore, his work in the field of observational learning has made a vital contribution to comprehending how people learn helpful and harming ways of thinking and acting. Additionally, he details the processes of cognitive concepts that are worthy of serious study by all counsellors.

▌ ⌄ 16 Rational emotive behavioural counselling: Albert Ellis

Albert Ellis was born in 1913 in Pittsburgh, Pennsylvania, but grew up in the city of New York. His father was frequently away from the home and his mother was more interested in her own pursuits than in Ellis and his brother and sister. At the age of four Ellis nearly died of tonsilitis and nephritis (a chronic kidney inflammation). He was in and out of hospital for the next few years, and at the age of 12 he found out that his parents had divorced. Although a shy boy he was successful at school, and at the age of 19 managed to beat his shyness with women by talking to a hundred girls one after the other in the Bronx Botanical Gardens in New York. He achieved a BA in business administration from the City University of New York and later entered the clinical psychology programme at Columbia University, where he received an MA. He went on to set up a private practice in marital and sexual counselling, and was awarded a PhD by Columbia University for his thesis on personality questionnaires. He trained in psychoanalysis and went to work for the New Jersey Mental Hygiene Clinic while maintaining his private practice. He rebelled against psychoanalysis and preferred to call himself a psychotherapist. It was the development of his ideas that led to the emergence of rational emotive therapy.

Theoretical assumptions

Fundamental and primary goals

There are three fundamental human goals: to survive, to be relatively free from pain and to be reasonably content or satisfied. In addition there are six sub- or primary goals that relate to human happiness: people want to be happy when alone, with other people, intimately with a select few, informationally and educationally, economically and vocationally, and recreationally.

Rational living

The goals listed above are preferences or choices rather than necessities. Rational living depends on feeling, thinking and behaving in a manner that promotes achievement of the goals, while irrationality means feeling, thinking and behaving in ways that hamper their achievement. Rational living involves finding a balance between the short-term pleasures of the here and now and the long-term pleasures achieved through discipline. Put simply, rationality is the use of reason when choosing short- and long-term hedonistic pleasures.

Thinking, emotion and behaviour

Rational emotive therapy is based on three fundamental hypotheses:

- Thinking and emoting are closely related.
- They are so closely related that they normally go hand in hand in a cause and effect relationship, so that thinking becomes emotion and emotion becomes thought.
- Thinking and emoting take the form of internalised sentences or self-talk that become a person's thoughts and emotions. These internal thoughts generate and modify emotions.

Thought or cognition, emotions and behaviour are rarely if ever totally separable. Thinking and emotion interact with behaviour in that individuals normally act on the basis of thoughts and emotions. Moreover their actions influence how they think and feel.

Cognitions

Cognitions can be divided into hot, warm and cool. Hot cognitions create and influence more intense feelings than do warm or cool ones. They involve highly evaluative thoughts and usually incorporate strong feelings. They can be held occasionally or constantly, loosely or strongly, blandly or vividly, mildly or intently, softly or loudly, and be limited to one setting or held generally. Warm cognitions are rational beliefs or preferential thoughts, including evaluations of cool cognitions. These evaluations range from weak to strong, as do the feelings they create and influence. Cool cognitions are descriptive and contain few if any feelings.

- Cool cognition: 'He's got that music on too loudly.'
- Warm or preferential cognitions: 'I don't like his loud music, I wish he wouldn't do it. It really annoys me.'
- Hot cognitions: 'I hate his damned music! He's got to stop it. He's a bloody nuisance! I'll kill him!'

Appropriate and inappropriate emotions

Emotions are appropriate when they are accompanied by rational or sane beliefs that do not prevent effective action and the achievement of fundamental and primary goals. To achieve a balance between short- and long-term hedonistic goals a balance is needed between short- and long-term appropriate pleasurable emotions. If emotions are not appropriate they will hamper achievement of the necessary balance between short- and long-term hedonistic goals.

Anxiety and overconcern are inappropriate emotions because they are based on insane beliefs and/or irrational thinking, and this can impede the attainment of goals. The sane part of hostility requires acknowledgement of annoyance and discomfort as this provides the basis for action to deal with the problem in question. The insane part of hostility is blaming others and the world in general to the extent that effective action is prevented, personal happiness is reduced and hostility from others is increased. Even enjoyable emotions can be inappropriate, for example when people feel immense pride when praised because they have an insane need for the approval of others.

Biological tendencies

According to Ellis (1993) there is tension between two innate and opposing creative tendencies in humans: the tendency to create, develop and actualise themselves as rational, goal-achieving, healthy human beings; and the tendency to have irrational cognitions, inappropriate emotions and dysfunctional behaviours. Humans have an inherent tendency to be destructive of themselves and others. They also tend to be illogical and make the same mistakes time and again. This is the case regardless of education and culture. This fallibility and failure to accept reality is manifested in emotional disturbance.

Individuals have some choice over the extent to which they make themselves emotionally disturbed in that there is an interaction between the influences of heredity, environment and choice. They can use their biological tendency to help as well as to damage themselves.

They can do this in two ways: they can decide to think differently and more effectively about the situations they encounter, and they can acquire and maintain the cognitive skills needed to contain and counteract their irrationality, simply because humans can think about how they think.

Ellis's ABC theory of personality

There are two types of belief (B): rational beliefs and irrational beliefs. If people's goals are hampered or blocked by an activating event (A) they respond consciously or unconsciously. This has appropriate or inappropriate consequences (C), both emotional and behavioural. Their response to activating events is normally the result of a mixture of rational and irrational beliefs, though one of these will dominate. If the response is emotional disturbance, those concerned have allowed irrational beliefs to gain the ascendant.

The ABCs of rational thinking and living

If people think rationally about activating events they are engaging in preferential thinking. Such events can aid or confirm, or sabotage or block goals. Preferential thinking, as opposed to demanding thinking, involves explicitly and/or tacitly reacting with people's belief systems in ways that are realistic. They experience relevant emotional and enacting goal-directed behavioural consequences. For example:

- An activating event is seen as assisting or confirming a goal.
- The belief system responds with 'This is good! I like this activating event.'

- The consequences are pleasure or happiness (emotional) and an attempt to recreate the activating episode (behavioural).

Alternatively,

- The activating event is seen as sabotaging or blocking a goal.
- The belief system responds with 'This is bad! I dislike this activating event.'
- The consequences are unhappiness and frustration (emotional) and an attempt to avoid or eliminate the activating event (behavioural).

The ABCs of irrational thinking

There are four categories of irrational belief, as follows.

1. *Primary demanding beliefs*. These involve people's main commands and demands in response to an activating event. As these beliefs are usually expressed as musts, ought to's, shoulds, got to's and so on, Ellis (1989) has labelled them 'musturbation'. There are three main types of primary demanding belief, each of which has inappropriate emotional and behavioural consequences:

- 'I must do well and win approval for all my performances.'
- 'Others must treat me considerately and kindly.'
- 'The conditions in which I live must be arranged so that I get practically everything I want comfortably, quickly and easily.'

The following is an example of how an emotional disturbance is created in ABC terms:

- An activating event is seen by an individual as preventing the achievement of a goal.
- The belief system demands that the goal be realised.
- The emotional consequence is hostility or anxiety, and the behavioural consequence is over- or underreacting to the activating event in a self-defeating manner.

2. *Derivatives of primary demanding beliefs*. Individuals usually make over-generalised and unrealistic inferences in response to their absolutistic demands. For example:

- Awfulising, terribleising, horribleising: individuals feel that it will be extremely awful or bad if their cherished goals are not unblocked and achieved.
- I can't stand it-itis: individuals feel that they will not be able to stand it if their desired goals are not unblocked and achieved.
- A feeling of worthlessness and self-hatred: individuals feel worthless and stupid if they fail to unblock and achieve their goals.
- Prediction of continuous failure: individuals feel that if they are unable to unblock and achieve their personal goals they will always fail to get what they desire, and will only get what they do not want, both now and in the future.

Two types of neurotic problem arise from the three primary demanding beliefs and their derivatives: ego disturbance (self-damning) and low frustration tolerance, which is also known as discomfort disturbance.

Ego disturbance comes about when individuals believe they must do everything well if they are to avoid feeling undeserving and inadequate. Ellis saw this as godlike grandiosity because the individuals concerned expect themselves to be outstanding, special and perfect.

Low frustration tolerance arises from individuals' ego disturbance belief that they are special and perfect. Because of the latter they feel they should be treated with kindness and consideration, and that the conditions in which they live should be arranged in such a way that they can get anything they want without hitches.

3. *Secondary demanding beliefs*. When individuals become miserable about a consequence they make it worse by becoming miserable about being miserable, that is, they convert the negative consequences of the primary demanding belief into an activating event for a secondary level demanding belief and consequence (ABC). For example a primary ABC might be:

- A: 'I did badly in my exam this afternoon.'
- B: 'This is dreadful because I must do well.'
- C: 'I feel anxious, guilty, worthless and depressed.'

Following on from this, the secondary ABC is:

- A: 'I feel anxious, guilty, worthless and depressed.'
- B: 'This is dreadful because I mustn't have these feelings.'
- C: 'I feel even more anxious, guilty, worthless and depressed.'

4. *Derivatives of secondary demanding beliefs*. There are three derivatives of secondary demanding beliefs. First, individuals can choose to derive awfulising, feelings of worthlessness, I can't stand it-itis and predictions of failure from both their primary and secondary demanding beliefs. Second, they can have two negative consequences and their derivatives for the price of one. Finally, they can intensify their unhappiness in a worsening spiral.

The interaction of As, Bs, Cs and goals

According to Ellis (1991) activating events, beliefs, consequences and goals are in collaboration with one another. He gives the example of eating food to ensure the goal of survival, which has a number of elements:

- Cognitive element: food is good and nourishing so it is essential to get it.
- Emotional element: eating good food is pleasurable, eating bad food is unpleasant.
- Behavioural element: cooking the food.
- Physical elements: sight, smell, touch and taste.

As and Bs interact and reciprocate in the following way. Individuals might see an activating event (A) as loss of approval. If they believe (B) 'I like to be approved of, but I don't need to be' they will probably take the loss of approval as a minor affront. However if they believe (B) 'I am worthless if I am not approved of' they might see the same event (A) as an intentionally cruel attack on them. In Ellis's view, people have a tendency to build cognitive, emotive and behavioural elements onto A. Once this has happened several times, these irrational beliefs become what are called basic philosophies and appear to be absolutely right. This means that instead of B following A, it comes before A and is brought into new As.

Bs and Cs interact and reciprocate as follows. Preferential beliefs (Bs) lead to consequences (Cs) that reciprocally influence Bs. So if people are rejected and consequently feel depressed they avoid anyone who may reject them because they have constructed the belief that 'he is an idiot and isn't worth bothering with'. If a belief strongly interacts with emotional and behavioural consequences they are said to be cognitive emotive.

The acquisition of irrational beliefs

Irrational beliefs can be the result of innate or biological tendencies (as discussed above), or they can be acquired through social learning or choosing irrational cognitions.

Social learning

Children are dependent on the thinking and planning of others. Young children cannot think clearly and want immediate rather than future gratification. Furthermore children cannot accurately distinguish imagined fears from real ones. These problems diminish with age in the normal child. Children's demands can be appeased by magic, for example by the commonly used, 'leave it for now and we'll write to Father Christmas to bring it.' Other members of the family, including parents, have irrational tendencies, superstitions, prejudices and attitudes that they instil into their children. This situation is aggravated by the mass media, and further irrationality can be fostered by culture or religion.

Irrational cognitions

Individuals tend to create their own emotional disturbances by not developing and using their capacity for rational choice. It is not necessarily what happens to them that matters but how they handle it, so people can have a negative experience but choose not to disturb themselves about it. Conversely, even people with favourable social learning can form irrational beliefs. In short social learning can influence us in a favourable or an unfavourable way, but we have the ability to choose our response.

The maintenance of irrational beliefs

People become irrational, stay irrational and even become more irrational because it is difficult to remain rational in an irrational world. People acquire irrational standpoints and continually repeat them because they have a powerful urge to reindoctrinate themselves with self-defeating notions. People remain irrational for the following reasons.

1. *Biological reasons.* Humans' tendency for irrationality is part of their genetic inheritance and therefore does not go away with maturity. They are unconsciously predisposed to prolong mental dysfunction and to make it a habit, even though they will 'fight like hell to give it up' (Ellis, 1987). Furthermore there is a

tendency to embrace short-term hedonism rather than try to balance the long and short term, and this is a main cause of resistance to change.

2. *Emotional causes.* Absolutist musts are 'hot' cognitions that are difficult to change because they contain powerful evaluative feelings that are strongly held. Individuals form derivatives of primary irrational beliefs and secondary irrational beliefs. This has the effect of raising their emotional plane, which in turn fosters greater irrationality. Then, by failing to see how upset they are, they neglect to reality test and challenge their irrational standpoints. In other words:

- Unrealistic beliefs cause disruptive feelings, which in turn aggravate unrealistic beliefs.
- Unrealistic beliefs also cause dysfunctional behaviours that make the unrealistic beliefs worse.
- So irrational beliefs make people worse, not better.

3. *Inadequate scientific thinking.* Individuals should always observe and check facts to see whether they have changed, or indeed whether they were ever true in the first place. Scientific method does not posit absolute standards of good and bad, and evidence is required to prove or disprove any given theory. Once people have decided to aim for a goal, scientific method can to some extent allow examination of whether of not they are achieving it. Irrational beliefs are maintained because people do not scientifically or objectively investigate whether they are realistic, true or logical.

4. *Reinforcing the consequences.* Irrational beliefs can be cognitively, emotionally and behaviourally reinforced. Strong feelings resulting from primary beliefs include anger and depression, which can make the beliefs seem true. Beliefs are reinforced cognitively and behaviourally, the method depending on the belief. For example people who need social approval will avoid taking social risks and are convinced that it would be dangerous and difficult to do otherwise. This is reinforced by the resulting sense of emotional relief. Hence they are made more rather than less socially anxious by their emotional, cognitive and behavioural reactions. Angry people justify and reinforce their self-disturbing beliefs by exaggerating the faults of those they hate. This can turn into a self-fulfilling prophecy in that their attitude can provoke an angry reaction by the objects of their dislike. In time people may try to correct their emotional disturbances, but if they fail they simply give up.

5. *Looking to the past.* Some people maintain their emotional disturbances by looking for causes in the past. The past cannot be changed, so they instead need to concentrate on the present and future. Focusing on the past can also result in overemphasis on other people's actions relative to one's own, and can obscure our responsibility for our own emotions, cognitions and behaviour when we should really be bringing these into focus.

6. *Unrealistic attitudes towards change.* There is a tendency to think that change can be achieved with a minimum amount of work and discomfort, that changing thoughts, feelings and behaviour should not be difficult, that there will be no setbacks during change, and that change will be quick and profound. When

this proves not to be the case individuals are willing to function as they are at present because further change is considered impossible.

7. *Rigidity*. Rigid thinkers may admit to having irrational beliefs, but will tenaciously hold on to primary beliefs and their derivatives.

8. *Ignorance*. Some people fail to see that they are creating their own emotional disturbances. They fail to distinguish between what are appropriate or inappropriate feelings, thoughts and behaviour, and consequently believe that it is healthy and normal to be unnecessarily upset.

9. *Defensiveness*. It is human nature to avoid dealing with problems directly. Problems are denied and distorted by a variety of methods, and people conceal behaviours of which they are ashamed.

10. *Changing the situation rather than addressing the problem*. One example of this is to divorcing one's partner rather than changing oneself. People may feel better by changing the situation in which their behaviour has been self-defeating, but the behaviour and its potential to cause problems remain the same.

11. *Pollyannaism and indifference*. People who suffer from extreme anxiety and have a serious physical illness may cope by denying its seriousness. Such an approach can prevent physical recovery and psychological change.

12. *The use of palliatives*. Some people try to find ways of diminishing the seriousness of their emotional problems rather than deal with the causes. Palliatives include:

- Yoga, meditation, relaxation techniques and so on.
- Superficial positive thinking.
- Deep involvement in politics, religious cults or a cause of some sort.
- Alcohol and drugs.

Most people are natural resisters and find it easy to block change but difficult to resist their resistance.

Rational emotive behaviour counselling

Although most people can benefit from REBC (juvenile delinquents, the mildly disturbed, those with borderline personality disorders and high-grade mental deficiencies, and psychotics with some contact with reality) it is most effective with people who are mildly disturbed or have one major symptom. It is less effective with strongly disturbed clients because the causes of primary demanding beliefs and emotional disturbance are mainly innate. It is also inappropriate for anyone who has lost contact with reality, or is autistic, manic, in the lower ranges of mental deficiency or brain damaged.

Length and goals of counselling

Sessions normally last 30 minutes and take place once a week. The number of sessions can vary from five to 50. For clients who want short-term counselling or have specific or mild problems, between one and ten sessions will suffice. Clients with severe problems participate in individual and group counselling for at least six months as this gives them time to practise what they have learned.

The goals of rational emotive behaviour counselling (REBC) are as follows:

- To overcome emotional blocks and disturbances in order to become more fully functioning, self-actualised and happier.
- To gain profound philosophical change by ending rigid primary thinking and replacing it with preferential thinking. The focus is on changing thoughts, emotions and behaviour. Specifically, becoming more rational and ending childish demandingness, which is the main cause of emotional difficulty; feeling more appropriate emotions; and acting more effectively to reach primary and fundamental goals.

Self-actualisation

REBC aims to overcome emotional blocks and help the client to become self-actualised or fully functioning and happy. Self-actualised people are characterised by:

- Self-interest: they will compromise their own interests for loved ones, but not completely as they value their own interests.
- Self-direction: they take primary responsibility for their lives.
- Social interest: they are interested in social survival and the needs of others.
- Flexibility: they do not have rigid rules for themselves and others, and are open to change and think flexibly.
- Tolerance: they accept the right of others to be wrong. Even if they dislike other people's behaviour they refuse to damn them as people.
- Acceptance of uncertainty: they accept that there is a lot of chance and uncertainty in this world, and although they enjoy a fair degree of order they do not demand it.
- Self-acceptance: they unconditionally accept themselves, and do not measure their worth by what others think of them. They prefer to enjoy rather than prove themselves.
- Commitment: they are committed to things outside themselves, and believe that maximum fulfilment and happiness are achieved by pursuing a long-term, absorbing interest.
- Scientific thinking: their thinking is governed by logic and scientific method, and is objective and rational.
- Creativity and originality: they have at least one major creative interest, and are innovative and creative about ordinary and artistic problems.
- Acceptance of human animality: they accept the animal nature of themselves and others.
- Long-term hedonism: they are not obsessed by immediate gratification, but balance long- and short-term considerations when pursuing happiness and avoiding pain.
- High frustration tolerance: they change conditions that can be changed, accept those which cannot, and know the difference between the two.

- Risk taking: they are willing to take calculated risks when pursuing goals, but adventurously rather than foolishly.
- Non-utopianism: they recognise that the perfect situation is not possible, and nor is the total absence of negative emotions. They refuse to strive unrealistically for total happiness.
- Self-responsibility: they acknowledge responsibility for some problems instead of blaming others and social conditions.

Philosophical change

The degree of philosophical change depends on whether the goals of counselling are 'inelegant' or 'elegant'.

Inelegant change involves some kind of symptom removal. Counselling focuses on thoughts, emotions and behaviours that go hand in hand with dysfunctional behaviour such as avoiding social situations or public speaking, and self-defeating feelings such as depression and anxiety. The aim is to remove these and replace them with appropriate feelings, rational beliefs and desirable behaviours.

Elegant change involves more than just symptom removal. It also aims to reduce clients' disturbability and help them to find and follow an effective philosophy of life, emotionally, cognitively and behaviourally. Those who successfully make the change are able to think in preferential, flexible ways as opposed to rigid, primary ones. They exhibit disciplined, goal-oriented reactions to unpleasant activating events. They think scientifically and struggle against arbitrary and narrow-minded intellectual/emotional/behavioural restrictions.

The client–counsellor relationship

Counsellors' main role is that of teacher of self-help skills to promote appropriate feelings, rational thoughts and effective behaviour so that clients' chosen goals can be achieved. They employ empathic listening techniques, including reflective listening, to build a rapport with their clients. They engage in two types of empathy: affective empathy to understand how clients feel, and philosophic empathy to understand the thinking behind clients' feelings. Clients are non-judgementally accepted as fallible human beings.

Counsellors are careful not to collude in clients' need for approval, so no undue warmth is shown to most clients. Instead they are encouraged to face their problems and find warmth and happiness for themselves. Counsellors do most of the talking in the early sessions and confront their clients with the fact that they are contributing to their own unhappiness. Illogical thinking by clients is forcefully disputed and debated, and they are taught how to do this for themselves.

As long as it is not harmful to their clients, counsellors self-disclose and freely share their opinions. Humour is used, but never at the clients' expense because it is recognised that they take themselves and their woes very seriously. Humour is useful in attacking disturbance-forming ideas. Counselling content and style vary, for example a forceful, hard hitting counsellor may be more gentle and passive with certain categories of client. In general counsellors are authoritative but not authoritarian.

Clients are tutored in how to be their own therapist once the counselling sessions are over. Early on in therapy clients are told about the ABCs of how people disturb themselves, and also how REBC works. They are taught how to dispute their beliefs, and are provided with skills, philosophies and insights that can be applied between and after counselling sessions.

The counselling process

Uncovering irrational beliefs

Irrational beliefs can be uncovered emotionally, cognitively and behaviourally within the ABC system. Emotionally, irrational beliefs are revealed by inappropriate feelings. Cognitively, they are revealed by subtle or overt signs of demandingness that are characterised by 'shoulds', 'musts', 'have to's' and so on and reveal primary demanding beliefs. Derivatives of primary and secondary demanding beliefs are indicated by phrases such as 'I can't stand this' or 'That's absolutely awful'. Behaviourally, irrational beliefs are revealed by self-defeating actions.

Counsellors help clients to distinguish irrational from rational beliefs and to see how rational beliefs lead to positive outcomes while irrational beliefs cause inappropriate feelings and self-defeating behaviours. Homework reports are often used to facilitate the process.

Disputing irrational beliefs

The musts and their derivatives cannot be made to disappear merely by acknowledging them. They must be disputed by counsellor and client together. The technique of disputing is the most commonly used method in REBC and involves questioning and challenging clients' hypotheses about themselves and the world in general. Usually a few irrational ideas and their derivatives are pinned down so that these can be disputed and clients can learn to dispute their central irrational ideas. Feelings, thoughts and behaviours interact when people form and sustain their irrational beliefs, so counsellors have to work on all three.

There are three cognitive disputing techniques, as follows.

Scientific questioning

This is the main disputing technique. To support their beliefs, clients use logic, reason and facts, so the aim is to show them when, why and how their beliefs are irrational. Questions are asked in the first person singular in accordance with the self-help nature of REBC. Examples of questions are:

- What irrational belief do I want to challenge and give up?
- Can I logically sustain this belief?
- Is there any evidence for the truth of this belief?
- What is the evidence for the falseness of this belief?

- Why is it terrible?
- Why can't I cope with it?
- How does this make me a dreadful person?
- Must I always perform badly in future?
- What would be an effective new belief to replace my irrational belief?

The desired outcomes are a sound set of effective new philosophies or preferential beliefs related to each belief. Stemming from and interacting with the effective new philosophies should be desirable emotional and behavioural effects. If a client desires elegant change, the outcome is an effective new philosophy that is applicable now and in future.

Homework techniques

Irrational beliefs must be continually challenged by clients, so disputing techniques need to be learnt and practised. Homework techniques include the following.

1. *Cassettes of sessions.* Clients are encouraged to tape sessions and listen to them several times at home.

2. *Self-help forms.* Clients fill these out and counsellors check them for their efficacy in disputing beliefs.

When clients wish to identify an activating event and the consequences or conditions they would like to change the form consists of three columns.

In the first column clients circle which of 13 irrational beliefs lead to which consequences; they may add other relevant irrational beliefs. In the second column there is space for them to dispute every circled irrational belief. In the third column they insert effective rational beliefs to replace irrational beliefs. On the far right there is space to describe the feelings and behaviours that come with their new effective rational beliefs.

Another self-help form is the DIBS or disputing irrational beliefs form. The questions are about:

- The belief to be disputed.
- Whether the belief can be rationally supported.
- The existing evidence for the belief.
- The existing evidence against the belief.
- The worst that could happen if the object of the belief is achieved.
- The good things that could happen if the belief is not achieved.

3. *Reminder cards.* Clients write down rational self-statements on postcards and repeat them between sessions.

4. *Visualising.* Clients are taught how to picture themselves successfully addressing situations they are afraid of.

5. *Listing disadvantages.* Clients write down ten disadvantages of avoiding a given behaviour. These are reviewed daily.

6. *Practising REBC on others.* Clients practice talking their friends and relatives out of their disturbances.

7. *Bibliotherapy.* Self-help books are read by clients.

8. *Self-help cassettes*. Audio and video cassettes are available on topics such as how to be happy, solving emotional problems and how to stop worrying.

Emotive techniques

There are five emotive techniques, as follows.

1. *Vigorous disputing*. Counsellors may do this with their clients, or the clients may do it for themselves. The hot cognitions that go with many irrational beliefs need very strong disputing and the shaky logic of clients' standpoints needs highlighting. For homework clients make cassettes that they play to themselves and their counsellor, and to their group when applicable. With reverse role play the counsellor plays the part of the client and defends his or her irrational beliefs, while the client attacks them.

2. *Rational emotive imagery*. As homework clients imagine the worst possible consequence to emerge from an activating event and the problems it would bring. Then they get in touch with the negative emotions that are likely to stem from the consequence (anger, anxiety, depression and so on) and try to feel them. They should not feel what they think they are supposed to feel, but what they actually feel. When they feel inappropriately upset they hold on to this emotion for a couple of minutes, then change their disturbed negative feeling to a pres- cribed appropriate negative feeling consequence, such as regret, displeasure, disappointment and so on. This is done by repeating rational and sensible beliefs or coping statements such as 'Yes, I've been treated badly, and I wish they hadn't done it, but then there is no reason why they should treat me fairly, no matter how desirable it is to me.' Clients persevere with the rational statements and imagery until they have changed their inappropriate feelings to appropriate feelings. This normally takes a few minutes. This type of homework takes 30 days and is executed on a daily basis for each disturbed feeling.

3. *Unconditional acceptance*. Counsellor's unconditional acceptance of their clients as people, despite any negative characteristics, helps them to see that they are accepted and worthwhile.

4. *Humour.* Applied carefully, humour can help the fight against irrational beliefs and self-defeating behaviours. Exaggeration, puns, witticisms, amusing anecdotes and so on are used to counteract clients' tendency to take things too seriously.

5. *Rational role playing*. This helps clients to see their false ideas and how they affect their relationships with others. If clients feel anxious during role play they are encouraged to ask 'What am I telling myself right now to make myself anxious? What can I do to think and feel away this anxiety?'

Behavioural techniques

There are four behavioural techniques.

1. *Assignments that challenge demandingness*. When clients have primary demanding beliefs about approval and derivatives about the awfulness of re- jection they are encouraged to socialise or pluck up the courage to ask someone out on a date. (Ellis himself was afraid of public speaking and meeting new women, but overcame these problems by giving political talks and chatting to

women on a park bench.) Clients are also encouraged to believe that rejection is inconvenient rather than awful. When clients have a fixation with perfection they might be asked to make a serious attempt to speak badly in public.

Whatever the assignment, clients are expected to do it repeatedly. For example a client with speech anxiety would be asked to engage in public speaking as often as possible. Other clients may be asked to do assignments floodingly, that is, to stay in a situation they regard as dangerous until they realise that the danger is imaginary. For example clients who fear trains and buses in the rush hour are encouraged to immerse themselves in rush hour travel.

2. *Exercises that attack shame.* Feelings of shame, guilt, humiliation and embarrassment are closely related to ego anxiety. It follows that clients are less likely to be disturbed if they confront the irrational beliefs behind these feelings. They are encouraged to do humiliating things in public, such as loudly asking for condoms in a pharmacy or shouting in a public place. The aim is to show that in themselves the behaviours are not shameful, and that they can be done with self-acceptance and relatively comfortably. In tandem with this the clients attack their feelings of shame by disclosing what they believe, and what they believe that others believe to be shameful.

3. *Skills training.* There is an imprecise boundary between behavioural and cognitive skills. When counsellors assist clients with behavioural skills they also train them to dispute the irrational beliefs and derivative self-statements that go with them. Clients may also be asked to engage in outside skills training courses, for example in assertiveness training or public speaking.

4. *Rewards and penalties.* These are used to motivate clients to do their homework and put their self-change programmes into action. Ellis (1991) says that one of his clients rewarded himself by listening to one of his favourite CDs. His penalty was to talk to a boring aunt for half an hour – he only needed to impose the penalty twice!

Problem solving

Goals are brought by clients to the activating events in their lives. There are practical or reality problems associated with these goals that clients either have to solve or remain upset about. If they choose the latter they will have an emotional problem about their reality problem. Clients are helped to detect and actively dispute these irrational beliefs prior to tackling the practical issues. The steps to success take place in the following order:

- State the problems and goals clearly.
- Identify and work through emotional difficulties.
- Generate and evaluate alternative strategies.
- Outline the steps to attain the goals.
- Identify resources and supports.
- Develop the necessary practical skills.

Examples of goals include a good education, getting a job, succeeding at work and finding a husband/wife/partner.

Removing resistance to counselling procedures

Ellis (1986) lists three irrational beliefs held by clients:

- I must do well at changing myself.
- You must help me to change.
- Changing myself must occur quickly and easily.

With resistant clients, negative consequences stem from such beliefs. Examples include self-pity and depression. Behavioural consequences include withdrawal and procrastination. They also use awfulising, which is a derivative of irrational beliefs. There are four techniques for overcoming resistance.

- Disputing: clients are taught to find and dispute the main irrational beliefs that are contributing to their resistance.
- Referenting: clients list the advantages of making an effort in counselling and the disadvantages of resisting. These lists are regularly reviewed and considered.
- Rational and coping self-statements: clients say that counselling does not have to be easy, and that they can enjoy the challenge and the difficulty it presents. They formulate statements to this effect and continually reiterate them.
- Proselytising others: clients persuade others to use REBT and practice the techniques of the approach on relatives and friends.

Maintaining change

Work and practice are vital to the establishment and maintenance of change. Homework helps clients to develop skills that can be used outside and after the termination of counselling. If clients start to regress into old patterns they return to the ABCs to find why this has happened. Next they dispute these irrational beliefs until they are securely replaced by effective new philosophies.

Other applications of REBC

Group counselling

This can be conducted instead of individual counselling or in tandem with it. Group members are taught the process of uncovering and to dispute each other's irrational beliefs. In addition, by disclosing material they regard as risky they practise attacking their ego disturbing irrational beliefs. They also take part in role playing to improve their self-assertion and communication skills.

Marriage and family counselling

Couples are seen together so that their complaints can be aired and discussed. They are taught that although their grievances relate to an activating event their feelings of upset at the consequences are not justified. Primary demanding beliefs that cause a feeling of hostility are particularly focused on. Partners are taught relating and compromising skills. Parents and children are taught tolerance of their own behaviour and that of others, irrespective of how appalling a behaviour might be.

◼ ⋁ **17** Personal construct therapy: George Kelly

George Kelly received a degree in physics and mathematics in 1926 and was later awarded an MA in educational sociology and a B.Ed. He received his doctorate in psychology in the early 1930s and became professor and director of clinical psychology at Ohio State University in 1946. As a result of his training his model of the person is expressed in scientific language, as is his entire theory. His science is based on the philosophy of 'constructive alternativism', in which there are no 'facts', only support for current hypotheses. Such hypotheses will eventually lead to others as new events occur, but people never learn everything because they are in a constant state of motion and change, like the universe they live in. In fact Kelly sees the person as a form of motion. His approach is about action, prediction and change. Kelly (1969) says that he sat through lecture after lecture in his psychology course watching an endless procession of 'Stimulus→ Response' pairs being written on the blackboard and hoping that someone would explain the nature of the arrow in between. No one ever did.

Theoretical assumptions

One of Kelly's unique contributions to our understanding of the person is his belief that we should view all behaviour as if it were a scientific experiment and study people as though we were scientists. That is, we should develop theories about why things happen, then form hypotheses from the theories and test them to prove or disprove the predictions that arise from them. Kelly's formulation of the psychology of personal constructs is linked to the image of the person in that we can understand human beings, ourselves and others, in psychological terms by analysing the personal constructs we have formed to help us predict what will happen in our personal existence. Human beings approach the world as it appears to be, but what it actually is might be quite different. We are constantly construing and predicting, not just with our minds but with our bodies as well. For example when we anticipate food our stomachs produce gastric juices and our taste buds cause us to accept or reject the food depending on whether or not it conforms to our expectations.

Dualistic thinking hinders understanding of the person. It is as important to ask what people are feeling as it is to ask what they are thinking. The reason for this is that many constructs (that is, discriminations between events) are formed before we formulate the words to express them. In short, personal construct theory is a theory of human experiencing. For example children discriminate between types of voice. A deep, gravelly voice may be associated with feeling reassured and a big body to cuddle up to before bedtime. A softer, smoother one can be comforting, but it may equally generate unease, particularly if it is especially soft. In the latter case, when children have grown up they may dislike women with a soft, smooth voice, but may not understand why. Here preverbal construing is being applied in adult life.

The conceptualisation of psychological disturbance and ill-health

Kelly disapproved of the use of medical models to deal with psychological disorders – people with psychological problems are not ill and therefore do not need treatment from a doctor. Furthermore medical models hinder attempts to understand people and deal with their problems. In short, there is no illness and no health.

Kelly's concept of functioning: construing, validation and invalidation

To be fully functioning, individuals must be able to construe the world in a way that can be validated. If there is invalidation they deal with it by reconstruing to achieve validation and the mistake is put down to experience. An example of this is misjudging the character of a new associate after only superficial contact, only to be disillusioned and forced to make a new assessment of him or her. People who are incapable of coping with invalidation could become anxious about facing an event they cannot construe. Moreover, they may find that they are increasingly unable to predict their behaviour. This can be traumatic, and with repeated predictive failures they may come to believe they have a problem.

Hostility is a way of coping with invalidity. In this context hostility means extorting validational evidence for a social prediction that has failed, or making things work out as predicted. For example we may construe a selfish person as helpful, and so we pick up a pile of boxes and appear to be struggling. The person in question may briefly give some assistance, and so we are validated. Hostility is not wrong, it simply serves to deal with events when our construing fails us.

Fully functioning people do not usually resort to hostility to deal with invalidation and are rarely confronted by events that they cannot construe. Their system for construing the world updates potentially troublesome preverbal constructs, that is they are capable of exploring early childhood discriminations in order to question, for example, the validity of an adult having an instant dislike of people with a particular type of voice, manner of dress, hair colour and so on.

The acquisition of psychological disturbance

Kelly's system does not recognise a mind/body dichotomy – the person is an integrated, indivisible whole. Many people do not have such a conception of themselves and are therefore dualists. According to personal construct theory we act on the world and predict (or construe) events, hence we cannot 'acquire' a disturbance. For example a client may construe fainting as a bodily symptom acquired as a result of a stressful psychological event. The counsellor will focus on understanding this construing. The fainting is as much a construct as the way in which the client describes it, and the counsellor will examine the client's construing system in verbal and non-verbal terms, as well as the context of the fainting. Two questions the counsellor might examine are (1) 'What experiment is my client carrying out when she faints?', and (2) 'What answers does she want from me and others when behaving like this?' The behaviour is an experiment by the client, so fainting is a way of questioning her world. A possible scenario is that she is growing up to be like her mother, a woman who is successful but emotional and manipulative. She does not want to be like her mother, and perhaps if she is prone to fainting she will not grow up and will remain a child. The fainting leads to her being treated differently. This client has not acquired a disturbance but has, according to her construing, conducted a successful experiment. So she is successful, but not in the same way as her mother. All this is not consciously formulated as much experimentation is done at the unconscious level.

The perpetuation of psychological disturbance

Psychological disturbance is perpetuated because it 'works' for some people, and predictions by the child are validated if maturation is prevented. Disturbances also tend to develop their own meaning. For example, 'As I'm unwell I can't live the sort of life that would make me successful.' Such people do not see themselves as personally unsuccessful, but as not yet successful. Long-standing problems may become entangled in individuals' 'core-role' construing, for example they may conceive of themselves as a 'fainter', a 'stutterer', a 'hopeless failure' and so on. The longer the problem goes on the more likely it is to become entrenched in the construing of the self, and to persist.

The invalidation of important notions of self usually comes from others, and our experiments in life succeed or fail according to our comprehension of the understanding others have of us. However invalidation can come from within if we find acceptable alternative ways of dealing with the world.

The organisation corollary of personal construct theory

This states that constructs are organised into a system, so it is not only core-role construing that takes place at the superordinate level, although most constructs are ordinate. The more abstract a superordinate construct is the more implications or ordinate constructs it has, and the more resistant it is to being changed.

Implicative dilemmas happen when individuals have not worked out the meaning and implications of some or other superordinate construct. If subtle changes of meaning in a variety of contexts are not obvious then useful predictions are difficult to make, and this can lead to invalidation. Sometimes lines of implication may exist but they conflict.

Change

In personal construct theory individuals are in a constant state of motion and change, so change is built into the theory, which has three elaborative corollaries to describe the theoretical structure that underpins change.

1. *The experience corollary.* This states that individuals' construction systems vary as they successively construe the replication of events. Just being in a situation does not amount to having an experience. It becomes an experience when one of its aspects is construed differently from the way in which it was construed before. Learning is not a separate psychological process; it is synonymous with all psychological processes. It is not something that occasionally happens to someone; it is what makes them an adult in the first place.

2. *The choice corollary.* This states that 'a person chooses for himself that alternative in a dichotomized construct through which he anticipates the greater possibility for extension and definition of his system' (Dryden, 1991, p. 133). This is a basic motivation construct. Individuals try to make their world a more predictable and meaningful place. Although they may not like their personal world they prefer it to the uncertainty of change. Hence they choose to remain where they are, and childhood problems such as stuttering are carried through into adulthood. This is how they make sense of their world; it is meaningful to them personally. The same is true of depression to the depressed, smoking for the smoker, obesity for the obese and so on. If the problem was removed they would find life chaotic.

3. *The modulation corollary.* This states that any variation in a construing system is limited by the permeability of the constructs within whose range of convenience the variants lie. If a number of personal constructs are not open to receive them, then new events will be difficult to construe. Individuals with a problem know exactly how people will respond to them, and they will have difficulty employing new constructions of these interactions.

Cycles of movement

These describe the process of change.

The cycle of creativity

This involves loosening how events are construed and tightening them when a different pattern has emerged. When we have a problem we construe loosely, that is, we mull over ideas that occur to us. When something suitable occurs to us we tighten up again so that we can assess whether or not we have a solution to the problem. When we loosen we release facts that are normally regarded as self-evident. This allows them to be seen in a new light, which kick-starts the creativity cycle.

The cycle of experience

This about the actual process of reconstruing. The first requirement is anticipation, because behaving is an experiment that tests our anticipation about what we are facing. It is important to be committed to this anticipation and to invest in our experiment. If we do not reconstrue in the light of the consequences of an experiment it is not a real experience. A major problem is that the same experiments are continually repeated without the last and most important part – reconstruing.

The cycle of pre-emption and control for decision making

This cycle does not require the tightening or loosening of construing. When we have a decision to make we weigh up the possible alternatives; in other words we engage in circumspection. Eventually we pre-empt the issue by choosing the best way. This puts us in a position to control the situation and take action.

Personal construct therapy

The goal of personal construct therapy (PCT) is to get clients moving again because they are seen as being stuck in an endless round of the same behavioural experiments. As Kelly (1969) says, 'The task of psychotherapy is to get the human process going again so that life may go on and on from where psychotherapy left off. There is no particular kind of psychotherapeutic relationship – no particular kind of feelings – no particular kind of interaction that is in itself a psychotherapeutic panacea.'

Client selection criteria

No construing person is deemed unsuitable for PCT because everything is seen as a construing process. The only limiting factors are the therapeutic location, because not all places are suitable for dealing with the violent, the catatonic and so on, and the psychotherapist, because it is a rare therapist who can deal equally successfully with all types of client and problem.

An important criterion is that the client must be willing to accept that the therapist does not have all the answers – in PCT it is held that the client has these answers. The therapist only has a theory about how people can set about making sense of themselves and their environment. Clients achieve most when they have an existing construct to do with psychological change.

When deciding whether change is most likely to take place as a result of one-to-one therapy or group therapy there are a number of factors to consider. For example, with a withdrawn adult the therapist needs to consider whether it would be best to see the client with one or more relatives, see the client and relatives on separate occasions, or split the session and see just the client in the first part, with the relatives joining in later. The decision hinges on how all parties view the problem. If the client is withdrawn owing to internal turmoil, then therapy is best conducted with only the client and the therapist in the room; if the problem is interaction and the client does not wish to communicate, then client and relatives will be seen together. The process is flexible, so as the client becomes less withdrawn the relatives will increasingly attend the sessions. If a client is having individual and group therapy the same therapist should not be involved in both, because the client will need to separate out the differing experiences. However the two therapists should collaborate closely to ensure that the client moves along a single path to reconstruing and to avoid conflicting processes such as one of them working on loosening the client's constructs while the other is concentrating on tightening them.

The qualities needed by therapists

A subsuming system of constructs

Counsellors should have a 'subsuming construct system' and be skilled in using it. All counsellors should have professional constructs in which to subsume their clients' personal system of constructs. For cognitive therapists this is defined in cognitive terms, for analysts it is defined in psychoanalytical terms and for personal construct therapists it is defined in terms of the theoretical constructs stated in the psychology of personal constructs. This approach should allow counsellors to understand the widely varying systems clients are likely to present.

Counsellors should be able to state exactly what constructs are being employed when a therapeutic decision is made. In the personal construct school of counselling the subsuming system is that which defines the theory itself. In psychotherapy the constructs most often used are called 'professional constructs'. One example is 'loose' versus 'tight': whether the client is using his or her constructs in a way that promotes loosened construing (varying prediction) or tight construing (that events will definitely be one way or the other). Counsellors must be able to work within the client's construing system, be this tight or loose.

Process differences must be comprehended both theoretically and experientially. Therapists will fail to help their clients to change if they do not have an adequate subsuming system of constructs, or if their level of skill precludes the use of such a system in an experiential way. If counsellors permit their own construing to come between their clients and themselves there is a strong chance that the clients will use them.

Creativity and aggression

Counsellors must be versatile, creative and aggressive. Every case demands techniques and constructs the counsellor has never used before, including a willingness to try unverbalised hunches and to view things in new ways. Being creative means taking on various roles and being aggressive when testing hypotheses because aggression is the active elaboration of construing. A fundamental tenet of PCT is that as we have created ourselves we can recreate ourselves if we choose. Psychotherapy demands that both parties in the therapeutic relationship be prepared to take risks and be aggressive.

Verbal ability

Counsellors should be observationally and verbally skilled. They should have a broad vocabulary as well the ability to speak the client's language. This is important because in order to avoid misunderstandings they must be able to comprehend the meanings that word-symbols have for their clients.

Therapeutic style

This is best understood by revisiting the model of the 'person as scientist' – both work to comprehend and solve the same problem. Like research supervisors, counsellors know about designing experiments and have some knowledge of the pitfalls inherent in any sort of research. In the end, only the research student can carry out the research. Both parties in the therapeutic relationship must be committed to solving the problem and to its attendant work and experimentation.

The credulous approach is adopted by counsellors within the research framework. It involves the suspension of all personal evaluations and judgements. In short, everything the client says is accepted as true.

Counsellors develop hypotheses about the nature of the problem in question as they gain increasing access to the world of the client. These hypotheses are then put to the test. Counsellors do not use a directive approach, even though the client's role is decided by them. Counsellors' construing of their clients' constructions leads to the conclusion that such a 'quiet' role is something that the client can make use of at this particular stage of therapy. Thus counsellors acts as the validator/invalidator of their clients' construing. An implication of counsellors acting as validators of clients' construing is that counsellors use the relationship as a tool for assisting clients' reconstructions, for example transference and dependency are not problems to be dealt with. It can be useful during certain stages of therapy, for example when a client tries to verbalise preverbal constructs, but at other stages dependence on the counsellor can block the client from conducting experiments outside the counselling room.

To sum up, therapeutic style is determined by the ways in which counsellors construe their clients' needs, bearing in mind that they are both experimenting and construing.

Therapeutic strategies and techniques

The repertory grid technique

This technique helps counsellors to evaluate the relationship between clients' constructs and those of people in their personal world. This has a place in psychotherapy but is not essential to it, and is only useful if therapists believe it to be. Therapists use it to validate hunches, monitor change over time and help clients to explore their construing of events more fully. In the case of the latter it becomes part of therapy if the results are shared with the client.

Laddering

This helps clients to explore the relationships between constructs at increasingly abstract levels. Questioning persists until construing has reached its limit. It is difficult to master the art of laddering, but the effort is worthwhile because it allows quick insight into clients' most important values in respect of themselves and others. It enables counsellors to learn about their clients, and clients can gain immense insight into their own construing.

Pyramiding

This is used to identify the more concrete levels of a client's construing system. Clients are asked 'How?' or 'What?' instead of 'Why?' This is useful when planning behavioural experiments. So clients may be asked how they know something or what they know, as opposed to why they know it.

The ABC technique

This searches out the advantages and disadvantages of each pole of a client's constructs to the client. This can then be used with constructs connected with the problem facing the client. The client's answers are not seen as truths but as guides for understanding and as springboards for further exploration. For example a person with a weight problem might be asked the following:

- What would be the advantage of being the desired weight? (Possible answers: to be able to wear nice clothes, to be attractive to the opposite sex and so on.)
- What are the disadvantages of being overweight? (Breathlessness when hurrying to catch a bus, difficulty finding nice clothes that fit, unattractiveness and so on.)
- What are the disadvantages of being normal weight? (Not being able to indulge in extra eating to maintain that weight, too great a choice of clothes and so on.)
- What are the advantages of being overweight? (Not being bothered by the opposite sex, being able to get away with overeating and so on.)

The self-characterisation technique

Here the client is asked to write a sketch of her- or himself as the principal character in a play. This is written in the third person as though by a sympathetic friend who knows her or him very intimately, perhaps better than anyone really could know her or him. When using this technique there is no formal method of analysis. The first sentence is a statement of where the client is now and the last is a statement of where she or he is going. It is important to look for themes running through the whole thing, and to go beyond the words and look inside at the person. Character sketches can be written from a number of different perspectives, such as what the client will be like when the problem has gone, or where she or he will be in five years' time.

Fixed-role therapy

This technique is the only one that is a tool in its own right. As such it is an example of the theory in action, based on self-characterisation. A second version of the client's original self-characterisation is written because the first can only lead back to where the client is now. It will not be the complete opposite of the first draft because that would be too drastic for the client to tackle. The client's fixed-role sketch is rewritten as orthogonal to the first. For example if the client has an *aggressive* rather than a *submissive* construct in relation to her or his employer, in the sketch this would be amended to *respectful*.

Together client and counsellor modify the sketch until it takes a form that the client can cope with comfortably, and the new life it contains is lived for a number of weeks. During this time the counsellor sees the client frequently. Sessions focus on the following:

- What the client sees as going on.
- What has gone well and what has not.
- What messages are being received from others.

The object of the exercise is to show that people can change themselves even if they are stuck at the moment. Fixed-role therapy is not suitable for everyone and for some a modified form may be more appropriate, involving a more limited application of the technique. For example they could try a particular behaviour as a one-off to see how effective it is. So clients with an aggressive/submissive construct could be respectful to their employer just once to see whether this affects the way in which the employer reacts to them.

In fixed-role therapy clients learn the following:

- Self-inventiveness.
- What happens when a particular behaviour is altered.
- Whether this can be pursued further or whether something different is needed.
- How the way in which they construe others and act towards them influences how the latter react to them.
- How to read messages from others – this is vital because the person invented in this process is largely the result of the way in which the reactions of others to the client have been construed.

The process of change

As there are no clear stages that can be applied to all clients during the change process, reference must be made to theory. The change process is determined by the reasons uncovered by counsellors as to why their clients cannot move forward. Some questions to considered are:

- How permeable is the client's construing in the area that is causing difficulty?
- If the client makes radical changes, what will be at stake?
- How loose or tight is the client's construing in those areas targeted for change?

Diagnosis is the planning stage for change, and theoretical guidelines are used to help the counsellor identify possible ways forward for the client. Diagnosis does not involve clients being given medical labels such as 'depressed' or 'schizophrenic'.

Impediments to change

The reconstruction process may be impeded by transition-related factors in clients' constructs. Change can involve feelings of threat, anxiety and hostility because clients sometimes find it difficult to construe the new behavioured areas being suggested for them. Also, when clients realise they are looking at changes in how they construe some essential aspect of their self they may experience a feeling of threat. If the proposed changes are too great for clients to contemplate they will relapse. This is a signal that an alternative is required, and should be seen as the clients' safety net and not as a negative event.

The problem of hostility

Clients may defend their position with hostility, in which case the therapy will fail; this is not their fault, it is the counsellor's. The best way forward is to find out what the client believes is important to preserve, and what sort of self the client wishes to become. An example is a client who wishes to find a way of becoming an adult without losing the child within, with its world of deep experiencing and rich fantasy.

Conclusion

An area that needs to be developed in this approach is group work. Although Kelly devoted a whole chapter to group work, in practice the focus has tended to be on the one-to-one. Apart from this, limitations tend to be in the therapist him/herself, rather than with the actual therapy. Practitioners find it easier to work with clients if they cooperate fully. It also helps if the clients are verbally fluent and of a similar culture to the counsellors, although neither is vital. Personal construct theory can be used by anyone if they accept that all people are experiencing, construing human beings.

Part Five

Eclectic and integrative counselling

Arnold Lazarus was born in Johannesburg, South Africa, in 1932, the youngest of four children. When he started university he intended to become a writer and journalist, but then he found out he could become a psychotherapist without formal medical studies and pursued his interest in psychology and psychotherapy. In 1956 he was awarded a BA in psychology and sociology, in 1957 a BA honours in psychology and an MA in experimental psychology and in 1960 a PhD in clinical psychology – all from Witwatersrand University in Johannesburg. He became a part-time psychologist with the Mental Health Society in Johannesburg in 1958–59.

Multimodal counselling was developed by Lazarus in response to the restrictions and limitations of traditional behavioural counselling. Its central tenet is that clients' needs are best served by an eclectic approach rather than rigidly adhering to one. It places great importance on selecting the best treatment techniques to suit the unique needs of each client.

Lazarus is an empiricist in that he has not developed a full theory of how people develop and maintain their strengths, weaknesses and BASIC ID modalities (see the section on modalities). He considers the theories and frameworks of others and adopts those which are suitable for his own work. It is important to remember that he does not integrate these theories and multimodal counselling is not a conglomeration of the various counselling theories. Although it is eclectic, for example it employs concepts from communication and systems theory, it is underpinned by a consistent social cognitive learning theory.

Eclecticism

There are two types of eclecticism:

- Unsystematic eclecticism, where the portfolio of techniques adopted by counsellors has no coherent rationale.
- Systematic or technical eclecticism, where counsellors use a particular technique or theory but also borrow from other approaches. Multimodal counsellors' preferred theory is Bandura's social and cognitive learning theory.

Technical eclecticists use procedures from various sources without necessarily subscribing to the theories or disciplines from which they derive, while systematic technical eclectics do not select techniques just because they 'feel right', nor do they move from theory to theory.

Technical eclecticists make use of prescriptive treatments based on empirical evidence and the needs of the client. This takes precedence over any personal or theoretical predispositions. Cognitive-behavioural techniques and ideas are most often used. They also draw on the following schools, but without actually embracing them: Adlerian, Eriksonian, Gestalt, Rogerian, psychodrama, reality and transactional analysis. The addition or expansion of explanatory principles is seen as unnecessary.

Integrationism

This approach uses techniques from various schools and tries to combine the various theoretical standpoints. Lazarus (1992) warns that this should be done with caution because of the danger of merging theoretical ideas that are fundamentally incompatible. Another danger is that counsellors will attach more importance to labelling their work theoretically than to determining the best procedure for each client.

Theoretical assumptions

Thresholds

Thresholds refer to people's differing capacity to tolerate frustration, stress, pain and other negative stimuli. People are less prone to anxiety if their autonomic nervous system is stable. The effectiveness of psychological interventions is limited by innate thresholds. An example is the limited effectiveness of hypnosis and other psychological methods on people with low pain tolerance – their pain tolerance can be raised, but their innate tendency to overreact to pain stimuli remains.

Modalities

The concept of modalities is the cornerstone of multimodal assessment and therapy. There are seven distinct dimensions or modalities. These are in a constant state of reciprocal interaction and flux, and are interconnected by complex sequences of behaviour and other psychophysiological processes. The acronym BASIC ID is made of the first letter of each modality, as listed in the multimodal self-assessment questionnaire (Lazarus, 1992, pp. 244–5):

- Behaviour: 'Some people may be described as "doers" – they are action oriented, they like to busy themselves, get things done, take on various projects. How much of a doer are you?'
- Affect: 'Some people are very emotional and may or may not express it. How emotional are you? How deeply do you feel things? How passionate are you?'
- Sensation: 'Some people attach a lot of value to sensory experiences, such as sex, food, music, art and other "sensory delights". Others are very much aware of minor aches, pains, and discomforts. How "tuned in to" your sensations are you?'

- Imagery: 'How much fantasy or daydreaming do you engage in? This is separate from thinking or planning. This is "thinking in pictures", visualizing real or imagined experiences, letting your mind roam. How much are you into imagery?'
- Cognition: 'Some people are very analytical and like to plan things. They like to reason things through. How much of a "thinker" and "planner" are you?'
- Interpersonal: 'How important are other people to you? This is your self-rating as a social being. How important are close friendships to you, the tendency to gravitate toward people, the desire for intimacy? The opposite to this is being a "loner".'
- Drugs/biology: 'Are you healthy and health conscious? Do you avoid bad habits like smoking, too much alcohol, drinking a lot of coffee, overeating etc.? Do you exercise regularly, get enough sleep, avoid junk foods, and generally take care of your body?'

Some important points about modalities

Behaviour is specific to particular situations and times. During the first ten years of life individuals develop tendencies that favour some modalities over others. Modality tendencies determine the quality and tone of how they function. For example individuals who are 'imagery reactors' will have the visual modality as their predominant modality, and will be inclined to respond to and organise the world in terms of mental images (although they do not do this all the time); 'cognitive reactors' use intellect to respond to the world; and sensory reactors are categorised by the predominance of each of the five senses.

Knowing and understanding other people requires full access to their BASIC ID, plus insight into the accompanying interactive effects. There are interactions between thresholds and preferred modalities, so that a person who has moderate activity and low frustration tolerance, and is highly analytical (cognition) and capable of only forming fleeting images will be at the opposite end of the spectrum from a person with low pain tolerance, high frustration tolerance, vivid imagery and high activity.

The acquisition of behaviour

Social learning

Association is vital to all learning processes and can take the form of events happening simultaneously or in close succession. A lot of human behaviour is derived from classical and operant conditioning, and from modelling:

- Classical conditioning is responsible for many aversions. Lazarus (1989) relates the story of a man in hospital who was suffering from post-operative nausea. He was in bed next to someone who repeatedly played a tape of *Moonlight Sonata*. Every time he heard that music afterwards he felt sick.
- With operant conditioning the probability of a behaviour recurring is mediated by its consequences. For example people who suffer from depression may avoid social contact, but this only serves to reinforce their depression. Another

common example is the person who comes to realise that his headaches are largely due to the fact that his spouse only shows him tenderness when he is in pain.

- With modelling or vicarious learning individuals observe and imitate the behaviour of others. The process includes perceiving both the positive and the negative consequences of this behaviour.

Perception

Individuals respond to their perceived environment, not the real environment. Factors that influence perception are:

- Expectations.
- Personal use of language.
- Selective attention.
- Goals.
- Problem-solving ability.
- Performance standards.
- Values, attitudes and beliefs.

Unconscious processes

A lot of what we learn is neither conscious nor deliberate. According to Lazarus (1992) we have different levels and degrees of awareness, and subliminal or unrecognised stimuli influence feelings, thoughts and behaviour. In altered states of consciousness we have access to memories and skills that are not available to conscious recall.

Defensive reactions

People learn unnecessary defensive reactions through their social learning experiences. The purpose of defensive reactions is to avoid pain, discomfort, guilt, depression, shame, anxiety and other negative emotions. People deny or distort their perceptions, mislabel their feelings and lessen their awareness. Examples of defensive reactions are denial, overintellectualisation, over-rationalisation, displacement (for example aggression against other people, animals or objects) and projection, or wrongly attributing personal feelings to others.

Misinformation and missing information

Individuals acquire erroneous assumptions and beliefs about life and the living of life, partly because of the perfectionist beliefs held in Western societies. Many also fail to see that their lives are controlled as much by how they perceive and think as by external events. Examples of erroneous beliefs are:

- Fame and fortune lead to happiness.
- It is good to give vent to your anger.
- It is important to please others.
- It is better to play safe and avoid risk.

- People should confess if they feel guilty.
- Romantic love always makes a good marriage.

While misinformation causes people to form erroneous ideas, missing information means that people lack the information needed to acquire the basic skills that are essential to successful living, such as conducting oneself at a job interview in such a way as to create the right impression to get the job. Phenomena such as international terrorism and drug dealing can be tied to extreme misinformation and missing information about the values and skills required to make the world a happier place.

The maintenance of personality and behaviour

Human personality is acquired and maintained through the interplay of genetic inheritence, socialisation and environmental influences. Genetic inheritance persists in the form of differing thresholds and favoured BASIC ID modalities. Social learning influences the maintenance of personality in three ways:

- Through a variety of associations and unfortunate combinations of events people learn maladaptive habits or acquire conditioned emotional reactions. Irrespective of whether these habits are complex or simple they continue to undermine happiness.
- Conditioning and modelling lead to the adoption of certain behaviours and to ideas about self-efficacy, goals and performance standards that individuals sustain for better or worse.
- The environment offers reinforcements and models that contribute to the maintenance of people's feelings, thoughts and behaviours.

Unconscious processes also play a part in personality maintenance. Individuals may be quite unaware of the feelings, thoughts and behaviours they have learned and keep learning from others, and therefore it is difficult to change them.

Defensive reactions are part of and serve to maintain unhelpful aspects of people's BASIC IDs. Once learned, these become habits that prevent people from achieving full awareness of how they and other people behave. The problem with defensive reactions is that they make it difficult to work on problems and their consequences because the individuals concerned lack insight into their defensive reactions and the resulting negative consequences.

Misinformation and missing information are the bedrock of behaviour maintenance. Gaps in people's repertoires mean they are poorly equipped to deal with the demands of society. Such gaps exist because they have not been given necessary information and therefore lack essential coping skills.

Three other contributory factors are:

- Conflicting and ambivalent feelings and reactions: avoidance–avoidance or approach–approach conflicts result in extreme indecisiveness, boosted by prior learning experiences. Indecisiveness is self-perpetuating and contributes to people's inability to change aspects of their functioning.

- Interpersonal inquietude: excessive hatred, misplaced love and undue dependency cause many people to remain upset. This has its roots in skills deficits and the unrealistic demands we impose on each other.
- Poor self-acceptance: negative feelings are maintained because individuals fail to differentiate between accepting their totality as a human being and the need to evaluate specific shortcomings and personal limitations. Self-acceptance means being able to make mistakes and accept a lack of skills without feeling crushed as a person.

Multimodal counselling

Multimodal counselling has six distinctive features:

- Comprehensive attention to the BASIC ID.
- The use of second-order BASIC ID assessments.
- The use of structural profiles.
- The use of modality profiles.
- Investigation of the modality firing order.
- Deliberate bridging procedures.

Its ultimate goal is long-term hedonism, but people need to achieve a balance between long-term and short-term pleasure. In short, a major goal for most people is to have fun during their lifetime.

There are seven subgoals:

- Behaviour: taking effective action to achieve realistic goals.
- Sensation: being in touch with and enjoying one's senses.
- Imagery: using coping images and being in touch with one's imagination.
- Affect: acknowledging, recognising and clarifying feelings; enhancing positive feelings and coping with negative ones.
- Cognition: having adequate and accurate information, and thinking realistically.
- Interpersonal: having good relating skills such as conversational and assertion skills, plus a capacity for healthy interdependency.
- Biology: taking proper care of one's physical health, and eating and drinking alcohol in moderation.

Individuals can be deficient in one or more of the seven subgoals but still be happy. The aim is for clients to accept their fallibility and be self-accepting while working towards reducing their fallibility. The counselling goals are unique to each client, taking into account their basic beliefs, goals, situational contexts, affective reactions, coping behaviours and resistances.

There is no rigidity in counselling, assessment and goal setting, and it may be necessary to assess all of the BASIC IDs and construct a modality profile of the problems in question, possible treatments and suggested outcome goals. With regard to the latter, if, say, depression is one of the problems listed in the affect section of a client's modality profile, an outcome goal would be a lessening of the client's depressed feelings.

The counselling relationship

The counselling relationship is based partly on universal principles and partly on factors tailored to individual clients. The need to develop a collaborative counsellor–client working alliance is one universal principle. Another is never to attack clients' dignity, although maladaptive behaviour is challenged. In Lazarus's view (1993) 'techniques of choice' are just as important as 'relationships of choice', so multimodal counselling aims to match both of these with the clients' varying needs at different stages of counselling. There are four ways of varying the counsellor–client relationship as follows.

The relationship continuum

The relationship continuum ranges from a formal, businesslike relationship at one end to tight bonding at the other. The relationship has to reflect the expectations and preferred modalities of each client, so one client may like a businesslike approach while another may prefer warmth and empathy.

Matching the client's style

In order to match the client's style the counsellor has to decide the following:

- Whether to be cold, warm or tepid.
- When and whether to be casual and informal rather than professional.
- When and when not to be confrontational.
- Whether or not to self-disclose.
- Whether to use a gentle or a tough approach.
- How to adjust the levels of supportiveness and directiveness.

Supportiveness and directiveness

Counsellors continually weigh up how supportive and directive they need to be with individual clients. There are four possibilities:

- High direction–high support.
- Low direction–low support.
- Low direction–high support.
- High direction–low support.

An effective counsellor will utilise all four modes as and when necessary. Lazarus personally favours the high direction–high support mode because in his view counselling is an educational process where the counsellor acts as a clinical teacher. Furthermore clients change most rapidly when there is high direction and high support.

Tailoring the technique to the client

Techniques are drawn from the work of Freud, Adler, Perls, Rogers, Haley, Ellis and the behaviourists to suit the individual needs of each client. Examples include Gestalt psychodrama and imagery techniques, Rogerian reflection and behavioural assertiveness training.

The two most important variables to consider when selecting the relationship of choice are the clients' readiness for change and their resistance level. Lazarus (1993) tells of a shy and timid young woman who had strong feelings about her dealings with loud, pushy or obnoxious people. Lazarus dealt with this by taking a gentle approach in which he was almost whispering. This worked and she cooperated with him, whereas she had had poor relationships with her two previous counsellors.

The flexibility of the multimodal counselling relationship is illustrated by an enhancement technique called 'bridging', whereby counsellors tune into their clients' preferred modalities and then help them to cross bridges into potentially more productive modalities. Counsellors respond first within their clients' preferred representational system because this gives them a sense of being understood, which in turn encourages them to move into less preferred modalities. For example a client might be asked how he feels about his father leaving home. If he replies that his father had put his own needs first and ignored the needs of him and his mother, the counsellor will join him in this cognitive modality rather than try to move him into the affective modality. After a few minutes the counsellor bridges into a modality that is less threatening than the affective modality. If the sensory modality is chosen the client is asked to tune into sensations in his body. After discussing these sensations the counsellor bridges into the affective modality by asking how the client feels about what his father has done. With this approach the client should become far less defensive about owning his feelings.

Assessment

The initial interview

This begins informally and basic information is collected on such things as address and phone number. This is followed by a more detailed enquiry, with two main questions being asked about the client's presenting problems: 'What has led to your current problems?' and 'Who or what is maintaining them?' Counsellors also look for signs of organic problems, depression and psychosis. Details of the modalities of BASIC ID that apply to the client's problems are also noted.

The client's expectations of counselling are assessed, the client's strengths and positive attributes are noted, and a decision is taken about the best style of counselling relationship to adopt. Specific interventions such as cognitive disputation may be used in the initial interview. At the end of the interview adult clients are given a 15-page multimodal life history inventory, which asks questions about previous events and maintaining factors; the answers are divided into BASIC ID categories.

Referral

It is important for counsellors to recognise their own limitations and to refer clients to other counsellors when the latter have skills that they themselves lack. The same is true if another counsellor has a more appropriate personal style for a particular client. Referrals are best carried out before a bond forms between client and counsellor. Finally, clients may be referred to an appropriate self-help group, such as Alcoholics Anonymous or Parents without Partners.

The modality and structural profiles

Modality profiles and structural profiles are the cornerstone of multimodal assessment. The modality profile is a BASIC ID chart that lists the problems and possible interventions for each modality. It is used when unforeseen problems arise and when counselling is not making sufficient progress. After two sessions the counsellor will have gathered enough information to draft a preliminary modality profile for the client. Sometimes clients are asked to draft their own profile for comparison with the counsellor's. Client modality profiles are regarded as hypotheses and are shared and discussed with clients.

The structural profile is drawn up towards the end of the multimodal life history inventory process and yields useful information on clients' interactions with the world. Clients rate themselves on a seven-point scale for each of the BASIC ID modalities and the data is converted to a bar graph.

There is also a 35-point standardised structural profile inventory, which is of particular value in couple counselling. Profiles uncover the reasons for misunderstanding and can facilitate discussions of how to deal with them.

Tracking

Tracking involves assessment of the order of the chain reaction between the various modalities. Although there are individual variations, clients have reasonably consistent modality patterns in respect of the creation of negative affect. They may, for example, generate negative emotions by focusing first on sensations (S) (such as a pain in the chest) that generate cognitions (C) ('Is it my heart?'), which in turn generate aversive images (I) (a picture of themselves collapsing with a coronary attack) that lead to maladaptive behaviour (B) (extreme withdrawal). Here the 'firing order' is SCIB, but patterns such as CISB (cognitive–imagery–sensation–behaviour) are also possible.

The purposes of tracking are to give clients insight into the processes that generate negative effect so that they can make a suitable intervention, and to help counsellors to choose and prioritise treatment techniques. Lazarus (1989) provides the following example.

An agoraphobic woman had a CISA firing order in which: the cognition (C) 'What if I pass out?' led to mental images (I) of herself hyperventilating and fainting. This in turn led to sensations (S) of sweaty palms and feeling faint, causing feelings (A) of anxiety and tension. Based on this firing order her counsellor provided her with self-instructional training to combat her self-defeating cognitions. She was then taught coping imagery in which she imagined herself staying calm in frightening situations such as shopping. To help this process the counsellor also taught her differential muscle relaxation and slow abdominal breathing. She was sent to practise her training 'in the field'. When shopping she followed a sequence of positive self-instructions (C) followed by coping imagery (I) and abdominal breathing while relaxing muscles not in use at the time (S). If the client had had a different firing order the counsellor would have employed a different sequence for her to use in real life.

Second-order BASIC ID assessment

This gives a more detailed picture of behaviours, cognitions, affective responses, sensory reactions, images, interpersonal factors, and drug and biological factors. It is conducted when there is an impasse in treatment.

Selection of techniques

Multimodal counselling is based on the assumption that clients have a multitude of problems and these should be dealt with by a multitude of treatments. Therefore counsellors need to be familiar with and have skills in a wide variety of techniques.

When selecting techniques there must be research data to support them and counsellors are expected to study research findings in the literature. The following are also taken into account: clients' priorities, clients' firing orders, the desirability of early success experiences, and clients' answers to three questions in the multimodal life history questionnaire:

- 'In a few words, what do you think therapy is about?'
- 'How long do you think your therapy should last?'
- 'What personal qualities do you think the ideal therapist should possess?'

The selected techniques are fitted to the unique nature and needs of clients to ensure they persevere with the therapy. If the chosen techniques are unsuccessful the counsellor draws on other well-researched techniques. Second-order BASIC ID may be used to investigate whether important factors were overlooked during the initial assessment. The following techniques are commonly employed.

Behavioural techniques

Behaviour rehearsal

The counsellor begins by playing the part of the client and showing how to behave in a given situation. The dialogue is recorded and then played back. In due course the client will practise these skills in a real life situation.

Modelling

Here the counsellor enacts particular behaviours and the client imitates them. A real setting may be used, such as going back to a shop to make a complaint.

Non-reinforcement

The counsellor and others in the client's world help to eliminate specific client behaviours by not attending to them.

Positive reinforcement

Praise, recognition, encouragement and other social reinforcers are used to strengthen particular behaviours. Tangible reinforcers such as food or money are used with children and adolescents. Tokens exchangeable for tangible rewards may also be used.

Recording and self-monitoring

Clients are encouraged systematically to record and chart their targeted behaviours.

Stimulus control

Related to the frequency of behaviours is the presence or absence of certain stimuli. Students wishing to improve their study behaviour can remove distracting stimuli from their desks and only sit at them when actually studying. Likewise someone who is trying to lose weight can ensure there are no desserts and snacks in the home.

Systematic exposure

Clients are encouraged to face their feared situation step-by-step. To combat avoidance, additional techniques such as coping imagery and goal rehearsal are employed.

Affect techniques

Anger expression

This technique involves helping clients to own and express their anger. Behaviour rehearsal may be employed to encourage them to express their anger assertively, for example saying 'I am angry' with increasing loudness. They can also kick and punch cushions or inflatable objects.

Anxiety management training

This begins with general relaxation training and coping imagery or goal rehearsal. The client is then shown how to have anxiety-causing thoughts and imagery, followed immediately afterwards by relaxation. The client is taught to concentrate on calm sensations and serene images, to nurture optimistic and relaxing thoughts and to dispute irrational ideas.

Feeling identification

An important part of counselling is the accurate labelling of feelings. For example clients may have anxiety symptoms but say they are depressed. The counsellor focuses on exploring the client's affective domain to facilitate the identification of unclear or misdirected feelings.

The empty chair

The client sits and faces an empty chair and pretends that it is occupied by a significant other. The client begins a dialogue with the other person, then switches chairs to continue the dialogue as the other, and so on, with help from the counsellor. This technique helps clients to appreciate the viewpoints of others as well as to own and express their feelings.

Sensation techniques

Biofeedback

Biofeedback is devised to help clients to monitor and modify physiological factors such as heart rate, galvanic skin response and muscular tension. For example the counsellor may attach electrodes to the jaw of a client who has painful jaw tension. The machine to which the electrodes are attached provides a tonal feedback that increases in volume with increasing tension. The client then learns to achieve a low tone level, or even eliminate it altogether.

Focusing

While in a relaxed and meditative state, clients are encouraged to focus on their spontaneous thoughts and feelings until a major bodily expression emerges. From this period of intense focusing, clients are asked to isolate something new from their sensations, emotions and mental images.

Hypnosis

Hypnotic-induction techniques involve some type of sensory fixation, such as focusing on a spot on the wall or ceiling and monotonously repeating a phrase such as 'relaxed and mellow'. Some counsellors learn several methods of inducing a trance in clients in order to increase their chance of success with them.

Meditation

During meditation clients gradually close their eyes and repeat a mantra, perhaps inwardly saying 'in' as they breathe in and 'out' as they breathe out. Thoughts float in and out of their minds during the sessions, which vary from two 20-minute sessions a day to two- or three-minute sessions several times a day.

Relaxation training

Total relaxation involves progressively tensing and then letting go of each muscle area, while differential relaxation involves learning to relax muscles that are not in use when carrying out a certain task.

Sensate focus training

This technique is used with sexually dysfunctional couples and relates to sensual rather than sexual pleasure. The partners take it in turns to give pleasure to each other by touching and stimulating those parts of the body they enjoy most. Sexual activity is not permitted.

Threshold training

This is used to treat premature ejaculation. The woman manipulates the man's penis until he feels an orgasm approaching, at which point he stops her until the sensation has declined. The process is then repeated. Advanced variations are employed later, including manual stimulation with the use of a lubricant, and vaginal penetration with withdrawal before ejaculation. These techniques result in an ability to delay ejaculation for extended periods.

Imagery techniques

Anti-future-shock imagery

This technique is used to prepare clients for predicted changes in the coming months or years, and involves them imagining themselves coping with these changes. Common examples are parenthood, promotion and/or moving to a different area.

Associated imagery

When clients have unaccountable emotions the counsellor gets them to focus on any image that comes to mind and to picture it as vividly as they can. Any new images that appear are also strongly visualised. If none occur the first image is zoomed back on. This process may elicit images that are suitable for tracking, and clients often gain important insights through the use of this technique.

Aversive imagery

This involves learning to associate unpleasant images with unwanted, self-reinforcing behaviours, such as overeating, alcohol abuse and sexual deviation. For example clients who have a problem with overeating can be trained to imagine that their food is covered in vomit.

Goal rehearsal or coping imagery

This technique requires clients to break down the various steps involved in difficult forthcoming events. They visualise themselves wavering and then coping with each step.

Positive imagery

Clients imagine a pleasant scene – real or fantasised, past, present or future. This has the effect of reducing tension and anxiety and increasing enjoyment.

Step-up technique

Clients who are anxious about a forthcoming event are asked to visualise the worst possible scenario, and then to imagine themselves coping with and surviving it. Some clients may need self-instructional training to accompany this technique.

Time projection

Projection can be forward or backward and is also known as 'time tripping'. It enables the client to relive and work through past events and/or envisage future events. For example clients for whom life holds little meaning could imagine being successful at rewarding activities, and visualise how their present situation might look at a more successful time in the future.

Cognitive techniques

Bibliotherapy

According to Lazarus (1989, p. 243) a good self-help book 'can be worth more than a dozen sessions'. The chosen books should be properly studied and discussed during the sessions.

Correcting misconceptions

Misconceptions about society can be corrected by providing the client with factual information. The counsellor needs to learn the relevant information, and bibliotherapy can play an important role here too.

Ellis's A-B-C-D paradigm

Ellis's (1991a) paradigm involves A (activating event), B (beliefs), C (consequences), D (disputing) and E (effects). Clients are taught to identify their irrational beliefs about activating events that cause negative consequences. Disputing irrational beliefs is intended to have the effect of reducing or even ending negative consequences.

Problem solving

In this technique clients apply basic scientific methods to their personal problems. Hypotheses are put forward and are tested against relevant factual information. The consequent decisions are therefore based on fact rather than supposition or speculation.

Self-instructional training

To improve their coping skills clients replace negative self-statements with task-oriented ones. For example to cope with a worrying future event they may:

- Instruct themselves to develop a plan for handling the event one step at a time.
- Instruct themselves to pause and take a few deep breaths when anxious.
- Acknowledge that fear does not have to be eliminated, merely managed.
- Focus on what needs to be done.
- Try to identify the link between controlling self-talk and controlling fear.

Coping tends to become easier each time the self-instructions are used.

Thought blocking

This is aimed at eliminating intrusive and obsessive thoughts. The client mentally shouts 'STOP' over and over again. Some clients find it helpful to visualise a huge sign bearing this ward, or to flick themselves with an elastic band as they scream 'STOP'.

Interpersonal techniques

Communication training

Role playing and behaviour rehearsal are regarded as particularly useful in communication training. Clients are also trained to send and receive communications. Sending skills are eye contact, body posture, voice projection and the use of simple concrete terms. Receiving skills are active listening and rewarding the senders of communications.

Contingency contracting

Clients agree to make rewards or penalties dependent on maintaining, increasing or reducing a certain behaviour. Penalties are normally self-imposed.

Friendship training

Here clients are taught to behave in affectionate, prosocial ways, and to avoid competitiveness and self-aggrandisement. Important skills include showing caring and concern, empathy, positive reinforcement, self-disclosure and give-and-take.

Graded sexual approaches

Partners engage in sexual and sensual activity while enjoyable feelings are to the fore, and end it as soon as anxiety appears. Anxiety recedes with each encounter, and thus greater intimacy and sexual arousal can be achieved.

Paradoxical strategies

A common parodoxical strategy is symptom prescription, where the counsellor prescribes an increase in undesirable behaviours, which may parodoxically result in a decrease in these behaviours. Yet another approach is to ban a desired behaviour, for example a client who has difficulty achieving an erection may be banned from having penetrative sex without permission. This is sometimes enough to overcome the problem.

Social skills and assertiveness training

Behaviour rehearsal and modelling are two important techniques in this training. Clients are trained in four response patterns or abilities: saying 'no', expressing positive and negative feelings, asking for favours and making requests, and continuing or ending conversations.

Health and lifestyle

Clients are encouraged to take responsibility for their health by eating properly, exercising and taking part in recreational activities. If counsellors suspect an organic problem or a need for antidepressant medication they will refer their clients to their doctors.

Other applications of multimodal counselling

Multimodal counselling can also be useful in the following areas:

- Marital work.
- Group work.
- To provide a framework for career counselling.
- Working with children in classroom settings.

- Helping adolescents to develop particular gifts and talents.
- Working with people in mental hospitals.
- Parent training.
- Counsellor training.

Conclusion

This approach is an interesting contrast to the theoretical schools in that it is a technically eclectic approach employing a wide variety of techniques selected from the consideration of empirical evidence and client need rather than from the dictates of a theory. Thus the counsellor can be best described as an 'authentic chameleon' who varies his/her approach to best suit individual clients. The importance of this cannot be overemphasised as every human being has a unique psychological profile and circumstances.

◪ Glossary

Actualising tendency Movement towards the achievement of potential and the development of trusting relationships with others.

Ambivalence Contradictory feelings and attitudes towards a person or object. In psychoanalysis ambivalence almost always refers to love–hate feelings towards another person.

Anal character A psychoanalytic term for an adult with characteristics that result from being fixated at the *anal stage* of development. The anal retentive person's characteristics include extreme tidiness, meticulous attention to detail, orderliness, punctuality, parsimony, obstinacy and a tendency to hoard and make collections. The anal expulsive character is untidy, generous and pliant.

Anal stage The stage where the 2–3 year-old infant gains pleasure from retaining and releasing faeces. This stage is important in the development of the libido and the ego. Early socialisation involves learning to control the anal sphincter. Harsh toilet training can cause excessive frustration, resulting in the infant becoming an adult with an anal character.

Angst The German word for anxiety, worry or fear. In existential counselling it is used to describe the mental anguish of someone who realises that the human condition is one in which essential personal decisions have to be made in a meaningless world. In psychoanalysis it is used synonymously with 'anxiety'.

Anima The Latin word for soul. In Jungian psychology anima has two meanings. Jung used it in his early writings to refer to the true inner self or psyche, which is in touch with the unconscious. He later used it in connection with the idea that essentially female and essentially male elements are present in both men and women. In this context anima means the feminine archetype that is present in the male unconscious.

Animus The Latin word for spirit and anger, among other things. In Jungian psychology it refers to the masculine archetype found in the female unconscious. In general psychological use it refers to an enduring and intense dislike.

Anonymity The counsellor does not exist as a person but as a 'mirror' for the patient. The counsellor brings no information to the session.

Anticathexis In Freudian analysis this refers to energy that blocks the discharge of *cathexes* or instinctual energy.

Anxiety Freudian. Signal anxiety is a reaction to danger from realistic situations in which the ego is in a state of tension and is warned to construct a defence mechanism to protect it from primary anxiety, which causes nightmares. The same applies to moralistic situations (superego) and neurotic situations (id). Existential anxiety is the equivalent of *angst*. In learning, anxiety is seen as an acquired drive that motivates an avoidance response (a movement, mental or physical, away from a goal). The avoidance response is reinforced by a reduction in anxiety.

Archetype Greek for 'original pattern or model'. In Jungian theory it is part of Jung's theory of the collective unconscious. Archetypes are innate, unconscious human ideas that manifest themselves as images and symbols, such as religious or geometric symbols, and are the material of myths and fairy stories. They can appear in dreams, especially when an individual is in a state of heightened emotion.

Attachment An emotional bond between two people. In particular it is used to describe the relationship between an infant and its closest adult(s), where the infant feels safe when with them and anxious when separated from them.

Attachment behaviour   Initially the child remains very close to the mother or mother figure but gradually becomes capable of leaving her proximity for increasingly longer periods of time. The child returns to the mother for safety and security, and when the mother goes the child experiences strong emotions and intense anxiety.

Attachment figure   A trusted, supportive person who acts as a companion and a secure base from which to operate. Individuals need a secure base throughout their lifetime.

Attachments   These are formed in early childhood to satisfy the physical and psychological needs of the child, such as the containment of strong feelings of anxiety and guilt, which are the result of the love–hate conflict. The greater the anxiety, the greater the guilt and fear of punishment for loving and hating the same person. Such feelings elicit a strong need for reassurance and love, and if these are not forthcoming there is further guilt, hate and aggression.

Autonomy   In transactional analysis this is marked by the release or recovery of three capabilities: awareness, spontaneity and intimacy.

Aversion therapy   Changing undesirable behaviour by employing conditioning techniques and unpleasant stimuli, usually drugs or electric shocks. For example an alcoholic may be given medication that, in combination with alcohol, produces nausea.

Awareness   In transactional analysis this refers to living in the here and now as part of *autonomy*. In Gestalt it permits choice but is not a must or a should. The here and now is the only contact with reality and is in the present. The past and future, memories and expectations are only of concern when they are experienced in the present.

Basic trust/mistrust   This is an Eriksonian concept. Basic trust is established at birth. If an infant is cared for by a loving, reliable and confident person during its first 18 months it will acquire a feeling of security and a basic trust in itself and its environment. If it does not it will have a basic mistrust of itself and its environment, and will feel suspicious of others and suffer anxiety.

Behaviour disorders   Conditions characterised by unacceptable and aberrant behaviour that is severe enough to warrant treatment. Examples include aggression, truancy, stealing and self-destructive behaviour.

Behaviourism   School of psychology founded by Watson. Its proponents hold that psychology can study only objective, observable behaviour, and because it is not possible to verify the introspective study of emotions, feelings and so on they are of no interest to psychology.

Behaviour modification   This involves the use of conditioning techniques in the treatment of psychological disorders and phobias. The associated theories are not concerned with the underlying causes of problem behaviour but focus instead on the overt behaviour being presented. As behaviour is learned it can be changed by relearning and reconditioning techniques.

Behaviour therapy   See *behaviour modification.*

Birth trauma   According to the early Freudian psychoanalyst Otto Rank, all anxiety arises from the trauma of birth, when the infant is expelled from the security and comfort of the womb. The resulting anxiety is reactivated by all experiences of separation from the mother, loved people and objects.

Bisexuality   According to Freudian theory everyone is born bisexual, and both sexes have the sexual characteristics of the other sex. Sexual, homosexual and incestuous urges are to be found in psychic life.

Body image   This refers to the view individuals have of their body and how it looks to other people. This image frequently fails to keep pace with actual bodily changes, such as those caused by ageing or illness. Although this is not abnormal, distorted or inaccurate body images, such as that found in anorexia nervosa, is symptomatic of disorder.

Body language   Non-verbal signals between people that transmit unconscious information on emotions and attitudes. Examples include posture, facial expression and gestures.

Bonding   The formation of a close link between people, especially between a newborn child and mother. It is often used synonymously with the term attachment to describe the longer-term relationship.

Breakthrough   An advance in a client's psychotherapy after a long period of no progress. It is frequently used to describe the overcoming of resistance to thinking about a particular difficulty and achieving an insight into its causes.

Castration complex A Freudian term for the universal male anxiety about losing the genitals. It arises from the childhood fear that sexual fantasising and masturbation may be punished with castration. In females it is the belief that castration has already happened, their lack of a penis being seen as evidence. The term castration anxiety is now used by psychotherapists for the more general and symbolic threat perceived by men with regard to their genitals and masculinity.

Cathexes Freudian. Charges of instinctual energy seeking discharge (see also *anticathexis*).

Censorship Freudian. The repression of unconscious desires, thoughts and ideas to stop them emerging into the conscious state. The theory of the superego developed from this.

Claustrophobia Extreme fear of being confined in enclosed places. The sufferer experiences acute anxiety and a feeling of suffocation in caves, lifts, small rooms and so on. Derives from the Latin *claustrum* (cloister plus phobia).

Client-centred counselling A type of psychotherapy in which the counsellor is completely non-directive and non-judgemental. What the client says is unconditionally accepted. Counsellors encourage and clarify their clients' ideas, thus helping the clients to solve their own problems. It is especially associated with Carl Rogers.

Clinical psychology The application of psychological methods to the diagnosis and treatment of emotional and behavioural disorders. Clinical psychologists differ from psychiatrists in that they do not usually undergo medical training.

Cocounselling Two or more counsellors working in a team to counsel a single client or a group of clients. The counsellors usually work at the same time, but they can work consecutively. The benefit of this method is that the different counsellors complement each other by having a different approach, or by being of different sex.

Cognitive behaviour modification See *cognitive therapy*.

Cognitive dissonance The state of tension that results from a person holding two inconsistent (dissonant) beliefs, attitudes or ways of thinking (cognitions), or where there is conflict between beliefs and behaviour. There is strong motivation to change because this is an emotionally painful situation.

Cognitive therapy A type of psychotherapy that aims to modify cognitive processes such as attitudes, beliefs, expectations and self-image. Apart from counselling and psychotherapy, techniques such as self-monitoring and self-evaluation are used to help people to comprehend the attitudes that govern their behaviour.

Collective unconscious Jungian term for the inherited part of the unconscious that is shared by all human beings. It is also called the racial unconscious. It has evolved in the human brain over the centuries and is not related to personal or individual characteristics. The contents of the collective unconscious are the archetypes or primordial universal images that appear in dreams and religious symbols and in the imagery of different cultures down the ages.

Compensation Making up for deficiencies in one area by developing strengths in another. It has a slightly different emphasis in the different types of psychoanalytic theory. In Freudian theory it is seen as a defence mechanism to prevent deficiencies from reaching consciousness. In Adlerian personality theory it refers to the way people deal with inferiority feelings and failure by means of self-assertion, achievement and the exercise of power. If compensation is more than required, overcompensation takes place and the individual becomes aggressive, domineering and overbearing.

Complex Psychoanalytic term for a group of repressed and emotionally charged memories and ideas that conflict with an individual's other ideas and have a powerful influence on personality and behaviour. Jung was first to use the word in this way. It was also used by Freud (Oedipus complex) and Adler (inferiority complex).

Compulsion An irresistible urge to behave in ways that are contrary to individuals' conscious wishes and against their interests. Such behaviour tends to be irrational, repetitive and long term.

Conditioning Divided into classical conditioning and operant conditioning, this refers to the learning in humans and animals that takes place under experimental conditions, and in which the subject learns to respond in a given way to a stimulus. The term is also used in a more general way to describe similar learning outside the laboratory. For example children who have had a painful experience at the dentist may dread going there for the rest of their lives. Similarly children who are rewarded for doing well at school are encouraged to continue to work hard, thus securing further reward.

Confusion   Used in its normal meaning by psychologists, and as a euphemism for dementia by professionals who work with old people.

Conscious   In psychoanalysis, the area of mental activity of which individuals are aware.

Conversion   In psychoanalysis, a disorder in which psychic conflict is transformed into physical symptoms. Also called hysterical conversion, conversion reaction or conversion disorder.

Coping   Overcoming and dealing with problems. Counselling focuses on helping the client to tackle the source of the problem instead of ignoring it or using defence mechanisms.

Counselling   Guiding individuals or groups of people to make decisions and solve problems by means of advice and information, therapeutic discussion, suitable activities and so on.

Countertransference   In psychoanalysis, the analyst's transference onto the client. This is thought to be a disturbing development that might distort the course of the analysis. More generally it refers to the analysts' feelings and attitudes towards the client, and their emotional involvement in the therapy. In this sense it is not seen as having negative effects, but as normal and even helpful.

Crisis intervention   Short-term counselling to combat acute psychological stress caused by rape or other violence, attempted suicide, the effects of drug or alcohol abuse and so on.

Death instinct   In psychoanalysis, the drive towards destruction and death. It is manifested by aggression, denying oneself pleasure, and self-destructive behaviour. In Freud's theories it is known as Thanatos (after the Greek god of death) and is the opposite to the life instinct. In Kleinian theory aggression is regarded as a projection of the instinct for self-destruction.

Death wish   The unconscious desire for death typified by people who engage in dangerous activities and situations. It is also used to refer to the death instinct.

Defence mechanism   Freudian. Unconscious activity by the ego to protect itself from memories, thoughts or situations that cause anxiety. It is also used to describe thoughts and behaviour that are unconsciously employed as a defence against anxiety or threats to self-esteem. Defence mechanisms include repression, denial and projection.

Delusions   Erroneous beliefs held despite evidence and logical arguments to the contrary. Delusions are not the same as hallucinations or illusions.

Denial   A defence mechanism against anxiety-provoking or painful thoughts, facts and experiences. It is an unconscious process in which unbearable feelings and thoughts are disavowed and unpleasant experiences are not recognised as having happened.

Dependence   This term is used in a variety of ways. In psychoanalysis it refers to a child's helplessness and dependence on its parents and other adults, and to the adult's continuing fixation on the parents. In psychiatry it refers to abnormal reliance on others, to the extent of being unable to make independent decisions (dependent personality disorder). In social psychology it refers to excessive reliance on others to support one's personal opinions and views of reality.

Depression   In common parlance depression refers to low feelings. In psychiatry it is used when such feelings are chronic. Depression embraces the following symptoms: sadness, despondency, inadequacy, pessimism, low self-esteem, lethargy and reduced responsiveness. It may also be accompanied by anxiety. Its causes can be psychological and/or biochemical.

Desensitisation   Reduction in sensitivity to a stimulus after frequent exposure. It is more often used to describe a technique of behaviour modification (also called desensitisation procedure or systematic desensitisation) aimed at reducing anxiety, especially in connection with phobias.

Developmental psychology   The psychological, physical, cognitive and social changes that happen throughout an individual's lifetime.

Developmental stages   The stages in the human developmental process, each of which is characterised by certain behaviours and mental attributes. Stage theories include Freud's theory of psychosexual development, Piaget's work on the progressive stages of a child's cognitive development and Erikson's eight stages of man. Other theories account for the development of morality and sensory-motor development

Displacement   In psychoanalysis this refers to the redirection of feelings from one mental image to another, as manifested in the symbolism of dreams. It is also used to describe the substitution of one behaviour or response for another, and the shifting of emotions from their original object to a less threatening or more suitable one.

Dissociation   This happens when a set of mental processes, activities or emotions are separated from the rest of an individual's personality and function independently of it. In amnesia the memory is dissociated. Dissociative disorders involve the breakdown of the integrity of the personality and loss of the sense of personal reality.

Double-bind   In this situation individuals receive conflicting messages from someone in a position of power over them, and cannot find a response that will be acceptable to that person. The parent–child relationship is fairly typical of this: a child's demands for affection may be refused but the parent continues to demand the child's affection. It is thought that the resulting stress and confusion may be a cause of schizophrenia in later life.

Dream analysis (or interpretation)   A psychoanalytic technique whereby clients' dreams are analysed to uncover their underlying meaning. Clients relate their dreams and then use free association to interpret them. Freud saw dreams as disguised wish fulfilments when wants and desires are repressed. The term dream work describes (1) the unconscious process in which the raw material of dreams is transformed into the dream, and (2) work to reveal the real meaning of a dream.

Drive   An urge to acquire satisfaction. A drive is distinguishable from a need in that a need does not necessarily involve motivation to satisfy the state of deprivation. Thus need states are thought to produce drive states.

Ego   Freudian. The ego is the portion of the id that is modified by the real world. It is the intermediary between the id and the world, and it has common sense and reason.

Ego ideal   Freudian. The model to which the ego wishes to conform; the positive standards and ambitions to which an individual aspires. It is formed through identification with parents or parent figures who are admired. Failure to conform to the ego ideal causes a feeling of shame and a sense of inferiority.

Electra complex   Jungian. Female equivalent to the Oedipus complex.

Empathy   The ability to understand and be sensitive to the feelings, ideas and actions of another person without feeling the same feelings. It can be depicted as putting oneself in another's shoes but not forgetting that one has a pair of one's own.

Engulfment   In Laingian psychology, the anxiety experienced by those who do not have a firm sense of their own identity. Such individuals see relationships with others as a threat to their identity. Hence the love and affection of others is more disturbing than hatred because it brings with it the threat of being engulfed by the loving person and losing one's identity.

Envy   Kleinian. The infant's ambivalent feelings towards its mother's breasts are central to its psychic development. The infant has an innate envy of the mother's breast and its creativity. Envy is not the same as jealousy because the latter involves a third party.

Eros   In Freudian psychoanalysis Eros (named after the Greek god of love) is the symbol of erotic or sexual love and refers to all the life-preserving instincts. It is a synonym for *libido*.

Existential counselling   A counselling theory based on existential philosophy. It states that individuals have free will and are responsible for their choices in an unfathomable world. Unconscious causes of human behaviour are not accepted as the emphasis is on the conscious mind and its experiences. Clients are not regarded as being sick, rather the purpose of counselling is to help clients to analyse their conscious self and immediate reality to reach a state of self-awareness.

Externalisation   Attributing one's thoughts and behaviour to an outside agency. In psychoanalysis it is synonymous with projection.

Extinction   The weakening of a conditioned response. In operant conditioning it is considered to have happened when reinforcement continually fails to accompany the conditioned response. In classical conditioning it happens when the conditioned stimulus is constantly presented in the absence of an unconditioned stimulus.

Extravert (or extrovert)   Derives from the Latin *extra* (outside) and *vertere* (to turn). In Jungian personality theory it refers to individuals who have turned outside themselves. Extraverts are gregarious, impulsive, outgoing, responsive to others, and more interested in the outside world than in their own mental state. They are sociable and confident in unfamiliar surroundings and with strangers. On the negative side, extreme extraverts are overly dependent on group acceptance and aggressive when opposed.

Facilitation   Often considered to be the counsellor's most important task, facilitation involves enabling clients to recognise the nature of their problems and the choices they can make, and helping them to reach decisions about changes to their lives. Non-directive counsellors often refer to themselves as 'facilitators'.

Family counselling   It is assumed that the whole family is involved in a given problem and therefore should work together to find a joint solution. Some family therapists consider that the problems of the individual are caused by his or her relationships within the family, while others see the individual's problems as symptomatic of the neurosis of the whole family.

Fantasies   Images and events created in the imagination. They are related to wish fulfilment and tend to be produced spontaneously. Indulging in fantasy is seen as normal and psychologically healthy, but it becomes a problem when the fantasies are more important to the individual than real life and/or are linked to delusions or drug abuse. In psychoanalysis they are seen as happening in conscious daydreams and unconscious dreams.

Fear   An emotion caused by a current or anticipated danger. It is characterised by physiological changes, agitation and the desire to hide, flee or attack. It differs from phobia, which is irrational, and anxiety, which is more general and undifferentiated.

Fear of failure/success   Fear of failure is associated with those who are under pressure to succeed, and especially to those with a strong need for achievement. Fear of success is linked to the expectation of negative consequences.

Fetish   An inanimate object or body part that has become the focus of sexual excitement. With fetishism sexual arousal is dependent on the fetish. The most common fetishes are clothing, such as underwear, and body parts such as hair or feet.

Fixation   Freudian. Fixation occurs when the libido becomes stuck at a particular stage of development, rather than moving on to the next stage. There is a persistent attachment to an object or person more appropriate to an earlier stage of life. It is often related to the Freudian psychosexual development stages. For example an individual may be said to be fixated at the oral stage. The fixation is often on a parent, for example mother fixation. Fixated adults are immature and neurotic in that they have an infantile ambivalence towards the object of fixation. This hampers their future relationships and obstructs the development of mature attitudes towards others.

Flight into health   Individuals seem to recover completely when faced with the prospect of attending psychotherapy. Hence flight into health is a defence mechanism to avoid the painful self-examination involved in psychotherapy.

Flight into illness   Individuals develop symptoms in order to escape from or avoid conflict. It was originally used in Freudian analysis to refer to patients who developed new neurotic symptoms to avoid examination of the central problems in their lives.

Flooding   This involves flooding a client with a particular experience in order to produce aversion or habituation. Clients are encouraged to indulge in the antisocial or unhealthy habit they want to cure until they are nauseated by it and lose their desire for it. Flooding can also be used to combat phobias. In the latter case it is more like an extreme form of desensitisation in that clients confront the phobia-inducing situation until they become used to it. This can be carried out in the imagination as well as in reality. The theory is that when the client's anxiety level reaches its zenith, thereafter it can only fall.

Focal therapy   In psychotherapy this involves focusing only on clients' presenting problems, rather than their entire life.

Folie a deux   French for 'madness of two'. Two people in a close, long-term relationship share the same delusions, which are often of a paranoid nature.

Free association   A psychoanalytic technique involving the free expression of all thoughts and images that come into the client's mind. There must be no guidance from the therapist and the client must have no reservations or constraints, and exercise no concentration or intellectual control. The aim is to uncover the client's unconscious conflicts. The term is also used for a type of psychological test in which those doing the test report the first thought that comes to mind when given a stimulus such as a word or phrase.

Free-floating anxiety A vague state of anxiety that seems to have no particular cause. In psychoanalysis it is assumed that a particular cause has become detached from the original circumstances and generalised.

Free-floating attention Therapists let themselves go when listening to the client and avoid any analysis of the client's disclosure so that they can concentrate on the overall tone of the session.

Freudian slip Literally 'faulty action', this is the popular term for parapraxis. In Freudian theory it refers to mistakes in speech and behaviour that the individual would not normally make. Such errors are caused by the intrusion of repressed wishes and unconscious conflicts. Such slips are also common among people who have no particular psychological problems.

Functional analysis The Skinnerian form of behaviourism in which behaviour is analysed without examining its structure or underlying motivation.

Functional disorder A disorder that is psychological in origin and has no identifiable physical cause.

Gender identity disorder Failure to identify with the sex to which one was born. The disorder involves feeling discomfort with one's body and the gender role that society expects. There is a preference in childhood for the clothes, toys and activities of the other sex and in adulthood it manifests itself as transvestism and transexualism.

Genital phase The arrival of puberty and exploration of sexual activity with partners. At this stage incestuous object choices are overcome. There can be a break from parental authority because individuals establish their own adult relationships. It also refers to the stage at the age of four or five when children become interested in their sexual organs and the differences between the sexes, and form an attachment to the parent of the opposite sex.

Gross stress reaction The general term for a reaction, usually anxiety and/or sleeplessness, caused by an extremely stressful experience such as trauma or combat. It is not applied to the ordinary stress reactions experienced in everyday life.

Group therapy Psychotherapy carried out with a group of individuals who help each other by engaging in group interactions and sharing experiences. The counsellor acts as facilitator. A variety of techniques are employed, ranging from morale raising and mutual self-help in groups such as Alcoholics Anonymous, to group analysis where psychoanalytic theory is used to interpret the interactions between the members of small groups.

Guiding fiction Adlerian. The unconscious principles and ideas that govern the way in which people direct and evaluate their behaviour and experiences throughout their lives. The degree to which the guiding fiction is consistent with reality depends on the mental health of the individual.

Guilt In psychoanalysis guilt is a result of conflict between the superego and the individual's aggressive and sexual drives.

Habituation The waning of a response to a stimulus when it becomes increasingly familiar after repeated presentations. In relation to drug abuse it describes psychological dependence on a drug.

Halo effect The tendency to generalise one likeable trait in a person to his or her whole personality; or the attribution of many admirable qualities to a person we happen to like. On the negative side, a person may be considered unreliable because of one negative trait.

Holding When counsellors and therapists talk of being 'held' or feeling 'held' they mean the feeling of warmth, security and acceptance found in a close relationship that provides the security felt by an infant cradled in its mother's arms.

Holism The theory that people cannot be understood by analysing their parts and should be seen as a whole. Counselling methods based this view are described as holistic.

Humanistic counselling This focuses on normal rather than neurotic behaviour, and on the attributes that make human beings unique among living creatures. This approach is largely associated with the work of Carl Rogers.

Hypochondria   Also called hypochondriasis, this is an excessive preoccupation with personal health, with minor symptoms of illness being seen as dangerously serious. Many people have mild hypochondria and it is only a sign of psychiatric disorder when it becomes an extreme preoccupation and is overwhelming the individual concerned, to the point of delusion.

Hysteria   Derives from the Greek *hystera* (womb). A psychiatric disorder whose symptoms include dissociation, hallucinations, amnesia, somnambulism (sleep walking), facial tics and physical symptoms with no physiological cause. It is no longer seen as a single disorder and hysteria is not used as a diagnostic term – an individual with the classic symptoms mentioned might be diagnosed as having a dissociative disorder or conversion hysteria.

Id   Freudian. The part of the psyche that strives to gratify instinctual needs, operating on the pleasure principle.

Idealisation   This has two meanings in psychoanalysis. (1) The elevation of individuals to the perfect ideal while denying any negative characteristics they have. There is often identification with the idealised image – this is often a partial refusal to recognise ambivalence. (2) Some theorists, particularly Kleinians, see idealisation as a defence mechanism that involves the splitting of an object of ambivalence into two aspects: an ideally good one and thoroughly bad one.

Idée fixe   French for 'fixed idea'. An obsessively held, persistent and irrational idea that dominates the mind for long periods and is quite unaffected by logical arguments against it or proof of its irrationality.

Identification   The establishment of a close link between oneself and someone with whom one feels an emotional bond. Psychoanalytically it means to assimilate another person's attributes, using that person as a model.

Identity crisis   Acute loss of the sense of identity. Human identity is equated with a person's essential self that the person recognises as an individual with particular characteristics and roles, and having a continuous existence over time, that is, how the person sees him/herself.

Imago   Latin for 'image'. In psychoanalysis imago is an unconscious, frequently idealised view of another person, usually formed in early life, continuing into adult life and influencing relationships. The subject is normally a parent.

Implosion   Bursting or collapsing inward. In Laingian theory it refers to the fear of loss of identity experienced by individuals who are insecure about their existence. Such people feel that they are like a vacuum and are terrified that reality will impinge and the world will crash into their emptiness, destroying their identity. They long for the vacuum to be filled, but their fear of having their identity destroyed forces them to withdraw from reality.

Implosion therapy   See *flooding*.

Impulse-control disorder   The inability to control a need to carry out an antisocial act, such as engaging in violent behaviour towards people and/or property, pyromania and kleptomania.

Inappropriate affect   An inappropriate response, such as laughing at a very serious situation. It is an indicator of severe psychiatric illness.

Individual psychology   A term used to describe Adlerian theory. It can also be applied to any theory that focuses on the striving of an individual's personality as the main element in human development.

Infantile amnesia   The inability to recall the experiences of early childhood. In psychoanalysis it is seen as the extension of repressed memories of infantile sexuality to all early childhood memories. Other theoretical approaches relate it to failure to encode events in the memory owing to lack of language ability.

Infantile sexuality   Freudian. The capacity in all children for sexual experience and desire.

Inferiority complex   An Adlerian theory, the feeling of inferiority and inadequacy. It is an almost universal experience, and may be wholly or partly unconscious. It is a response to physical defects, inferior physique, ill-treatment, parental neglect or being a small and powerless child. The strategies adopted to cope with this complex influence personality development. The main motivating force is to compensate for inferiority and strive for superiority. The mature adult has successfully compensated for this inferiority feeling.

Failure can lead to overcompensation, aggression, antisocial attitudes and behaviour, illness and neurosis.

Inhibition   The restraining or prevention of a process through the operation of internal or external influences. It refers to the situation in which one basic emotion or drive blocks another. In cognitive psychology it means the reduction of performance, especially of the memory due to the presence of other information. Psychoanalysis holds that the superego causes inhibition by controlling the instinctive impulses of the id. Unlike repression, in inhibition the impulse is blocked and never reaches the conscious.

Insight learning   In Gestalt, a form of problem solving in which insight into a problem is achieved by the sudden reorganisation of its elements, that is, the disparate parts suddenly form themselves into a pattern and the solution becomes clear. This is called the 'aha reaction'. In psychotherapy it is the breakthrough that comes when the client realises the significance of a pattern of past events, leading to self-knowledge and the solution of problems.

Instinct   The innate motivating force behind behaviour. In Freud's view there is a dualism or polarity between two sets of instincts and this causes conflict. The two basic instincts are the life instinct and the death instinct.

Intellectualisation   The use of abstract, logical terms to deal with situations and problems without involving emotions. In psychoanalysis it may be used by clients to resist the attempts of the analyst to put them in touch with their feelings and fantasies.

Internalisation   The process by which individuals accept external attitudes, beliefs and standards of behaviour as their own. In psychoanalytic theory the superego is the result of the unconscious process by which individuals internalise the principles and values of their parents. This is sometimes called introjection. In social psychology it is the opposite of externalisation, that is, attributing one's behaviour to internal motivation rather than external influences.

Introvert   Derives from the Latin *intro* (inward) and *vertere* (to turn). In Jungian personality theory it describes individuals who are preoccupied by their mental life. Such people are withdrawn, unsociable and prefer reflection to action. They are also shy, cautious about forming relationships, and have a dislike for large social gatherings and new social situations. Introverts can be imaginative, thoughtful and sensitive, but on the negative side they can be inward-looking and so passive that they are unable to form relationships.

Isolation   A defence mechanism involving the unconscious isolation of an occurrence or event to stop it from connecting with the rest of the individual's experiences. This does not mean that individuals forget the event, but that they keep it separated from the emotions and impulses to which it is connected. They also refuse to recognise it as a memory source. Isolation is particularly characteristic of obsessive-compulsive disorders and is sometimes associated with the use of rituals and formulas.

Jealousy   As an emotional state jealousy involves anxiety about a loved object. This is caused by insecurity about the reciprocal love of the person concerned. It differs from envy in that it involves a rival third party. If it becomes pathological it leads to delusions and paranoia. In Freudian theory jealousy is linked to the Oedipus complex.

Kleptomania   From the Greek *klepto* (to steal) and mania. This impulse-control disorder is characterised by the inability to resist stealing. Typically, kleptomaniacs have no economic need to steal, and they tend to steal things that are of no use to them rather than things they need or want.

Latency   Occurs between the ages of five and twelve, when sexual energy is largely sublimated to cognitive and social development. It marks the end of infantile sexuality and dissolution of the Oedipus complex.

Latent content   In dream analysis, the 'real' meaning of a dream, as revealed in its interpretation. The meaning is hidden as repression and censorship cause the dream to be presented in code.

Learned helplessness   The theory that the feeling of being helpless and unable to control one's situation is learned from previous failures. Individuals feel that there is no connection between their behaviour and what happens to them, so they cease to make an effort to avoid negative outcomes. They also have an external locus of control and attribute their success or failure to luck, the whims of others and so on.

Libido Freudian. The psyche is an energy system and the energy it produces, libido, is instinctual and sexual and so drives humans to reproduce as a species. Freud later changed his definition of libido to a more generalised form of life energy or psychic energy that accompanies all strong desires or drives.

Life instinct Freudian. All the drives aimed at the preservation of life.

Little Albert The 11 month-old boy used in an experiment by the behavioural psychologist J. B. Watson to prove his theory that basic emotions such as fear are the result of conditioning. Albert was made to fear rats and other furry creatures by being shown a rat at the same time as a loud, unpleasant noise was made.

Little Hans Pseudonym used by Freud for a five-year-old boy who had a phobia about horses. Freud said that this was related to his Oedipus and castration complexes.

Locus of control Individuals with an internal locus of control believe they are responsible for their actions, that events are being mainly determined by their own behaviour, and that they can control what happens to them. Those with an external locus of control believe that events are in the hands of outside forces and other people, and they see success and failure as a matter of luck or fate. Such people lack the motivation to pursue personal success.

Machiavellianism Named after the Italian political theorist (1469–1527), this refers to the manipulation of others and the use of devious methods to gain personal advantage.

Magical thinking The belief that there is a link between what one thinks and wishes and what actually happens. In adults in Western cultures it is seen as a symptom of alienation and psychological disturbance.

Mania Literally: 'madness'. An abnormal state characterised by extreme excitement and activity. It can also be accompanied by a feeling of elation or euphoria. Manic individuals may have delusions and be violent. Mania is present in affective disorders such as manic depression.

Manifest content The overt content of a dream remembered by the dreamer upon waking.

Masochism The achievement of sexual pleasure from humiliation and physical pain. It also refers to individuals with a tendency to turn hostile and destructive impulses in on themselves, or to seek punishment to alleviate guilt.

Maternal deprivation Lack of love and care from one's mother or carer during infancy. This causes anxiety and emotional and physical retardation.

Melancholia An outdated term for depression. Sometimes used to describe the depressive phase in manic depression.

Mirroring and matching Counselling techniques that are used to demonstrate empathy with a client. In mirroring the counsellor matches the behaviour of the client, for example uses the same body posture, tone of voice and words. Matching is similar but the client's behaviour is approximated rather than precisely mirrored. The use of these techniques should be subtle enough not to be apparent to the client.

Multiple personality A psychiatric disorder in which the personality becomes fragmented into two or more subpersonalities. Also called split personality. Dual personality means two distinct personalities.

Narcissism In psychoanalysis this is the continuation into adult life of the early stage of psychosexual development when the libido is directed towards the self. Narcissitic individuals are drawn to autoerotism or masturbation rather than a sexual relationship with another person. If they do manage to love someone else, this will be someone with similar looks or characteristics to themselves. In psychiatry narcissism is a personality disorder in which individuals have an exaggerated regard for themselves. They also overestimate their looks and abilities, are hostile to criticism, and have an excessive need for admiration but are unable to direct love towards others.

Negative reinforcement In conditioning, training a response by using an aversive stimulus, for example an electric shock. A desired response is made more likely or more frequent by removing the aversive stimulus (for example rats can be trained to press a lever by giving them an electric shock; the shock is stopped when they press the lever). Negative reinforcement differs from punishment in that in the latter the aversive stimulus follows undesirable behaviour (the rats are trained to avoid pressing a lever by giving them an electric shock if they touch it).

Neo-Freudians A group of US analysts and their followers who place greater emphasis on the social and cultural aspects of personality development than on biological instincts.

Nervous breakdown A disabling attack of emotional disturbance that is often severe enough to need treatment in hospital. It is a neurotic rather than psychotic disorder.

Neurosis Derived from the Greek *neuro* (pertaining to the nerves), a neurosis is a psychological disturbance with no organic cause. Its usage started with Freud, who identified a number of types, such as anxiety neurosis, obsessive-compulsive neurosis, hysteria and phobic neurosis. According to Freud, all neuroses have their origins in the emotional conflicts of childhood. Psychiatrists now refer to neurotic disorder rather than neurosis.

Non-directive counselling In this approach the counsellor concentrates on showing empathy with clients, has no preconceived interpretation of their problems, gives no direct advice, does not guide what the clients say, and does not evaluate what is said. The focus is on helping clients to clarify their thoughts so that they can solve their own problems. It is based on the theories of Carl Rogers and is related to client-centred therapy.

Nymphomania Excessive sexual desire in women. True nymphomania is a rare condition in which satisfaction is never achieved and enjoyment does not matter. It is a symptom of a severe psychological disorder.

Object relations theory A psychoanalytic theory on relationships with objects outside the self. The stress is normally on fantasised objects and relationships, not on actual relationships. It differs from classical Freudian theory because it moves away from the idea of instinct being central to the explanation of motivation and personality.

Obsession The persistent, unwilled intrusion on the conscious mind of inappropriate or abnormal thoughts and ideas. Obsession is often linked with compulsion, the latter focusing on behaviour rather than thought.

Obsessive-compulsive disorder Once known as obsessional neurosis, this disorder is characterised by obsessive thoughts and compulsive behaviour. In psychoanalytic theory the problem is linked to fixation at the anal stage.

Oedipal stage Freudian. Boys become attached to their mother but fear of their father's revenge (castration) prevents them from loving her. The relinquishing of the mother enables them to form other relationships and identify with their father. Girls become attached to their father but think they have been castrated by their mother and desire a penis of their own. The resulting disappointment enables them to let go of their father and form their own relationships.

Oral character In psychoanalysis this refers to individuals who are fixated at the oral stage of development. Such individuals get pleasure from oral activities such as eating, drinking, thumb-sucking and excessive talking. They are optimistic and generous, and show elation and dependence on the one hand, and pessimism, aggression and depression on the other. The good characteristics are linked to good experiences at the oral stage, and the negative characteristics arise from bad experiences and early weaning. Both sets of traits are often found in the same person. Some psychoanalysts believe that the mood swings of manic depression are associated with the oral character.

Oral stage In psychoanalysis this refers to the first stage of psychosexual development. In the infant's first year erotic pleasure is gained from the sensations associated with feeding.

Organismic trusting Coined by Rogers, this term refers to trusting relationships and the ability to make decisions.

Overdetermined In psychoanalysis this is usually applied to dreams or neurotic symptoms. These are said to be overdetermined if they express more than one unconscious drive or conflict. Classical Freudian theory states that almost all behaviour is overdetermined.

Panic disorders Anxiety disorders characterised by frequent panic attacks that seem to have no obvious cause. Feelings of fear and unreality are combined with physical symptoms such as sweating and palpitations.

Paranoia   Derived from the Greek *paranous* (disorder of the mind), this term is specifically applied to a psychotic disorder characterised by delusions of persecution and intense, irrational jealousy. Occasionally these are accompanied by delusions of grandeur.

Passive-aggressive   This has two meanings. (1) The passive-aggressive personality is very dependent, does not initiate action but will react aggressively to events. (2) Passive-aggressive behaviour is displayed by individuals in a subservient position towards those in a superior position. Here the aggression is not manifested in overtly hostile actions. For example workmen who resent their employer may deliberately waste raw materials, steal from their employer and take turns to be absent.

Passivity   Displayed by Freudian analysts, who speak only when interpreting. There is no attempt to establish a social relationship in the therapy session.

Penis envy   Freudian. The hypothesis that all women have a repressed desire to have a penis. This is related to the female castration complex, which results from girls discovering they are anatomically different from boys and imagine they have been deprived of their penis.

Persona   Jungian term derived from the Latin for person, but specifically meaning an actor's mask. In Jung's theories it is individuals' public face, the personality they project in their social relations. The mask disguises the anima or true self.

Personality disorder   A mental disorder in which individuals' distorted perceptions and thoughts impair their functioning and social relationships. Examples are megalomania, narcissism and obsessive-compulsive disorder.

Person perception   The ways in which individuals perceive others. Includes the way in which impressions of other people are formed, the characteristics attributed to them, and prejudices about them.

Phallic character   In psychoanalytic theory, an individual who is fixated at the phallic stage, usually because of an unresolved Oedipus complex. The individual defines sex in terms of potency and performance, not in terms of personal relationships.

Phallic stage   Between the ages of three and five children discover the pleasure of their own genitals and masturbation.

Phallic symbol   Anything that can be thought to represent the penis. In psychoanalysis it is used with reference to symbolism in fantasies and dreams.

Phobia   Derives from the Greek *phobos* (fear). An excessive and irrational fear of a particular situation or object. The feeling of fear is accompanied by anxiety symptoms such as sweating, palpitations and the desire to flee.

Phobic character   In psychoanalysis, a person who deals with threatening or anxiety-inducing situations by avoiding them. Counterphobic characters look for dangerous situations and activities that would cause most people anxiety.

Placebo effect   Any situation in which people react positively to being given some form of attention or experimental treatment. It is believed that the effect is caused by the attention given rather than by the treatment itself.

Pleasure principle   Freudian. The theory that mental functioning is controlled by the desire to gain pleasure by satisfying the drives of the id, and to avoid unpleasure or pain.

Pollyanna mechanism   A defence mechanism characterised by unrealistic optimism and unfailing cheerfulness. Individuals deny there is anything wrong with their situation or themselves when other people can see that there is.

Positive reinforcement   Presenting a reward to increase the likelihood of a given response or behaviour happening again in the same circumstances.

Positive transfer   This is where the knowledge and skills acquired by carrying out a particular task help to improve performance when learning a different task.

Post-traumatic stress disorder   A psychological disorder caused by experiencing an accident, a crime, terrorism and so on. Symptoms include recurrent distressing images and recollections, nightmares about the event in question and flashbacks. There are attempts to nullify the experience through loss of memory, detachment, estrangement, numbed emotions, irritability and insomnia. Situations that prompt recall of the episode cause an anxiety reaction.

Preconscious A term used in psychoanalysis for the thoughts, emotions and images that are not in a person's consciousness at a given time, but are accessible. Such thoughts and emotions are not repressed, and therefore are easy to recall.

Primary gain The gain or benefit to a client from developing a disorder. In psychoanalysis it is the gain from developing a neurosis and reducing anxiety.

Projection Kleinian. The externalisation of an instinctual impulse, for example I am calm but she is angry.

Projective identification Kleinian. A powerful form of projection in which individuals have an unconscious need to make others aware of what is being communicated non-verbally and what needs to be responded to.

Psyche Freud used this term to denote the mind or the self. In psychoanalysis it means 'mental'.

Psychiatrist A qualified medical doctor who specialises in psychiatry. Unlike psychologists and psychotherapists, psychiatrists can prescribe drugs for their clients.

Psychiatry The branch of medicine that deals with mental disorders.

Psychoanalysis The type of psychotherapy invented by Sigmund Freud. It is also a theory of human behaviour.

Psychoanalyst Someone who practises psychoanalysis and has received full training at an institute of psychoanalysis.

Psychologist A practitioner, theorist or researcher in psychology. It is unusual for psychologists to undergo medical training. They first take a degree in psychology and then embark on further training in academic psychology, applied psychology, or abnormal or clinical psychology.

Psychopathic personality The term psychopath was once used to describe anyone with a severe mental disorder that needed treatment, but was then amended to 'psychopathic personality' and applied to people once known as 'moral imbeciles', that is, people with no sense of social or moral obligation who disregard the rights of others. They also experience no guilt or anxiety about their behaviour.

Psychosis A severe mental illness with physical as well as mental causes. The most important characteristic is loss of reality, involving the misinterpretation of thoughts and perceptions and of external reality. Psychotics also refuse to admit they are ill. Symptoms include hallucinations, delusions and inappropriate affect. The major types of psychotic disorder are manic depression, paranoia and schizophrenia.

Psychosomatic disorder Derives from the Greek *psyche* (mind) and *soma* (body). With psychosomatic disorders physical symptoms arise from emotional causes such as stress. They include asthma, migraine and stomach ulcers.

Psychotherapy A term that covers all types of treatment of emotional and psychological disturbances or disorders by psychological rather than physical methods. It is based on talking and the client–therapist relationship, and can be carried out individually or in a group.

Rationalisation In psychoanalysis, a defence mechanism. Individuals try to hide their true motives and justify themselves by providing logical, rational explanations for their feelings and behaviour.

Reactance theory This states that individuals react to restrictions or attempts to control their options and decisions by pursuing whatever it is they are being diverted from. The 'Romeo and Juliet effect', in which the mutual attraction of two young people is strengthened by parental opposition to their friendship, is a good example.

Reaction formation In Freudian psychoanalysis, a defence mechanism. The ego acknowledges an impulse that is at variance to one it feels threatened by, for example the sex impulse is replaced by shame.

Reality principle Freudian. One of the two principles that govern mental functioning, this acts as a brake on and regulator of the other principle: pleasure principle. The child's ego develops the capacity to adapt and modify the id's desires so that the child will have a better chance of success in reality rather than by wish fulfilment.

Regression Freudian. The return to an earlier stage of development. This is a defence mechanism in psychoanalysis, its purpose being to avoid anxiety and conflict.

Release therapy   This aims to release bottled-up emotions by means of open expression of hostility, anger or grief.

Reparation   A defence mechanism that reduces guilt about destructive thoughts and fantasies by doing good to the object of hostility.

Repetition compulsion   In psychoanalysis, the client's desire to revert to a former emotional state as a resistance to the insights gained in therapy.

Repression   Freudian. Involuntary exclusion of painful impulses, memories or thoughts from awareness. The most common defence is ego censorship.

Resistance   Clients' resistance to repressed material being brought into the conscious by the analyst during psychoanalysis.

Resolution   The point where clients feel able to understand and cope with their problem or conflict.

Retroflection   Gestalt. This occurs when individuals cannot direct their behaviour towards others so direct it back at themselves.

Rule of neutrality   Respect for client autonomy. The absence of personal involvement gives client and counsellor the space unreservedly to seek the truth behind the client's symptoms.

Satyriasis   Obsessive and excessive sexual desire in men. Also called 'Don Juanism', it is the urge to be a serial seducer. Affectionate relationships are never formed and satisfaction is never achieved.

Scapegoat   A defence mechanism in which frustration, aggression and inadequacies are denied by blaming someone else for one's failures.

Screen memory   A childhood memory that is clear and striking but quite trivial in content. Such memories may be false or inaccurate but are important because they may be key elements of childhood experiences and cover repressed childhood fantasies or events.

Secondary gain   Using an established illness or neurosis to manipulate other people and avoid undesirable responsibilities and duties.

Self-actualisation   A term invented by theorist Kurt Goldstein to refer to the primary human motive to fulfil personal potential. Abraham Maslow used it to describe a level of development characterised by autonomy, independence and confidence in dealing with the world, and the ability to form deep, long-lasting relationships.

Self-concept   Everything that individuals think of themselves.

Self-esteem   How people value themselves. Psychological problems such as depression are often characterised by low self-esteem. In narcissism, self-esteem is too high.

Self-image   The self that individuals imagine themselves to be, which is often at odds with the actuality. Self-image is normally formed early in life.

Separation anxiety   Infantile anxiety about being separated from the mother or the mother substitute. It also refers to later separation fears in respect of home, parents or other carers. Separation anxiety disorder refers to children who fear leaving their home and parents because they worry what will happen to their parents while they are away. Such children often become 'school phobic'.

Sibling rivalry   Competition and/or rivalry between siblings, usually for the affection and attention of their parents. First-born children fear that younger brothers and sisters will be favoured by their parents, while younger children are jealous of the supposed abilities and privileges of their older siblings.

Significant other   A person who is important and influential in forming an individual's attitudes, values and self-image. It tends to be a person in a position of power, such as a parent or teacher.

Socialisation   Adapting to and fitting in with society. In psychoanalysis it involves a child internalising the values of its parents and developing a superego. Other approaches define it as children learning the values, customs and language of society. Children model themselves on others, who have previously modelled themselves on others, and so on.

Social learning theory   A theory based mainly on the work of Albert Bandura, it states that children develop their personality and learn their social behaviour and morals from observing others and modelling themselves on them.

Socially embedded   Adlerian. Humans are social beings who want to belong to and find a place in the group. Adler thought that all our problems are basically social problems or problems of interaction with others.

Social phobia Most people know what it is like to feel shy and anxious about speaking in front of a group of strangers, but those who have social phobia are incapacitated by their fear. Such individuals cannot work or eat in a public place and avoid such situations.

Sour grapes A defence mechanism in which individuals convince themselves that something they cannot have or achieve is not worth having.

Splitting This has several meanings in psychoanalysis. (1) For Freud, the splitting of the ego is a defence mechanism in which individuals see only one part of the self and dissociate themselves from the rest. (2) It also involves the splits in the ego found in fetishism and various psychoses. (3) In Kleinian terminology, 'splitting of the object' refers to the splitting of another person who is the object of ambivalent feelings. The splitting divides this person into 'good' and 'bad'. (4) The process of remembering good experiences and repressing bad experiences.

Stress Any strain or pressure that is caused by frustrating situations or pressure at work or home and results in psychological tension. It is manifested in anxiety, irritability and/or depression, and it can also cause physical symptoms.

Sublimation Freudian. The diversion of instinctual sexual impulses into socially acceptable activities such as art and sport. It is the best way to deal with the impulses of the id and is essential to civilised culture.

Superego Freudian. The part of the ego that is formed by parental and other significant influences, such as family and culture. It develops an internalised authority in the child, and issues commands such as 'must', 'should' and 'ought' via repression and identification during the time of the Oedipus complex conflicts. It also promotes the higher side of human existence: ego ideal and conscience.

Symbiosis Derives from the Greek *sumbioun* (to live together). The close relationship between people living together in an interdependent way. A good example is the relationship between a mother and her newborn baby. There can be a pathological dimension when there is excessive mutual dependence in, for example, parent–child or husband–wife relationships, in families where relationships depend on the members supporting each other's neuroses, and in sado-masochistic relationships.

Symbol In psychoanalysis a symbol is an unconscious disguise that covers the real meaning of the thing represented. Symbols are important in dream analysis, as in dreams repressed material is expressed in symbols.

Thanatos See *death instinct.*

Thought stopping A technique used in directive forms of behaviour modification, such as rational emotive therapy. Clients are asked to express thoughts aloud until they say something that therapy is meant to discourage, then the therapist shouts 'Stop!' Clients learn to interrupt their negative or counterproductive thoughts until they eventually stop altogether.

Transference The emotions of the client are transferred to the counsellor, especially emotions and attitudes associated with a very important person in the client's life, usually a parent. The transference relationship is called positive transference when the feelings are good, and negative transference when the feelings are hostile.

Trauma The Greek word for 'wound'. Experiences that cause psychological damage and shock, and the effect of the latter.

Type A personality Individuals who strive for achievement and success, are obsessive about punctuality, need to be in control and cannot tolerate the failings and weaknesses of others. They are always in a hurry and do not have the patience or time for self-reflection.

Type B personality Individuals who are easy-going, unambitious and given to self-reflection.

Unconscious The mental processes that individuals are not conscious of, and the part of the mind where they take place. In Freudian theory it is the place where the repressed impulses of the id operate. The repression and inhibition of such impulses cause neuroses.

Undoing A defence mechanism in which people try to undo something they have thought, said or done in the past, and which they have come to regret. Children may engage in the ritual of mentally and/or physically re-enacting the scene, changing the part they wish had never happened. Such rituals are the mechanism operating in obsessive-compulsive disorders.

Wishfulfilment The process by which the desires of the id are realised in the imagination, thus easing the tension caused by their non-fulfilment. It takes place in dreams and in fantasy, and manifests itself in neurotic symptoms and the Freudian slip.

Withdrawal Individuals remove themselves from their day-to-day routines, gradually withdraw from reality and become uncommunicative and uncooperative. Such symptoms are found in schizophrenia and similar disorders. Sufferers take refuge in drugs and/or alcohol to escape from reality.

Working through The process in which clients overcome their resistance, accept the implications of the therapist's interpretations and gain insights into their problems. The term is also used in the sense of coming to terms with a painful situation such as bereavement.

■ ⊻ Bibliography

Adler, A. (1912) *The Neurotic Constitution* (London: Kegan Paul, Trench Trobner).
Adler, A. (1917) *Study of Organ Inferiority and its Psychical Compensation. A contribution to Clinical Medicine* (New York: Nervous and Mental Diseases Publishing).
Adler, A. (1962) *What Life Should Mean to You* (London: Allen and Unwin).
Adler, A. (1964) *Superiority and Social Interest: A Collection of Later Writings*, edited by H. L. Ansbacher and R. R. Ansbacher (New York: Norton).
Alberti, R. E. and M. E. Emmons (1990) *Your Perfect Right: A Guide to Assertive Living* (San Luis Obispo: Impact Publishers).
Ansbacher, H. L. and R. R. Ansbacher (eds) (1956) *The Individual Psychology of Alfred Adler* (New York: Basic Books).
Bandura, A. (1986) *Social Foundations of Thought and Action: A Social Cognitive Theory* (Englewood Cliffs, NJ: Prentice-Hall).
Beck, A. T., A. Freeman and Associates (1990) *Cognitive Therapy of Personality Disorders* (New York: Guilford Press).
Beck, A. T. and M. E. Weishaar (1989) 'Cognitive Therapy', in R. J. Corsini and D. Wedding (eds), *Current Psychotherapies* (Itasca: Peacock).
Berne, E. (1961) *Transactional Analysis in Psychotherapy* (New York: Grove Press).
Berne, E. (1966) *Principles of Group Treatment* (New York: Oxford University Press).
Berne, E. (1975) *Games People Play* (Harmondsworth: Penguin).
Berne, E. (1978) *What Do You Say After You Say Hello?* (London: Corgi).
Berry, R. (2000) *Jung: A Beginner's Guide* (London: Hodder & Stoughton).
Buber, M. (1970) *I and Thou* (New York: Scribners).
Cautela, J. (1967) 'A Reinforcement Survey Schedule for Use in Therapy, Training and Research', *Psychological Reports*, vol. 20.
Dreikurs, R. (1971) *Social Equality: The Challenge of Today* (Chicago, Ill: Henry Regnery).
Dryden, W. (ed.) (1991) *Individual Therapy, A Handbook* (Milton Keynes: Open University Press).
Dryden, W. (1992) *Rational-Emotive Counselling in Action* (London: Sage).
Egan, G. (1994) *The Skilled Helper: A Systematic Approach of Effective Helping* (Pacific Grove: Brooks/Cole).
Ellis, A. (1986) 'Rational-emotive therapy approaches to overcoming resistance', in A. Ellis and R. M. Grieger (eds), *Handbook of Rational-Emotive Therapy*, vol. 2 (New York: Springer).
Ellis, A. (1987) 'The impossibility of achieving consistently good mental health', *American Psychologist*, vol. 42.
Ellis, A. (1989) 'Rational-emotive therapy', in R. J. Corsini and D. Wedding (eds), *Current Psychotherapies* (Itasca: Peacock).
Ellis, A. (1991a) 'The revised ABC's of rational-emotive therapy (RET)', *Journal of Rational-Emotive & Cognitive Behaviour Therapy*, vol. 9.
Ellis, A. (1991b) 'Rational-emotive treatment of simple phobias', *Psychotherapy*, vol. 28.
Ellis, A. (1993) 'Reflections on rational-emotive therapy', *Journal of Consulting and Clinical Psychology*, vol. 61.
Evans, R. I. (1989) *Albert Bandura: The Man and His Ideas: A Dialogue* (New York: Praeger).
Fordham, F. (1991) *An Introduction to Jung's Psychology* (London: Penguin).
Frankl, V. E. (1955) *The Doctor and the Soul: From Psychotherapy to Logotherapy* (Harmondsworth: Penguin).

Frankl, V. E. (1963a) *Man's Search for Meaning: an Introduction to Logotherapy* (London: Hodder & Stoughton).

Frankl, V. E (1963b) 'Existential dynamics and neurotic escapism', *Journal of Existential Psychiatry*, vol. 4.

Frankl, V. E (1975) *The Unconscious God: Psychotherapy and Theology* (New York: Simon & Schuster).

Frankl, V. E. (1988) *The Will to Meaning: Foundations and Applications of Logotherapy* (New York: Meridian).

Freud, S. (1935) *An Autobiographical Study* (London: Hogarth Press).

Freud, S. (1973) *New Introductory Lectures on Psychoanalysis* (Harmondsworth: Penguin).

Freud, S. (1976) *The Interpretation of Dreams* (Harmondsworth: Penguin).

Freud, S. and J. Breur (1956) *Studies in Hysteria* (London: Hogarth Press).

Glasser, W. (1965) *Reality Therapy: A New Approach to Psychiatry* (New York: Harper & Row).

Glasser, W. (1984) *Control Theory: A New Explanation of How We Control Our Lives* (New York: Harper & Row).

Hayes, N. (1994) *Foundations of Psychology. An Introductory Text* (London: Routledge).

Heidegger, M. (1962) *Being and Time* (London: SCM Press).

Hinshellwood, R. D. (1989) *A Dictionary of Kleinian Thought* (London: Free Association Books).

Hoffman, E. (1989) *The Right to be Human. A biography of Abraham Maslow* (Wellingborough: Crucible).

Hosford, R. E. (1969) 'Behavioural Counselling – a contemporary overview', *The Counselling Psychologist*, vol. I.

Howard, A. (2000) *Philosophy for Counselling and Psychotherapy* (London: MacMillan).

Hyde, M. and M. McGuinness (1992) *Jung For Beginners* (Cambridge: Icon Books).

Jung, C. G. (1953) *Collected Works* (London: Routledge & Kegan Paul).

Jung, C. G. (1971) *Memories, Dreams, Reflections* (London: Fontana).

Kadzin, A. E. (1993) 'Evaluation in Clinical Practice'. Clinically sensitive and systematic methods of treatment delivery', *Behavior Therapy*, vol. 24, pp. 11–45.

Kelly, G. A. (1955) *The Psychology of Personal Constructs* (New York: Norton).

Kelly, G. A. (1969), in B. Maher (ed.), *Clinical Psychology and Personality: The Selected Papers of George Kelly* (New York: Krieger).

Klein, M. (1932) *The Psycho-Analysis of Children* (London: Hogarth).

Klein, M. (1952) 'On the theory of anxiety and guilt', in J. Riviere (ed.) *Developments in Psychoanalysis* (London: Hogarth Press).

Klein, M. (1957) *Envy and Gratitude* (New York: Basic Books).

Klein, M. (1960) *Our Adult World and its Roots in Infancy* (London: Tavistock).

Krumboltz, J. D. (1966) 'Behavioral goals for counseling', *Journal of Counseling Psychology*, vol. 13.

Lazarus, A. A. (1989) *The Practice of Multimodal Therapy: Systematic, Comprehensive and Effective Psychotherapy* (Baltimore, MD: Johns Hopkins University Press).

Lazarus, A. A. (1992) 'Multimodal Therapy: Technical eclecticism with minimal integration', in J. C. Norcross and M. R. Goldfried (eds), *Handbook of Psychotherapy Integration* (New York: Basic Books).

Lazarus, A. A. (1993) 'Tailoring the therapeutic relationship, or being an authentic chameleon', *Psychotherapy*, vol. 30.

Lewisohn, P. M. and M. Graf (1973) 'Pleasant activities and depression', *Journal of Consulting and Clinical Psychology*, vol. 41.

Lewisohn, P. M. and J. Libet (1972) 'Pleasant events, activity schedules and depression', *Journal of Abnormal Psychology*, vol. 79.

Lewisohn, P. M., R. F. Munoz, M. A. Youngren and A. M. Zeiss (1986) *Control Your Depression* (New York: Prentice-Hall).

MacPhillamy, D. J. and P. M. Lewinsohn (1971) 'Pleasant Events Schedule', mime, University of Oregon.

Maslow, A. H. (1943) 'A Theory of Human Motivation', *Psychological Review*, vol. 50, pp. 370–96.

Maslow, A. H. (1954) *Motivation and Personality* (London: Harper & Row).

Maslow A. H. (1962) *Towards a Psychology of Being* (Princeton, NJ: Van Nostrand).

Maslow B. (ed.) (1969) *Abraham Maslow: A Memorial Volume* (Monterey: Brooks-Cole).

May, R. (1977) *The Meaning of Anxiety* (New York: Norton).

May, R. and I. O. Yallom (1989) 'Existential Psychotherapy' in *Current Psychotherapies*, ed. R. J. Corsini and D. Wedding (Itasca, IL: Peacock).

Meltzer, D. (1979) *The Kleinian Development* (London: Clunie Press).

Milne, A. (1999) *Teach Yourself Counselling* (London: Hodder & Stoughton).

Nelson-Jones, R. (1995) *The Theory and Practice of Counselling* (London: Cassell).

Pavlov, I. P. (1927) *Conditioned Reflexes: An Investigation of the Physiological Activity of the Cerebral Cortex* (Oxford: Oxford University Press).

Perls, F. S. (1969) *Gestalt Therapy Verbatim* (New York: Bantam Books).

Perls, F. S. (1970) 'For Lectures', in J. Fagan and I. L. Shepherd (eds), *Gestalt Therapy Now: Theory, Techniques, Applictions* (Palo Alto, CA: Science and Behaviour Books).

Powers, W. (1973) *Behavior: The Control of Perception* (Chicago, Ill.: Aldine).

Rogers, C. R. (1939) *The Clinical Treatment of the Problem Child* (Boston: Houghton Mifflin).

Rogers, C. R. (1942) *Counselling and Psychotherapy* (Boston: Houghton Mifflin).

Rogers, C. R. (1951) *Client-Centred Therapy* (Boston: Houghton Mifflin).

Sartre, J. P. (1956) *Being and Nothingness* (New York: Philosophical Library).

Sharpe, R. and D. Lewis (1976) *The Success Factor* (London: Souvenir Press).

Skinner, B. F. (1957) *Verbal Behaviour* (New York: Appleton-Century-Crofts).

Skinner, B. F. (1971) *Beyond Freedom and Dignity* (Harmondsworth: Penguin).

Stampfi, T. G. (1975) 'Implosive Therapy: staring down your nightmares', *Psychology Today*, February, pp. 66–73.

Storr, A. (1998) *The Essential Jung, Selected Writings* (London: Fontana).

Swan, G. E. and M. L. MacDonald (1978) 'Behavior Therapy in Practice: A national survey of behaviour therapists', *Behavior Therapy*, vol. 9.

Tillich, P. (1952) *The Courage to Be* (New Haven, CT: Yale University Press).

Turner, R. W., M. F. Ward and J. Turner (1979) 'Behavioral treatment for depression: An evaluation of therapeutic components', *Journal of Clinical Psychology*, vol. 35.

Watson, J. B. (1931) *Behaviorism* (London: Kegan Paul, Trench & Traubner).

Watson, J. B. and R. R. Raynor (1920) 'Conditioned emotional reaction', *Journal of Experimental Psychology*, vol. 3.

Wolpe, J. (1958) *Psychotherapy by Reciprocal Inhibition* (Stanford, CA: Stanford University Press).

Wolpe, J. (1982) *The Practice of Behaviour Therapy* (Oxford: Pergamon Press).

Wolpe, J. and D. Wolpe (1988) *Life Without Fear: Anxiety and its Cure* (Oakland, CA: New Harbinger Publications).

Yallom, I. D. (1980) *Existential Psychotherapy* (New York: Basic Books).

Zeiss, A. M., P. M. Lewinsohn and R. F. Munoz (1979) 'Nonspecific improvement effects in depression using interpersonal skills training, pleasant activity schedules, or cognitive training', *Journal of Consulting and Clinical Psychology*, vol. 47.

▪ ᵛ Index

Note: The 'founding fathers' of 'counselling (e.g. Sigmund Freud) have separate chapter within the look (e.g. Freud in Chpater 1).

contact boundary 88
contingencies of reinforcement 193
contracting 114
control theory 125
controlling parent ego state 103
conversion 20
counterscript 107, 108
countertransference 56, 59
courage 29
covert sensitisation 214
cycle of creativity 247
cycle of experience 247
cycle of pre–emption 247
cycles of movement 247

D
death 151
decatastrophising 184
decentring 185
decisions 107
decontamination 115
defence mechanisms 12, 17, 149, 153, 154
defensive reactions 260
deintegration 55
dementia praecox: see schizophrenia
denial 19
dependent personality disorder 180
depression 106, 164, 176
depressing 124
dereflection 167
determinism 192
developmental deficit model 112
development games 108
dichotomy 87
direct reinforcement 211
discipline 123
discounts 107
displacement 19
diversion techniques 187
dreams 24, 45, 46, 97, 166
Dreikurs, Rudolph 29
dysfunctional schemas 179

E
eclecticism 257
efficacy 223–4, 225
Egan, Gerard 1
ego 14, 17, 49, 56
egograms 111
ego–ideal 15
ego state analysis 110
ego states 101
Eigenwelt 145, 146
elegant change 237

Ellis, Albert 5, 6
eidetic images 39
emotional conditioning 192
emotions 229
emotive techniques 240
empty chair technique 97, 267
enactive attainment 224
enactive learning 219
Eros 13
existential counselling 4
existential frustration 164
existential guilt 145, 152
existential psychodynamics 147
existential vacuum 164, 165
experience corollary 247
extinction 195, 196
extraversion 56
extravert 48

F
five-stage model 2
fixation 19
fixed–role therapy 251
Fleiss, Wilhelm 11
flooding (implosive therapy) 214
Fordham, Michael 55
forethought 220
forethought capability 217
four-stage model 2
fourth force 137
Frankl, Viktor 5, 6
free association 22, 46
freedom 148, 152
Freud, Sigmund 4, 5, 6
fundamental OK position 100

G
genital 15
genital phase 17
Gestalt 87
Glasser, William 6
goal specification 203
group counselling 154, 242
guided discovery 183
guilt 145

H
helping relationship 1
historical diagnosis 110
histrionic disorder 180
holism 80
homeostasis 88
homework techniques 239
hyperintention 162
hyperreflection 162
hysteria 50